POSTINDUSTRIAL
POSSIBILITIES

POSTINDUSTRIAL POSSIBILITIES

A Critique of
Economic Discourse

FRED BLOCK

UNIVERSITY OF CALIFORNIA PRESS
BERKELEY   LOS ANGELES   OXFORD

University of California Press
Berkeley and Los Angeles, California

University of California Press, Ltd.
Oxford, England

© 1990 by
The Regents of the University of California

Library of Congress Cataloging-in-Publication Data
Block, Fred L.
   Postindustrial possibilities : a critique of economic discourse /
Fred Block.
      p. cm.
   ISBN 0–520–06813–0 (alk. paper).—ISBN 0–520–06988–9 (pbk. :
alk. paper)
   1. Economic forecasting.   I. Title.
HB3730.B57   1990
330'.01' 12—dc20
                                                    89–29622
                                                    CIP

67377

Printed in the United States of America
1   2   3   4   5   6   7   8   9

For Miriam and Judith

Contents

Preface

This small book has three large goals. The first is to restate and revitalize postindustrial theory. The second is to demonstrate the power of economic sociology as a method for understanding contemporary economies. The third is to offer an alternative framework for thinking about economic policy and social choice in developed capitalist societies. Clearly, any of these tasks alone is far too ambitious for a single volume. Moreover, the topics are so large that the substantive chapters only scratch the surface of the data and scholarship relevant to my argument, and new articles and books that should be incorporated into the analysis are appearing almost daily. Nevertheless, if it encourages others to take up these issues in a more sustained and systematic fashion, I think I am justified in publishing an essay—literally, an attempt—that is provisional and incomplete. Without this kind of intellectual chutzpah, there is a real danger that serious scholarship will confine itself to narrow questions that lend themselves to mastery by a single scholar, and that the great issues of our time will go unstudied.

I have incurred numerous debts in the preparation of this volume. The German Marshall Fund of the United States provided me with support during the 1986–87 academic year; without that year devoted to research and writing, this volume could not have been written. I am also indebted to the University of Pennsylvania's Program for Assessing and Revitalizing the Social Sciences for research support over several summers. Even more important, the arguments of this book reflect what I have learned from my colleagues in seminars sponsored by this program.

A number of individuals provided references or data that were critical; these include Paul Adler, Ann Miller, Patricia Roos, and Michael Weinstein. Many people read chapters or the entire manuscript and provided valuable comments; these include Daniel Bell, Nancy Folbre, Roger Friedland, Jerry Jacobs, Henrika Kuklick, Frances Fox Piven, Samuel Preston, Carmen Sirianni, Judy Stacey, Ann Swidler, and Robert Wood. The manuscript has also benefited greatly from the editorial work of Peter Dreyer and Naomi Schneider. As they have for the past fifteen years, five friends have been particularly important in the development of my thinking; they are Larry Hirschhorn, Karl Klare, Magali Sarfatti Larson, David Plotke, and Peggy Somers. I cannot express the depth of my gratitude to them.

My debts to my family are also formidable. I am deeply grateful to my mother, Jean Libman Block, and my father, Frederick H. Block, for their love and support. I am reluctant to engage in the rhetorical excesses that would be necessary to describe my debt to my wife, Carole Joffe. Suffice it to say that her love and wisdom have immeasurably enriched my work. The book is dedicated to my daughters, Miriam and Judith Joffe-Block, in the age-old hope that they will inherit a better world. This dedication is hardly adequate recompense for what they have given to me.

Chapter One

The Postindustrial Context

This is a strange period in the history of the United States because people lack a shared understanding of the kind of society in which they live. For generations, the United States was understood as an industrial society, but that definition of reality is no longer compelling. Yet no convincing alternative has emerged in its absence.

This confusion and uncertainty is reflected in both common-sense views and social theory. Contemporary social theorists tell us remarkably little about the kind of historical era in which we live.[1] Social theorists have become preoccupied with questions of meta-theory; much theoretical debate centers on defining the proper scope and ambition of social theory and on determining the kind of theory that should be created. Recent years have seen relatively few efforts to define the nature of contemporary societies and to delineate their major dynamics. It is almost as though such an effort

1. More accurately, they tell us little directly; their silence on the classical issue of defining the nature of the society is itself deeply revealing. There are exceptions to this prevailing silence, but an examination of the essays in a recent volume designed to reflect the state of the debate in social theory (Anthony Giddens and Jonathan Turner, eds., *Social Theory Today* [Stanford: Stanford University Press, 1987]) provides strong support for this conclusion. Important partial exceptions include the recent multivolume work by Roberto Mangabeira Unger, *Politics: A Work in Constructive Social Theory* (Cambridge: Cambridge University Press, 1987), and Anthony Giddens's own multivolume study, *A Contemporary Critique of Historical Materialism* (Berkeley: University of California Press, 1981, 1987). The second volume is entitled *The Nation-State and Violence*.

is now seen as an old-fashioned exercise, an anachronistic return to the lofty ambitions of nineteenth-century theorists.[2]

This silence of contemporary theorists has real consequences, because individuals cannot do without some kind of conception of the type of society in which they live. In modern societies, social theory plays an indispensable role in providing us with a roadmap to our social environment. While there are complex mediations between high social theory and everyday "common sense," the two are connected in important ways.[3]

In those periods when social theory fails to define the nature of our society, other ideas tend to fill the void of popular understanding. As Keynes said of economics, those who profess not to be influenced by any theory are usually enthralled by the ideas of some long-forgotten scribbler. In our own period, it is economic ideas—and, ironically, pre-Keynesian economic ideas in particular—that have filled the vacuum left by the silences of contemporary social theory. The remarkable revival during the 1980s of classical free-market economics has served to fill people's need for some kind of social understanding to guide their day-to-day actions.[4]

The relative silence of social theory is rooted in events of the 1960s and 1970s that critically weakened the previously dominant theories of post–World War II American social science. Structural-functionalism in sociology, pluralism in political science, and liberal Keynesianism in economics shared in common an evolutionary triumphalism that saw American society as having evolved new institutional arrangements that provided solutions to such historic problems of industrialism as class conflict, economic crises, and exploitation. All three approaches proclaimed the arrival of a new

---

2. This is, in fact, the position of many who have been influenced by post-structuralism. They see any attempt to create a unified theory of society as intellectually indefensible and as potentially coercive.

3. The classical source of the idea that social theory plays a critical role in shaping popular perceptions of reality is Gramsci. See Antonio Gramsci, *Selections from the Prison Notebooks*, vol. 1 (New York: International Publishers, 1971).

4. Fundamentalist religious ideas have also filled this space for many. There are, of course, affinities between free-market ideas and the Christianity of the Gospels. See Karl Polanyi, *The Great Transformation* (1944; reprint, Boston: Beacon Press, 1957), 249–58B.

stage in history in which enlightened state action and a spirit of consensus would make possible the gradual solution of the remaining social problems. All three of these approaches were unapologetically liberal in their political and social outlook.

These optimistic visions of American society were shattered by the political and social developments of the 1960s and 1970s. Theorists working within these traditions were unable to put forward persuasive accounts of these new developments, and the result was that their views were delegitimated both in the academy and in the broader society. The fact that *liberalism* has now become a term of derision in American politics is the most dramatic testimony to the crisis of the ideas that dominated social science discourse in the 1950s and 1960s.

For a brief moment in the late 1960s and early 1970s, it appeared that left-wing critics of these mainstream perspectives would be able to construct an alternative social theory that might become broadly influential in the society. However, this did not happen. For one thing, deep divisions on fundamental questions emerged among radical scholars as soon as their attacks on mainstream positions appeared victorious. For another, many on the left proved reluctant to move beyond classical Marxist formulations that had long since been overtaken by historical developments. The left was also unable to move beyond a critique of existing institutional arrangements; it failed to provide an alternative vision of how American institutions could and should be reorganized.

The crises of both mainstream and leftist social theories opened the way for the revitalization of the tradition of economic liberalism that had been largely quiescent since the Great Depression. It was almost as if people responded to the turmoil of the 1960s and 1970s by saying: "We may no longer know what kind of society this is, but *we do know* that it is a market economy, and the best way to make a market economy work is through a minimum of governmental interference." Increasingly, public debate has come to hinge, not on what kind of society we are or want to be, but on what the needs of the economy are. Hence, a broad range of social policies are now debated almost entirely in terms of how they fit in with the imperatives of the market.

This broad substitution of a particular type of economic theory for a more general understanding of society is unfortunate. It means, above all, the domination of our politics by claims of "false necessity"—arguments that market realities radically constrain our range of political and social choices.[5] We have been told repeatedly, for example, that our efforts to be compassionate to the poor through welfare programs have necessarily backfired because tampering with the operation of the labor market will always produce negative economic and social consequences.[6] The fact that the "free market" premises of such arguments have repeatedly been challenged over the past hundred years of intellectual history makes no difference. In fact, the utter defeat of "free market" ideas in the course of the Great Depression of the 1930s is now almost completely forgotten. This demonstrates that when social theories lose their power to make sense of people's experiences, even previously discredited theories can be resurrected and pressed into service.

Postindustrial theory has the potential to fill this gap in understanding by providing a persuasive map of contemporary societies. To date, however, this has not happened. Even among social theorists, postindustrial ideas remain at the margins of contemporary debate and their impact on broader public debates has been limited. If the reasons for this failure can be grasped and overcome, postindustrial theory could illuminate our present political and social circumstances.[7]

5. False necessity is a central category in the thought of Roberto Mangabeira Unger. See, in particular, *False Necessity: Anti-Necessitarian Social Theory in the Service of Radical Democracy* (Cambridge: Cambridge University Press, 1987).

6. For a full discussion, see Fred Block, "Rethinking the Political Economy of the Welfare State," in Fred Block, Richard A. Cloward, Barbara Ehrenreich, and Frances Fox Piven, *The Mean Season: The Attack on the Welfare State* (New York: Pantheon Books, 1987), 109–60.

7. While this book was being written, the concept of postmodernism came to broad prominence. Although originating in the analysis of art, it has been broadened to characterize all of social life, and it now competes directly with the concept of postindustrialism. What is interesting about the concept of postmodernity is that it explicitly acknowledges that we are living in a period in which the master concepts of social science, the meta-narratives of modernity, no longer make sense of people's experience. See Jean-François Lyotard, *The Postmodern Condition: A Report on Knowledge* (Minneapolis: University of Minnesota Press, 1984). Some theorists of the postmodern might question whether it is possible or desirable to fill this gap, but for others there is a clear need for a postmodern social theory. It would seem that the choice of the label *postmodern* or *postindustrial* to describe the intellectual project of constructing such a theory is arbitrary.

The Theory of Postindustrialism

Daniel Bell first formulated the concept of postindustrial society in articles published in the 1960s, and he elaborated it in *The Coming of Post-Industrial Society*, published in 1973.[8] In the same period, a series of other scholars also explored the idea of a parallel historical discontinuity—sometimes referring to the "information society," the "service society," or the "technetronic society."[9] In 1980 Alvin Toffler's popularized version of the postindustrial argument, *The Third Wave*, was a major bestseller.[10] Yet instead of invigorating the discussion, Toffler's book appears to have marked an ending. In the 1980s there have been relatively few major statements of the postindustrial position,[11] and figures such as Bell and Alain Touraine have turned to other questions. Moreover, there are also signs in the 1980s of an explicit rejection of the postindustrial framework. A widely reviewed 1987 volume by Stephen S. Cohen and John Zysman is subtitled *The Myth of the Post-Industrial Economy*.[12]

Even so, the term *postindustrial* has actually seen broad usage as a label, despite the fact that neither social theorists nor an educated public have taken up the idea seriously. The term is generally used as a relatively empty synonym for modernity; "postindustrial America" is a livelier way for journalists or academics to say "contemporary America." But these uses of the term do not involve any serious effort to make sense of the specific character of contemporary societies.

There is a reason for the wide appropriation of the term even while the theory has been marginalized. The term rests on the idea

---

8. References are to the paperback edition (New York: Basic Books, 1976).

9. See the references in Bell, *Coming of Post-Industrial Society*, 51–55. See also Alain Touraine, *The Postindustrial Society* (New York: Random House, 1971); Greg Calvert and Carol Nieman, *A Disrupted History: The New Left and the New Capitalism* (New York: Random House, 1971).

10. New York: William Morrow, 1980.

11. Among the significant exceptions has been the writing of Larry Hirschhorn. See, in particular, *Beyond Mechanization: Work and Technology in a Postindustrial Age* (Cambridge, Mass.: MIT Press, 1984) and *The Workplace Within: Psychodynamics of Organizational Life* (Cambridge, Mass.: MIT Press, 1988).

12. Cohen and Zysman, *Manufacturing Matters: The Myth of the Post-Industrial Economy* (New York: Basic Books, 1987).

of three great phases in human development—agricultural society, industrial society, and postindustrial society. Yet the current phase is not positively characterized; it is simply that which comes after industrial society. *Postindustrial* is a kind of marker that stands in place of the more substantive label that will presumably emerge somewhat later in the historical process. Just as the phrase *industrial society* did not become widely used until long after the beginning of the Industrial Revolution, it may be some years before this new phase of human history can be adequately characterized.[13]

There is also a deeper problem that accounts for the neglect of postindustrialism by many social theorists. The concept of postindustrial society carries much of the baggage of nineteenth-century evolutionary thought. The typology of agricultural, industrial, and postindustrial societies bears a close resemblance to many of the great nineteenth-century evolutionary schemas that delineated the stages of the development of human society to show how each stage gave rise to the next. The terms used to characterize a particular phase of human development by Comte, or Marx, or Spencer were not simply labels; on the contrary, they were designed to capture the essential features of that stage of human development. Moreover, the evolutionary impulse—the pressure to move to the next stage of development—was closely tied to the essential features of each historical stage. Hence, for Marx, it was part of the very nature of capitalism that it would produce its own gravediggers—the revolutionary proletariat.

Much of contemporary social theory is persuasively critical of these nineteenth-century traditions of thought. While it is generally recognized that these evolutionary schemas continue to shape—often unconsciously—our own modes of thinking, they have been systematically criticized for their essentialism, their optimism, and their determinism.[14] These theories tend to reduce a complex social reality to a single essence, but this is a highly problematic operation. How does one determine what is essential and what is epiphenomenal? Or to put it in other terms, contemporary

13. There have been many contenders for a more substantive term—*service society, information age, age of cybernetics,* and so on—but none of these convey the breadth of transformation implicit in *postindustrialism.*

14. This critique is one of the fundamental themes elaborated in Unger, *Politics.*

social scientists tend to be more self-conscious about the problematic relation between intellectual concepts and the reality that they are supposed to comprehend. The idea of "industrial society," for example, is a useful abstraction that highlights commonalities among otherwise diverse societies, but one would not expect the "industrialness" of these diverse societies to provide the master clue for understanding the future development of all of the societies that fit the category. The optimism of nineteenth-century thought has long since been brutally undermined by this century's experience with genocide, total war, and brutal statist regimes. Moreover, much contemporary scholarship has been sharply critical of the determinism implicit in these evolutionary schemes. The idea that social arrangements are largely determined by economic or cultural dynamics has been challenged by a vast body of work emphasizing the variety of historical contingencies that shape social development.

The problem, in short, is that postindustrial theory appears to be in conflict with the current emphases of social theory. It has been perceived as deterministic, evolutionary, and essentialist in a period when those are seen as serious intellectual errors. Some postindustrial theorists, particularly Daniel Bell, have sought to avoid these associations; he argues explicitly that his concept of postindustrialism was not meant to capture the inner dynamics of advanced societies, but was rather intended as a "speculative construct" against which future developments could be measured. Moreover, Bell has himself contributed to the current antideterminist emphasis in social theory with his argument that culture, politics, and economy each operate according to their own independent "axial principles," rather than one determining the others.[15] Nevertheless, Bell's work on postindustrialism has often been misread and other theorists fell directly into the trap of formulating postindustrial theory in terms of an inevitable process of social development.[16] As a result, postindustrial theory has come to be

15. This idea is developed by Bell in *The Cultural Contradictions of Capitalism* (New York: Basic Books, 1977), which was actually carved from the same 1,000-page manuscript as *The Coming of Post-Industrial Society*.

16. This criticism applies as well to Fred Block and Larry Hirschhorn, "New Productive Forces and the Contradictions of Contemporary Capitalism," in Fred Block, *Revising State Theory: Essays in Politics and Postindustrialism* (Philadelphia: Temple University Press, 1987), 99–126.

perceived as inextricably linked to evolutionary and deterministic assumptions.

It follows from these points that a revitalization of postindustrial theory must do two things. First, the theory must be reformulated in a way that definitively separates it from deterministic and evolutionary readings. Second, the theory must have more content; it must help us to make sense of our own society and of the choices that we and the society face. On one level, these are contradictory goals. The more room a theory allows for contingency, the less well it will serve as a guide to action. Yet at another level, these seemingly contradictory goals can be resolved.

Reformulating Postindustrial Theory, 1

The first step in such a reformulation is to recognize that social science concepts are not simply analytic abstractions, but are themselves cultural tools that play an important role in creating a semblance of order out of the potential chaos of social life. This insight makes it possible to redefine postindustrialism as the consequence of the collapse of the theory of industrial society.

Master concepts such as capitalism or industrialism are important guides to action in the shaping of social institutions and practices. Hence, for example, the particular way in which educational institutions have been constructed over the past century has had much to do with implicit or explicit ideas about what kind of society this is. Those educational reformers who succeeded in linking their proposals to widely shared views of the direction in which the society was moving tended to be more successful than those who were unable to connect their reform proposals to the master concepts of social science.[17]

These master concepts play a critical role in shaping perceptions of the relative degree of "fit" among the different institutions of society. There is an ongoing process of institutional selection through which people reshape and reform social institutions along particular lines; this is a political process—in the broadest sense—in which different groups with different interests struggle to in-

17. One of the most influential of these ideas has been the notion that this is a market society, and that other social institutions should contribute to market efficiency. This idea is criticized in chapter 3.

fluence the outcome. But the balance of forces among competing groups is itself influenced by ideas of what makes sense in this kind of society, and it is here that social theory plays a major role by helping to shape the way people think about particular institutions. Moreover, whatever the legacy of past struggles in a particular society, social theory can shape perceptions about the "fit" between different social institutions and practices. Since "objective" criteria for evaluating the degree of functional relation among institutions are inherently problematic, social theory has fairly wide latitude to define the reality as one of fit or lack of fit.

Through the last decades of the nineteenth century and most of the twentieth, the master concept of "industrial society" has played a central role in defining social reality in the United States and other developed societies. As Richard Badham writes, "Beyond the limited confines of academic discourse, the classical image of industrial society has played an important role in structuring contemporary social identity and political programmes."[18] The vision of a society organized around a continuing increase in the efficiency and scope of manufacturing has served as a kind of template for shaping social struggles and social reforms. In the Progressive Era, for example, the idea of industrial society served as the guiding principle in efforts to reshape American institutions. Similarly, reforms during the New Deal and in the immediate post–World War II period continued to rest on the assumption of the centrality of factory labor. To be sure, there have always been important aspects of social reality that were inconsistent with the concept of "industrial society"—such as the role of African-Americans in southern agriculture—but the idea of "industrial society" still served to give the appearance of coherence to American institutions.[19]

The capacity of social science concepts to define reality is not, however, unlimited; changes in society can create "theoretical anomalies" that become progressively more glaring and that can

18. Richard J. Badham, *Theories of Industrial Society* (New York: St. Martin's Press, 1986), 3.

19. There are strong parallels between the argument here and that of Scott Lash and John Urry, *The End of Organized Capitalism* (Madison: University of Wisconsin Press, 1987). In analyzing a number of advanced capitalist societies, they distinguish between a more coherent period of "organized capitalism" and the current, less coherent, period of "disorganized capitalism."

undermine the persuasiveness of long-accepted definitions of reality. Three social trends emerged in the 1960s that could not easily be explained or understood as part of industrial society. Each had long historical antecedents, but it was only in the late 1960s that they began to constitute anomalies. Moreover, these trends continued to accelerate through the 1970s and 1980s.

The first of these "postindustrial" trends is the growing importance of services in the economy, and the declining weight of goods production—manufacturing, farming, and mining—in total employment. Although the service category is highly heterogeneous and includes a multitude of different types of activity, the point remains that the factory floor has ceased to be the central locus of employment. But it is not just the statistical reality that is important; it is critical that the most dramatic social conflicts of the 1960s tended to occur in service institutions—universities, welfare offices, and hospitals.

The second trend is the arrival of computer-based automation. This emerged haltingly in the 1960s and has expanded since then. As Larry Hirschhorn and others have argued, computer-based automation tends to change both the organization and the experience of work in both blue-collar and white-collar settings.[20] In particular, the characteristic "industrial" pattern of work organization, in which workers are given narrowly defined repetitious tasks that can be done with relatively little attention, is fundamentally disrupted. Debate still rages over the precise impact of computerization on workers' skill levels, but there is considerable evidence that the new forms of work require higher levels of attention and concentration by employees (this issue will be addressed at greater length in chapter 4).

The third trend is the decline of patriarchy and the breakdown of the linear life course. Earlier patterns of female subordination, based on the restriction of most women to the domestic sphere, have given way to the massive entrance of women into the paid labor force. This movement has been accompanied by a full-scale critique of social inequalities based on gender. Although many of these inequalities remain, it is difficult to exaggerate the cultural significance of the recent changes in women's roles.

20. Hirschhorn, *Beyond Mechanization*, 113–69.

Moreover, the decline of patriarchal arrangements is linked to other changes in the adult life course. For some time, men's lives had been organized around the "one-career, one-marriage imperative"; men were supposed to remain married to the same person for life and remain in the same occupation.[21] Progress through the life course tended to be linear; men were supposed to proceed from education to work to retirement without interruptions or reversals. This pattern came apart—both marriages and occupational careers became more fluid as divorce rates increased and midlife career changes became more common. Now both men and women are more likely to move in and out of the labor force at various times in the course of their lives, the role of education and training has increased dramatically for people over twenty-five, and even the meaning of retirement has begun to change. Together, the changes in women's roles and the decline of the linear life course have fundamentally changed the individual's experience of adulthood.[22]

Each trend reverses patterns long identified as fundamental to industrialism, and postindustrial theory was initially developed by Daniel Bell and others in an attempt to explain these discontinuities in social development. "Postindustrial society" is the historical period that begins when the concept of industrial society ceases to provide an adequate account of actual social developments. This definition is meant to locate the key change as occurring at the level of ideas and understanding—that is, our loss of a persuasive master concept for making sense of our own society.

There are two special virtues to this way of defining the postindustrial era. First, such a definition does not assume a particular theory of how society is constituted or of which social dynamics are most fundamental. It is possible to recognize that the society has entered a postindustrial era even in the absence of a theory that

21. Seymour Sarason, *Work, Aging and Social Change: Professionals and the One Life–One Career Imperative* (New York: Free Press, 1977).

22. These changes in gender roles and the adult life course have been accompanied by the spread of a sensibility that holds that individuals should be free to develop their capacities in response to their own needs. The negative consequences of this sensibility have been a central theme for Daniel Bell, *The Cultural Contradictions of Capitalism;* Christopher Lasch, *The Culture of Narcissism* (New York: Norton, 1978); Robert N. Bellah, Richard Madsen, William M. Sullivan, Ann Swioler, and Steven M. Tipton, *Habits of the Heart: Individualism and Commitment in American Life* (Berkeley: University of California Press, 1985).

explains why those "postindustrial" trends have occurred. In short, postindustrial theory need not be wedded to one position or the other in the debate between materialist and idealist theories of historical change.

Second, this definition highlights the fact that postindustrialism is a period of transition in which efforts to define what kind of society this is and should be take on a special urgency and intensity. It is a period in which basic questions about the organization of society are "up for grabs" and the society can experience rapid shifts in political ideology. The rapidity with which liberalism has fallen from popular favor is an example of such a shift. In this kind of transition, those who are able to shape the definition of what kind of society comes after industrialism will have extra leverage in the struggle to shape social institutions.

Reformulating Postindustrial Theory, 2

This way of formulating the postindustrial problematic solves one problem, but it does not address the other. If postindustrial theory is to contribute to people's understanding of their society, it must provide more than the claim that there are important discontinuities in social development that undermine previous ways of thinking. It must begin to map out the patterns and characteristic conflicts of the emergent postindustrial society, so that individuals are able to recognize their situations and reshape their behavior and expectations accordingly. Yet this is the recurring paradox. Is such mapping possible without a return to deterministic formulations that assume that the future shape of things already exists in embryonic forms? Moreover, even the development of such a map can be seen as an effort to close off historical possibilities that might still be open.

Constructing social theories is, however, always a political act; there are implicit value positions embedded in any analysis of how social institutions operate and how individuals make choices in particular situations. Hence, there cannot be a purely objective effort to map out the patterns of an emergent social order. This does not mean that any proposed mapping is as good as another; different mappings can do more or less to make sense of the experiences of different groups of people who will struggle over the proper definition of social reality.

There is a methodology, however, that can minimize both the problem of subjectivism and the problem of prematurely closing off historical possibilities. This method has three steps. It begins with the close examination of actual trends and patterns observable in social life, while avoiding any effort to intuit abstractly the basic organizing principles of an imagined postindustrial future. The idea is simply to map emergent changes in social life. This procedure has pitfalls, because short-lived phenomena can always be seized upon as harbingers of new social arrangements. Moreover, social change occurs unevenly, and in some realms of social life, it might be impossible to detect new patterns of social organization. Nevertheless, the effort to build a theory of postindustrial society out of analyses rooted in the empirical world seems the only approach that can possibly be fruitful.

The second step is to demonstrate, where appropriate, how these observable patterns conflict with the system of categories that has organized social life in the industrial period.[23] Analyses of the decline of the linear life course, for example, show how few individuals are able or willing to organize their adulthood along established lines.[24] Studies of automated workplaces demonstrate that the historic distinction between work and learning as separate activities that take place in separate institutional arenas has increasingly broken down as work and learning become more closely intertwined.[25] The goal of such analyses is to demonstrate both the inadequacies of the older categories and the positive and negative consequences of their decay. As social action spills over the es-

23. Categories work imperfectly; there are always exceptions and anomalies and individuals or pieces of data that must be treated with some violence to fit where they are thought to belong. However, the argument here is that there are variations across time in the level and obviousness of these imperfections in systems of categories.

24. See Larry Hirschhorn, "Social Policy and the Life Cycle: A Developmental Perspective," *Social Service Review* 51, no. 3 (September 1977); Block and Hirschhorn, "New Productive Forces and the Contradictions of Contemporary Capitalism." See also Carmen Sirianni, "The Self-Management of Time in Post-Industrial Society: Towards a Democratic Alternative," *Socialist Review* 88 (October–December 1988): 5–56.

25. Hirschhorn, *Beyond Mechanization.*

tablished categories, it simultaneously opens up possibilities for human creativity and development and produces distress and dislocation.[26]

The third step is the one in which normative concerns become central; the task is to conceive of new categories and new patterns of organizing institutional life that can minimize the negative consequences and maximize the positive consequences of this transition. Hence, the idea of a developmental life course was theorized as a way of moving beyond the breakdown of the linear life course and the study of automated work settings has led to a discussion of institutional arrangements that could effectively combine work and learning.

A body of work built up along these lines would probably not cohere into the kind of unified theory of society developed by nineteenth-century thinkers. However, it could add up to a powerful social map that made sense of the society for individuals and groups and allowed them to understand their personal troubles in relation to historical processes.[27] The body of work would also chart a range of possibilities for a politics of restructuring social institutions.

The present study is intended to develop such a postindustrial analysis of economic life through the use of this method. The choice of economic life does *not* rest on a conviction that the economy determines the rest of social life. In fact, much of the argument takes issue with the tendency of both neoclassical economics and Marxism to treat the economy as an analytically separate and determining realm of society. Nor is my argument that the emergence of a postindustrial society depends most critically on economic changes. I am not taking a position on the relative role of cultural, political, social, and economic forces in creating a postindustrial society. All are important and, if anything, it is politics that is most critical, because people's political understanding of what kind of

26. For a powerful example of this method at work in describing the psychological consequences of traditional bureaucracy in the postindustrial era, see Hirschhorn, *Workplace Within*.

27. This is the now classic definition of the sociological project elaborated by C. Wright Mills, *The Sociological Imagination* (New York: Oxford University Press, 1959).

society they live in influences the way they mobilize or fail to mobilize to achieve certain goals.

The analysis of changes in the economy is developed through a critique of the central categories of neoclassical economics. Neoclassical economics developed in an effort to make sense of a specifically industrial economy, but recent trends have created serious anomalies both for neoclassical theory and for people trying to use that theory in their day-to-day lives.

There is historical precedent for the inability of an established economic tradition to cope with historical changes. Little remained of the tradition of physiocratic economics after the Industrial Revolution, and the classical economists built their system on quite different foundations. The argument of this book is that a similarly radical transformation in economic thought will be necessary to make sense of the economy in a period of postindustrial transition.

Since it has already been noted that a certain type of economic theory has come to play a dominant role in the society's understanding of itself, a critique of some central concepts of modern economics has important political implications. To be sure, economists are not a homogeneous group; they take a range of different positions on central questions of economic and social policy, such as how important is it to balance the federal budget, how much emphasis should be placed on "deregulating" markets, and so on. However, there are areas of broad consensus within the discipline of economics in the United States—such as the preference for market allocation, the emphasis on investment in tangible capital as a means for expanding output, and the tacit commitment to the idea that employees must accept the authority of their employers.[28]

However, if these kinds of consensual economic views are built on industrial foundations that are no longer sound, then there is a justification for a fundamental rethinking of how economic institutions should be organized in this society. Reforms previously dismissed as inconsistent with economic rationality would have to be reconsidered, as would many of the specific assumptions that shape policy-making in a broad range of different fields. The way would be

---

28. There are, of course, dissenters within economics who question each of these elements of consensus, but their influence is relatively limited.

open for radically new approaches to the organization of economic life.

This book indeed argues that the core positions of neoclassical economics have been weakened by postindustrial trends, and that there is a pressing need to develop a new framework for economic thought. Four key concepts in the neoclassical tradition—the market, labor, capital, and Gross National Product will be critically examined. On the basis of these critiques, the outlines of an alternative framework for thinking about questions of economic policy will be suggested.

Postindustrialism in International Perspective

At the outset, however, it is essential to say something about the relation between national societies and the international economy. Much of the argument elaborated in the rest of this book focuses almost entirely on the U.S. domestic economy. This is a glaring omission in a period in which many analysts have stressed the growing internationalization of the world economy. It hardly needs reiterating that many of the world's major corporations manage subsidiaries operating in a wide range of different countries and that trends in a particular country's balance of international trade and payments will have a significant impact on both its domestic economy and politics.

Part of the motivation for ignoring these trends and focusing the analysis in this study on the domestic economy is simply the need to make an already ambitious project more manageable. Yet there are also sound intellectual justifications for this narrower focus.

One justification is theoretical; it rests on a way of conceptualizing the international economy that differs from the conventional view. In the conventional view, the existence of an international economy is analytically prior to the domestic economy; each national economy is subject to varying degrees of pressure and constraints that flow from the dynamics of international transactions in goods and services, capital, and, to a lesser degree, labor. This view tends to naturalize the world economy—that is, to see it as having a life of its own independent of politics. Proponents of this view recognize that nations will interfere with the dynamics of that world economy by erecting tariff barriers or by subsidizing their foreign trade, but these measures are conceptualized as political interventions in an economic realm.

The alternative view is that the particular structure of the world economy—the rules of the game that determine international economic transactions—emerges out of political negotiations and conflicts among nation-states. The balance of political forces within and among nations shapes, and can reshape, the structure of the international economy. Moreover, there is wide latitude in the nature of such rules; the level of state involvement in influencing flows of goods and capital can vary enormously.

In the period since World War II, the United States has played the dominant role in shaping the rules of the game in the international economy.[29] The particular direction of U.S. influence has in turn been shaped by the relative power of different domestic social and political actors, as well as by the economic understandings that have dominated policy debates. It seems plausible that if both those economic understandings and the balance of social forces within the country were to change radically, U.S. influence over the structure of the international economy could be used to reshape the rules. Although the United States would have to win the support of other countries for such changes, there is good reason to imagine that this country would find allies among those who have long been dissatisfied with the status quo.

The point can clearly be seen with a concrete example. It is widely recognized that current rules allow an extraordinarily high degree of freedom for international capital flows. Huge pools of savings can almost instantaneously be transferred from one country to another. These transfers can have a highly disruptive effect on efforts to stabilize exchange rates and on the effectiveness of monetary policies at the national level. Moreover, the threat of massive capital outflows can discourage governments from pursuing certain domestic reforms that might be opposed by vocal segments of the international business community. The point is that this high degree of freedom for international capital flows is not a necessary and inevitable feature of a world economy. In fact, even the post–World

29. See Fred Block, *The Origins of International Economic Disorder: A Study of U.S. International Monetary Policy from World War II to the Present* (Berkeley: University of California Press, 1977) for an elaboration of this argument.

War II economic miracle in Western Europe occurred through 1958 within a system of exchange controls that limited international capital mobility. With a significant shift in U.S. policy, it is possible to conceive of international agreement on measures that would place new limits on the free movement of capital that would, in turn, give national governments greater control over their domestic economies.

The other reason for focusing exclusively on the domestic economy is empirical; theorists of internationalization have exaggerated the extent to which U.S. policy options are constrained by international economic competition. Those who are concerned with internationalization emphasize the tendency for American firms to shift production facilities abroad, particularly to low-wage areas in the Third World. This pattern is well documented in certain industries, but two points are frequently neglected. First, a much larger share of domestic job loss in manufacturing has occurred as a result of automation than through the shift of production to the Third World.[30] Second, there is now an important countertrend to the export of manufacturing jobs. Many firms that are shifting to more advanced production technologies are finding it economical to build production facilities in the United States, since labor costs represent a negligible fraction of total costs.[31] Moreover, the increasing use in the United States of Japanese techniques of inventory control that emphasize just-in-time availability of parts also militates against the globalization of production; such techniques require close monitoring of nearby suppliers.[32]

Theorists of internationalization also point to the growing U.S. trade deficit as further evidence that the U.S. economy is under pressure from low-wage economies in the Third World. Yet analysis of U.S. trade in manufacturing goods indicates that the bulk of U.S. imports still come from other developed capitalist countries that

30. This conclusion is rooted in a comparison of trends in output per person-hour in domestic manufacturing with trends in the growth of Third World manufacturing employment.

31. This trend is even apparent in the apparel industry. See "Why Made-in-America Is Back in Style," *Business Week*, November 7, 1988, 116–18.

32. Richard J. Schonberger, *World Class Manufacturing: The Lessons of Simplicity Applied* (New York: Free Press, 1986), 163–64.

have quite comparable standards of living. Third World imports dominate only among less sophisticated goods like apparel and textiles.[33] The problems in the U.S. trade balance reflect the growing difficulty of the U.S. economy in competing with Western Europe and Japan in the production of sophisticated manufactured goods. Yet these difficulties have less to do with such purely economic variables as wage levels and much more to do with the strength or weakness of institutional arrangements for managing innovation.

Yet even this problem of international trade competition is rarely understood in the proper context. The reality is that services such as housing, health care, restaurant meals, and transportation constitute the dominant and growing share of what consumers in the United States purchase.[34] It is in the nature of most of these consumer services that they are insulated from international trade; they can only be produced domestically. Hence, the intense international competition in manufactured goods represents a struggle over a diminishing share of the consumer dollar. The shift to services means that these developed economies actually become in some ways less international over time, since internationally traded goods represent a diminishing share of total consumption.

In short, the analysis that follows rests on the claim that the international economy represents a less important constraint on the structure of the domestic U.S. economy than is generally believed. First, since it played a disproportionate role in shaping the current rules of the game for international economic transactions, it seems plausible to imagine that the United States has the power to initiate a major change in those rules. Second, arguments about the pressures of international trade competition tend to ignore the fact that the bulk of the competition comes from other developed countries. Moreover, developments in production processes often militate against the export of jobs to low-wage production platforms. Finally, the growing role of services operates as a counterweight to the increasing international competition in goods production.

33. For the relevant data, see Block, "Rethinking the Political Economy of the Welfare State," 141.
34. By 1984, services represented 59.1 percent of all consumer purchases. Ibid., 145.

Outline of the Argument

Chapter 2 lays out the theoretical foundations for the critique of economic categories, showing how the tradition of economic sociology can be used to challenge the tendency of economists and other theorists to "naturalize" the economy—to see existing economic arrangements as natural and necessary. The next four chapters elaborate critiques of the concept of the market, of labor, of capital, and of Gross National Product. Chapter 7 brings these critiques together by elaborating an alternative approach to economic policy—a society organized around qualitative growth.

Chapter Two

Economic Sociology

This chapter lays out the foundations for the critique of economic categories that is developed in subsequent chapters. This critique is derived from the tradition of economic sociology, which has only recently reemerged as a significant area of scholarly work. Economic sociology provides a powerful means for bringing together the many criticisms of modern economics elaborated by Marxists, institutional economists, sociologists, and others.

Two different—albeit interrelated—critiques of economics are developed here. The first is a general critique of the methodology of neoclassical economics—namely, that neoclassical economics has never provided a fully adequate understanding of the economies that it seeks to analyze. The second is a historical critique that emphasizes that postindustrial trends have significantly undermined the key categories of neoclassical economics. The link is that recent developments have brought to the surface long-standing weaknesses in economic method.

The Critique of Economic Methods

The methodology of neoclassical economics rests on two basic building blocks. The first is the idea that the economy is an analytically separate realm of society that can be understood in terms of its own internal dynamics. Economists are perfectly aware that economic behavior is influenced by politics and culture, but they see these as exogenous factors that can be safely bracketed as one develops a framework that focuses on purely economic factors. Just as the physicist will ignore factors such as wind and rain in initial calculations of how fast a unit of a particular mass falls to earth, so the economist also begins by dealing with the most theoretically significant variables—those that are internal to the economy.

The second key foundation is the assumption that individuals act rationally to maximize utilities. Here, again, economists are acutely aware that individuals are capable of acting irrationally or in pursuit of goals other than the maximization of utility, but the strategy of excluding these deviations from the rationality principle is justified by the effort to identify the core dynamics of an economy. As with studies of the impact of exogenous factors, economists postpone any exploration of deviations from rationality until after they have successfully identified how economic actors are supposed to behave.

It is on these two foundations that marginalist economics built its magnificent structure—a model of the self-regulating market that integrates and harmonizes transactions in markets for products, labor, and capital. Since all commodities—including labor and capital—are bought and sold on competitive markets by actors interested in the maximization of utilities, price changes will equilibrate supply and demand. The result of the millions of transactions that are mediated by the price mechanism will be a general economic equilibrium in which all resources are utilized in the most efficient way possible.

This model is extraordinarily powerful because it depicts an economy in which utility is maximized and there is an optimal use of resources. Moreover, the model is also dynamic; it has the capacity to respond to change. When a shock occurs, such as a technological innovation that makes it possible to produce widgets with half the labor, the equilibrating mechanism works to restore order. The combination of the fall in the price of the displaced labor and the reinvestment of the increased profits in the widget industry will mean that some entrepreneur will put the displaced workers back to work producing a different product.

There are many problems with this model of a self-regulating market. For one thing, efforts to work out the mathematics of a general equilibrium model have run into serious obstacles.[1] But the

---

1. Frank Hahn, "General Equilibrium Theory," in Daniel Bell and Irving Kristol, eds., *The Crisis in Economic Theory* (New York: Basic Books, 1981), 123–38.

central issue here is not the model of market self-regulation as much as its methodological foundations. Economic sociology calls into question the basic strategies of explanation used by economists.

The tradition of economic sociology challenges the idea that the economy is an analytically separate realm of society that has its own internal dynamics.[2] On the contrary, economic transactions are seen to be continuously shaped and influenced by social, political, and cultural factors. The preferences of individuals in maximizing utility are one obvious example—how does an individual weigh the relative value of more money as against more leisure, or of a new automobile as against a new kitchen. Economists argue that such preferences are formed exogenously; they are recognized to be social in nature. But most economic analyses proceed on the assumption that regardless of how such preferences are formed, they quickly become fixed. This is a necessary assumption if the price mechanism is to produce a stable equilibrium between supply and demand. Yet there is ample empirical evidence of efforts to alter these preferences on a day-to-day basis; this is one of the key purposes of advertising. Moreover, one can imagine many circumstances in which individuals alter their preferences in response to the behavior of others, as Veblen long ago stressed in his analysis of conspicuous consumption.[3] In fact, there is often a strategic dimension to preference change where individuals deliberately alter their preferences in order to gain relative advantage over others, as when a style of clothing or furniture is abandoned by status groups because it has become too "common." Even changes in preferences that occur more slowly—such as the shift in married women's relative ordering of paid work and housework—can have such powerful consequences that it is folly to exclude them from analysis.

Another instance where economic transactions are obviously shaped by social factors is the relationship between employer and employees. Economists working in a neoclassical tradition have sometimes asserted that it makes no difference whether the work-

2. For a valuable recent survey of economic sociology that includes an explicit contrast of the two traditions, see Richard Swedberg, "Economic Sociology: Past and Present," *Current Sociology* 35, no. 1 (Spring 1987): 1–221.

3. Thorstein Veblen, *The Theory of the Leisure Class: An Economic Study of Institutions* (1899; reprint, New York: Mentor Books, 1953).

ers hire the capitalist or the other way around.[4] Marginalist theory argues that both factors of production—labor and capital—are rewarded commensurately with their marginal utility. Since prices are determined in a competitive market, there is no inherent advantage to being the capitalist.

Yet this position has increasingly been subject to serious criticism, as analysts have recognized that employees can vary the intensity of their work effort.[5] Such variations in work intensity make the social relations of the workplace a central variable in determining the efficiency with which economic inputs are transformed into outputs. However, the marginalist tradition systematically neglects the range of factors that influence the intensity of work effort.

Moreover, as Durkheim emphasized, even the contract itself—a basic element of any economic transaction—rests on noncontractual elements.[6] Both buyers and sellers require certain cultural understandings before it is possible for them to agree on terms. There is also a legal regime that plays a central role in influencing these transactions. There are different possible legal concepts of property and ownership, so that the particular legal regime will influence the kinds of transactions that take place. The legal regime also establishes the recourse that parties will have in the case of contractual violations, and this is another influence on the behavior of economic actors.

Parallel points can also be made about the second foundation of neoclassical economics—the assumption of rational action by individuals to maximize utilities. One strand of argument suggests that the model of "economic man" on which much economic analysis rests is itself a consequence of social arrangements. Karl Polanyi

4. Paul Samuelson, "Wages and Interest: A Modern Dissection of Marxian Economic Models," *American Economic Review* 47 (December 1957): 884–912, cited in Samuel Bowles, "The Production Process in a Competitive Economy: Walrasian, Neo-Hobbesian, and Marxian Models," *American Economic Review* 75, no. 1 (March 1985): 16–36.

5. See Bowles, "Production Process in a Competitive Economy"; George A. Akerlof and Janet L. Yellen, *Efficiency Wage Models of the Labor Market* (Cambridge: Cambridge University Press, 1985).

6. Emile Durkheim, *The Division of Labor in Society* (1893; tr. 1933, reprint, New York: Free Press, 1964), 200–219.

emphasizes that it is culture that sets out the goals of individual action that are then embedded in social arrangements:

Single out whatever motive you please, and organize production in such a manner as to make that motive that individual's incentive to produce, and you will have induced a picture of man as altogether absorbed by that particular motive. Let that motive be religious, political, or aesthetic; let it be pride, prejudice, love, or envy; and man will appear as essentially religious, political, aesthetic, proud, prejudiced, engrossed in love or envy. . . .

As a matter of fact, human beings will labor for a large variety of reasons as long as things are arranged accordingly.[7]

The point is that the elevation of material self-interest to dominance over all other motives was itself the consequence of a cultural process.

Another set of criticisms has emphasized the problematic nature of individual rationality. Herbert Simon has used the term *bounded rationality* to describe behavior that is "intendedly rational, but only limitedly so."[8] The problem is that individuals usually lack the information, the computational skills, and the time to act with perfect rationality. They will try to do the best they can in the circumstances, but this might be quite different from what an economic model might predict. Moreover, Oliver Williamson has stressed that under conditions of complexity and uncertainty, the gap between bounded rationality and perfect rationality can be substantial.[9]

Moreover, recent work has also emphasized that what constitutes rational action by an individual depends to a substantial de-

7. Karl Polanyi, *Primitive, Archaic, and Modern Economies* (New York: Doubleday, Anchor Books, 1968), 68.

8. Herbert A. Simon, *Administrative Behavior: A Study of Decision-making Processes in Administrative Organization* (New York: Macmillan, 1947), cited in Oliver E. Williamson, *Markets and Hierarchies, Analysis and Antitrust Implications: A Study in the Economics of Internal Organization* (New York: Free Press, 1975), 21.

9. Williamson, *Markets and Hierarchies*, 22–23. For extended discussions of the problem of rationality in economic theory, see Geoffrey Hodgson, *Economics and Institutions: A Manifesto for a Modern Institutional Economics* (Philadelphia: University of Pennsylvania Press, 1988), and Amitai Etzioni, *The Moral Dimension: Towards a New Economics* (New York: Free Press, 1988).

gree on the context.[10] Mark Granovetter, for example, has emphasized that while it might appear more rational for a purchasing agent to buy at the lowest possible price, a firm's need for good relations with suppliers over time might suggest another purchasing strategy altogether.[11] Similar findings have come from work in game theory that has explored the tension between formal rationality and substantive rationality. In a Prisoners' Dilemma game,[12] for example, the rational pursuit of self-interest by actors will generally lead to an outcome that is undesirable or substantively irrational for the participants. However, it has been shown that when the Prisoners' Dilemma is repeated a number of times—so that the participants are aware that their pursuit of self-interest is occurring in the context of an ongoing relationship—they are able to develop strategies that are rational in their outcomes. This finding is important because it emphasizes that the ongoing relationships in which people are embedded are extremely important in allowing individuals to act rationally.[13]

These criticisms of the two methodological foundations of neoclassical economics call into question the soundness of an approach that analytically separates the economy from the rest of society. Even more important, these arguments highlight the tendency of economic arguments to "naturalize" the economy—to treat economic arrangements that have a specific history and context as timeless products of the need to economize scarce resources. A method that obscures from view the social, cultural, and political determinants of economic action results in analysis that is ahistori-

10. See also Amartya K. Sen, "Rational Fools: A Critique of the Behavioral Foundations of Economic Theory," *Philosophy and Public Affairs* 6, no. 4 (Summer 1977): 317–44.

11. Mark Granovetter, "Economic Action and Social Structure: The Problem of Embeddedness," *American Journal of Sociology* 91, no. 3 (November 1985): 481–510.

12. In the Prisoners' Dilemma, the convicts have two options—to implicate the other or to remain silent. Each must make this choice with no knowledge of how the other one will act.

13. An even more fundamental critique is that the focus on rational action ignores the vast array of nonrational and irrational actions that occurs within all social settings—the economy included. For a discussion of the sociological tradition's neglect of the nonrational and irrational, see Alan Sica, *Weber, Irrationality, and Social Order* (Berkeley: University of California Press, 1988).

cal and, through a tautological procedure, continually rediscovers the centrality of purely economic motives.

Such a tendency to naturalize the economy has played a central role in social thought since Adam Smith. As Polanyi argues, both the liberal and Marxist traditions have been marked by their adherence to the "economistic fallacy"—the belief that the evolution of society has been principally determined by such economic considerations as the search for efficiency or greater profit.[14] Based on the belief that the pursuit of economic gain is a "natural" human inclination, the "economistic fallacy" imagines that capitalist societies do not have cultures in the way that primitive or premodern societies do. This, in fact, has been one of the central conceits of modernity; our institutions are supposed to be shaped by the dictates of practical reason rather than by the kinds of deeply held, but unexamined, collective beliefs that are known to dominate in less enlightened societies. But when we recognize that the pursuit of economic self-interest is itself a cultural creation, then it is apparent that we, too, are ruled by deeply held, but unexamined, collective beliefs.

Marshall Sahlins has pursued this critique of tendencies to naturalize the economy by elaborating the notion of bourgeois society as an anthropological culture.[15] He argues, for example, that our society's choices of clothing and food, while often defended in instrumental terms, cannot be understood as exercises in practical reason. Our views of which animals are edible and which are inedible, and of what kinds of clothes are appropriate to wear, involve the same kind of complex classification schemes that anthropologists discover among premodern peoples.

What is at stake in these arguments is the degree of freedom that societies have in shaping their economic institutions. For example, in analyzing a tribe of hunters and gatherers, it is possible to calculate the minimum amount of total labor necessary to assure that the

14. Karl Polanyi, *The Great Transformation* (1944; reprint, Boston: Beacon Press, 1957). For more on Polanyi, see Fred Block and Margaret Somers, "Beyond the Economistic Fallacy: The Holistic Social Science of Karl Polanyi," in Theda Skocpol, ed., *Vision and Method in Historical Sociology* (Cambridge: Cambridge University Press, 1984), 47–84.

15. Marshall Sahlins, *Culture and Practical Reason* (Chicago: University of Chicago Press, 1976).

tribe has enough food and other resources to reproduce itself over time. This amount of labor represents a kind of baseline of economic necessity. Yet the anthropological evidence makes clear that there are a multitude of different ways to handle that necessity; different ways of organizing the division of labor and different kinds of cultural practices. In fact, it is now generally recognized that in such societies, economic necessity does not predict the society's actual social arrangements.

Yet in the analysis of more complex societies, there is a strong tendency to believe that institutional arrangements have been dictated by considerations of economic necessity. This is deeply ironic, in that most developed societies are much more insulated from biological necessity than tribal societies, since they generally have substantial stocks of food. It should follow that their leeway in shaping the division of labor should be even greater than that of tribal societies.

However, this potential freedom is generally obscured by claims based on "false necessity," which are rooted in a naturalized view of the economy.[16] Such claims take the form of arguments that a particular change in economic arrangements will lead to such a loss of efficiency that the society's entire standard of living would be significantly reduced. For example, interference with market allocation or with an existing set of economic incentives is often said to have such dire consequences. Such claims gain their plausibility from a "naturalized" view of the economy that ignores the cultural context of economic behavior.

A more realistic view that avoided this tendency to naturalize would affirm instead that there are multiple different institutional configurations that could produce levels of output comparable to or better than those already achieved. In fact, economic history has taught us that late-developing countries have often developed "functional substitutes" for the economic institutions of earlier developers, and these have often proved superior to those that they

16. The concept of "false necessity" has been central for Roberto Unger. See Roberto Mangabeira Unger, *False Necessity: Anti-Necessitarian Social Theory in the Service of Radical Democracy* (Cambridge: Cambridge University Press, 1987).

replaced.[17] The reality is that advanced societies have even more leeway than tribal societies in shaping their economic institutions, even in those cases where their members are strongly committed to maximizing output. The range of choice in structuring economic institutions is far broader than a "naturalizing" economics would suggest.

A Contextualized View of Economic Institutions

An alternative to the naturalizing approach to the economy must be acutely sensitive to historical context, must be aware of "background" factors often ignored in conventional analyses, and must recognize the importance of conceptual understandings in shaping economic action.

Karl Marx remains one of the principal sources for the argument that economic arrangements are historically contingent. Marx continually criticized the classical economists for their tendency to assume that the economic patterns that they had identified would exist for all time. His analysis of the fetishism of commodities was a direct attack on a naturalized view of economic arrangements. He recognized that within capitalism, the social relations among human beings take the ghostly form of relations among things, as when abstract market forces are perceived as determining prices. He stressed that this tendency made it harder to change existing arrangements because people forget that economic institutions are social creations that could be recreated in different ways.

Yet despite the power of this insight, it was undermined by another aspect of Marx's thought. His effort to identify the essential dynamics of the capitalist mode of production meant that he, too, created a theoretical framework insufficiently sensitive to its own historical limitations.[18] In seeking to identify the "laws of motion" of

17. Alexander Gerschenkron, *Economic Backwardness in Historical Perspective* (Cambridge, Mass.: Harvard University Press, 1962).

18. A comparable problem that has plagued Marxist thought is the question of whether the method of historical materialism is specific to bourgeois society, as Lukács thought, or is appropriate for all historical societies. See discussion in Sahlins, *Culture and Practical Reason,* 17–18.

the capitalist economy, he ended up naturalizing what he sought to criticize. As a result, subsequent generations of Marxists have struggled with the intractable problem of reconciling the obvious changes in the institutional structures of capitalist societies, such as the increased role of the state and the rise of unions, with Marx's claims about the essential dynamics of a capitalist economy. The problem lies in the notion that there is a transhistorical essence to capitalism that will continue to exist regardless of changes in the specific institutional arrangements of the economy.

One way to pursue Marx's initial insight about the historical contingency of economic institutions is to focus on the "background conditions" that shape economic activity. These are background only from the point of view of economic analyses that tend to lump them into the category of *ceteris paribus*—other things being equal. However, when these background conditions change, they radically undermine all of the analyses that assume them to be constant.

One important example has been highlighted by feminist critics of economics who have stressed the importance to market economies of nonmarket work performed by women and other unpaid family members.[19] Much conventional economic analysis has simply assumed that this kind of unpaid labor will be abundant and will make it possible for the family to produce and reproduce a labor force. By neglecting the complex social and cultural arrangements that have led women to perform these unpaid tasks, economists are able to develop relatively simple models of the operation of the labor market. Yet when these background conditions change— when, for example, the willingness of women to perform unpaid work in the home declines, those simplified models of the labor market are thrown into disarray.

Legal rules and enforcement mechanisms are another example of "background" factors that are assumed to be constant in most economic analyses, but these are also subject to change. Morton Horwitz's classic study *The Transformation of American Law, 1780–1860*[20] shows how the courts redefined property rights during the nineteenth century with significant economic consequences. Simi-

19. See citations in Swedberg, "Economic Sociology," 182–87.
20. Cambridge, Mass.: Harvard University Press, 1977.

larly, different systems of labor law have significant consequences for the relative power of employers and employees. And if legal rules are important, so, too, obviously are factors that shape attempts to enforce those legal rules. Stephen Marglin has argued, for example, that the rise of the factory can be understood, in part, as a technology for enforcing existing property rules.[21] With decentralized cottage industry, producers were able to pilfer a significant share of the raw material from the merchants, but the centralized factory made it substantially easier to halt such theft.

Another type of "background" factor are the beliefs held by economic actors. While there is a temptation to imagine that these beliefs are simply a reflection of individual self-interest, the reality is that they can shape perceptions of self-interest themselves. For example, beliefs shape the preferences that individuals have for one or another type of product or for leisure relative to money; they set the framework in which individuals then proceed to maximize utility. Similarly, beliefs shape the expectations of economic actors, and these expectations have come to be recognized as a critical variable in economic analysis. Expectations about the future shape such macroeconomic variables as the level of investment, but these expectations, in turn, are influenced by other beliefs, such as adherence to a particular economic theory that predicts particular consequences from particular action. Such "theories" may be more or less "scientific" or academically respectable, but they have significant consequences regardless.

Perhaps the most striking way in which beliefs shape the perceptions of economic actors is through the role of accounting. Since the importance of accounting is often overlooked, it is worth developing this point at some greater length. It is striking as an illustration of Sahlins's point that the gap between modern and anthropological societies is smaller than we generally assume since accounting systems are actually quite reminiscent of the schemes premodern people use to organize reality. The dualism of double-entry bookkeeping bears a similarity to the complex kinship systems analyzed by structural anthropologists. In both cases, a typological system operates to defend against uncertainty and ambiguity, and it pro-

21. Stephen Marglin, "What Do Bosses Do? The Origins and Functions of Hierarchy in Capitalist Production," *Review of Radical Political Economy* 6, no. 2 (Summer 1974): 60–112.

tects people from having to consider a broader range of human possibilities.

This characteristic of accounting results from the fact that none of the basic categories of economic analysis—profit, loss, revenues, and so forth—have a transparent meaning in a complex economy. Whether or not a particular firm is profitable in a given quarter or a given year is not just a matter of whether it took in more money than it paid out; it depends, for example, on how one counts certain expenditures, since capital investments are treated differently from current expenses. The precise determination as to whether a particular cost falls into one category or the other depends upon the accounting rules in effect at the time. The seemingly objective economic facts of contemporary life are themselves shaped by accounting conventions.

The very phrase *accounting convention* is revealing as an indication that these rules are not the result of an "objective" scientific process. In many cases, because of the tensions between reality and any dualistic typology, they cannot be derived objectively. For example, the core distinction that economists make between investments and current expenses is inherently problematic; it is not at all clear where one should draw the dividing line. Moreover, many specific expenditures combine purposes—they are oriented both to long-term growth and to achieving immediate objectives, and there is no obvious way to measure the weight of these two components. Nonetheless, the logic of accounting requires that any particular expenditure go into the books under one heading or another. Accountants must have a rule for deciding on such cases; if they were allowed to decide each case on its own merits, the profession would lose its claims to objectivity. But the choices are limited—they can establish a rule that all expenditures of a certain type be classified as investment or current expenses, or they can decide that some fixed percentage of the cost be included in one category and the balance in the other. Since they cannot capture the actual combination of purposes in the specific expenditure, however, whatever rule they decide on will ultimately have an element of arbitrariness.

Systems of accounting, whether designed for a particular firm, for the public sector, or for calculating the whole society's Gross National Product, are built up out of these somewhat arbitrary conventions, which serve to create the appearance of certitude out of ambiguity and complexity. Out of the work of accountants come the findings that a firm is losing money or that the government's accounts are in deficit, and such information may become the basis for decisions with profound consequences for millions of people. It is only very rarely that anyone questions these findings or examines the conventions that might have produced that particular "social fact."[22]

This is not to say that the shift from one set of accounting conventions to another will turn black into white or cause a highly profitable corporation to go bankrupt. But accounting conventions can have more than a marginal impact in a situation where even relatively small differences in economic variables have broad ramifications. The point remains that one should not underestimate the power of beliefs—including the acceptance of particular accounting conventions—to shape economic action. Moreover, when such beliefs change—as they do from time to time—they can generate enormous problems for economic models that treat beliefs as another "background" factor that can be held constant.

The Tradition of Economic Sociology

The tradition of economic sociology provides the best foundation for developing a historically rooted analysis of economic processes. However, the evolution of economic sociology has been complex and confusing, and it is not possible simply to build on an already established theoretical framework. But a review of developments in the field can help us locate the outlines of an approach to economic sociology that is most fruitful in overcoming the weaknesses of the tradition of neoclassical economics.

In the early years of sociology, there was reason to imagine that economic sociology would be at the core of the new discipline. Auguste Comte, the founder of sociology, polemicized against the practitioners of political economy and saw sociology as a science

22. For exceptions, see William Alonso and Paul Starr, eds., *The Politics of Numbers* (New York: Russell Sage Foundation, 1987); Paul Attewell, "Imperialism within Complex Organizations," *Sociological Theory* 4 (Fall 1986): 115–25; Fred Block and Gene A. Burns, "Productivity as a Social Problem: The Uses and Misuses of Social Indicators," *American Sociological Review* 51 (December 1986): 767–80.

that would subsume the subject matter of economics. Moreover, the theorists who are now acknowledged to constitute the classical tradition of the field—Marx, Weber, and Durkheim—were centrally concerned with economic phenomena and sought to construct an intellectual framework that grasped both the social and the economic. But this early promise of economic sociology was not to be realized, particularly in the development of American sociology. The early attempts to institutionalize sociology in the American university system resulted in a fierce turf battle between sociologists and economists in the 1890s. Economists were opposed to giving space in the academy to another discipline that challenged their claim to exclusive jurisdiction over the study of economic phenomena. At first, sociologists sought to defend a broad definition of their field, but as the battle continued, they chose instead to strike a compromise. In exchange for the support of the economists, sociologists dropped their claims to jurisdiction over economic phenomena and accepted the dubious status of a "science of leftovers" that studied whatever aspects of society were not covered by economics or political science—basically social institutions such as the family, the community, and the city.[23] This initial division of labor between the disciplines remained largely unchallenged for almost three-quarters of a century. There were occasional scholars who saw the resulting academic division of labor as arbitrary and who contributed to the sociological analysis of economic processes. But these tended to be marginal figures whose work had little impact on the overall development of the field. Even when the development of sociology opened up areas that involved sociologists closely with economic issues, there were few direct challenges to the economists. So, for example, as industrial sociology developed as a distinct specialty within sociology, its practitioners were generally content to examine only the questions left over when the economists had completed their work.[24] Similarly, in the studies of Third

23. Mary O. Furner, *Advocacy and Objectivity* (Lexington, University of Kentucky Press, 1975), 291–312. Other scholars have stressed, however, that the boundary between sociology and other disciplines was not settled in the 1890s, but continued to be an issue in the twentieth century. See Henrika Kuklick, "Boundary Maintenance in American Sociology: Limitations to Academic 'Professionalization,' " *Journal of the History of the Behavioral Sciences* 16 (1980): 201–19.

24. Michael Burawoy, *Manufacturing Consent: Changes in the Labor Process under Monopoly Capitalism* (Chicago: University of Chicago Press, 1979), 3–12.

World modernization that proliferated in the 1950s, sociologists often worked in tandem with economists in a cooperative division of labor that distinguished between the economic and the social aspects of modernization.

The result of the compromise was that economic sociology had only the most tenuous existence within American sociology. While sociologists produced some significant work within the field of economic sociology, there was no systematic effort to develop a sociological understanding of the economy.[25] Even the phrase that was often used as a substitute for economic sociology was revealing; sociologists with a strong interest in economic phenomena described themselves as working in the field of "economy and society." This formulation implied the existence of two separate and distinct social realms—an economy governed by economic laws and a society governed by sociological laws.[26] The project of this subfield has been to understand what happens at the boundary between these distinct institutional jurisdictions.[27]

This historical compromise began to unravel during the 1960s. The challenge from the left by Marxist and other critical sociologists called into question the status of sociology as a science of leftovers. Sociology, it was argued, had to contend with the fundamental issues of power and distribution, and this required attention to the economic dimension of society. In addition, the need to explain inequality among nations required that sociologists come to terms with the dynamics of the international market. At the same time, the appearance of Barrington Moore's *Social Origins of Dictatorship and Democracy* both signaled and legitimated a revival of interest by sociologists in questions of large-scale historical development that necessarily involved an analysis of economic relations.[28] And, at the end of the 1960s, the emergence of a feminist critique of mainstream social science also called into question the division of labor between sociologists and economists. Specifically,

25. Swedberg, "Economic Sociology: Past and Present," 17–20.
26. This is not, however, what Weber had in mind in using the same phrase to title his major work.
27. For a lucid presentation of this approach to economic sociology, see Neil Smelser, *The Sociology of Economic Life* (Englewood Cliffs, N.J.: Prentice-Hall, 1976).
28. Boston: Beacon Press, 1966.

feminists posed the question of how it happened that activities such as housework, performed predominantly by women, could be defined as outside of the economy. By exposing the arbitrariness of the reigning definition of "the economy," feminists disrupted the historical compromise. They also opened up a broad range of new questions by developing a systematic critique of Western societies' narrow focus on instrumental action.

These diverse challenges opened up space for the expansion of economic sociology in the 1970s and 1980s. Both scholars influenced by Marxism and feminism and figures more in the mainstream turned their attention to the analysis of economic institutions. One important example is the body of work that followed on the heels of Immanuel Wallerstein's *The Modern World System*,[29] which has led sociologists into such previously neglected areas as studies of the operation of capitalism on a world scale and research into the behavior of multinational corporations.[30] In other cases, traditional areas of sociological investigation such as stratification and the sociology of organizations have come to focus more directly on economic issues. Hence, scholars of stratification increasingly focus on the analysis of labor markets, while sociologists of organization study corporate interlocks or the economic transactions within firms.

The breadth and diversity of this thrust toward economic sociology is impressive, but it is still the case that some of the people involved do not yet recognize themselves as doing "economic sociology." They are more likely to identify themselves with a theoretical approach—Marxist, Weberian—or with a particular area of inquiry—sociology of organizations or sociology of the professions. The return of economic sociology has occurred in a relatively inadvertent way as sociologists have pushed their inquiries in new directions that appeared logical.

As a consequence, there has been relatively little theoretical clarity in this reinvigorated field. In this respect, the subfield is no different from sociology in general, since all of the great theoretical systems have fallen into states of disrepair. But because there are

29. *Capitalist Agriculture and the Origins of the European World-Economy in the Sixteenth Century* (New York: Academic Press, 1974).

30. Swedberg, "Economic Sociology: Past and Present," 91–104.

radically different conceptions of what the subfield should be, the problems in economic sociology are even greater. The differences concerning the proper relationship between economic sociology and economics are particularly great.

A number of analysts have put forward the view that the two disciplines have much to learn from each other; that sociological work would be enriched by a better understanding of economic theory and vice versa.[31] This is a continuation of the tradition of "economy and society," with its emphasis on increasing cooperation between two distinct, but complementary, approaches. But there are also currents that call into question the idea of any meaningful boundary between the two fields.

Some economic sociologists have been strongly influenced by the work of Gary Becker and others who have used economic tools to analyze noneconomic phenomena. For this group, the core weakness of sociology is its lack of microfoundations—plausible models of individual behavior that can be used to construct analyses of large-scale social structures and processes.[32] For these theorists, the best way to provide microfoundations is by using the economic assumptions of individuals behaving as rational maximizers of utilities with fixed preferences. This version of economic sociology *is* economic analysis applied to noneconomic processes, so that by this definition Gary Becker is an economic sociologist.[33]

The final approach also denies the meaningfulness of the disciplinary boundary, but in quite a different way. For this group of

31. Smelser, *Sociology of Economic Life*; Mark Granovetter, "Toward a Sociological Theory of Income Differences," in Ivar Berg, ed., *Sociological Perspectives on Labor Markets* (New York: Academic Press, 1981), 11–47.

32. See Michael Hechter, ed., *The Microfoundations of Macrosociology* (Philadelphia: Temple University Press, 1983).

33. In fact, Becker has been given a secondary appointment in the sociology department at the University of Chicago. Scholars such as Becker and Mancur Olson are challenging this notion of a dividing line between the economic and the noneconomic through their insistence that both can be understood within the framework of the economizing of scarce resources. Ironically, such efforts to conquer new territory for economics might well undermine the power of the economic paradigm itself. The point is that when the object of inquiry is simply the economy, the mechanism of self-regulation is obvious—it is Adam Smith's invisible hand. But when the object of inquiry becomes all of society, what is the mechanism of self-regulation—how does the pursuit of self-interest in all of the diverse realms of society produce some form of order? It is, after all, the promise of order that gives the economic paradigm its initial appeal.

economic sociologists, "the economy" is an analytic abstraction because economic activity is always embedded in a larger social and cultural framework. Abstracting from this framework, as economic analysis tends to do, is bound to result in models that fail to grasp the actual complexity of the social world. In this view, economic sociology is a superior tool for understanding "economic" processes because it is able to grasp the full context in which such processes occur.

It is this latter view of economic sociology that provides the best means of overcoming a naturalized analysis of the economy, and the term *economic sociology* will be used here to refer only to this particular intellectual current. This approach allows sociologists to continue to learn from the literature of economics without themselves taking over either the assumptions or the limitations of economic analysis. In this perspective, the relationship between sociologists and economists is not unlike that between sociologists of religion and theologians. In both cases, the question of why the practitioners (economists or theologians) have accepted certain beliefs is a central one for sociological analysis. Moreover, the sociologist aspires in both fields to develop an account of why things happen that is richer than the typical accounts of those who have a stake in a certain tradition of religious or economic thought. And inasmuch as some theologians have learned from the sociology of religion and have adopted a more sophisticated understanding of religious processes, it may perhaps be hoped that economists will likewise be able to learn from economic sociology.[34]

For this approach to economic sociology, the towering figure is Karl Polanyi (1886–1968), a Hungarian refugee intellectual who produced his major works in the 1940s and 1950s.[35] Polanyi taught in the Department of Economics at Columbia University in a period when economic sociology was in eclipse, but in the twenty years since his death, his work has come to be widely read in sociology.

Polanyi made a fundamental distinction between two distinct

34. In fact, the names of the fields are revealing. *Sociology of religion* conveys a certain distance from the subject matter in contrast, say, to *religious sociology*. My preference would be for the term *sociology of economies*, but *economic sociology* is too well established by this point for such a quibble.

35. See Block and Somers, "Beyond the Economistic Fallacy."

meanings of the word *economic*. One meaning is the formal definition that centers on the economizing of scarce resources to make the most efficient use of what is available. The second meaning is the substantive—the meeting of material needs through a process of interaction between humans and their environment. It is only in the latter, substantive, sense that all human societies have economies—they must all provide for human livelihood. However, it is not the case that all human societies have economized scarce resources to increase the efficiency of production. On the contrary, through most of human history, the pursuit of human livelihood was structured by kinship, by religion, and by other cultural practices that had very little to do with the economizing of scarce resources. This means that the model of formal economics in which individuals maximize economic utilities through competitive behavior cannot easily be applied to such societies. In short, the claimed universality of economic theory is based on a trick of language that obscures the fundamental differences in social organization between capitalist and precapitalist societies.

Moreover, Polanyi also challenged the way economists analyze capitalist societies. The neoclassical insistence that the economy is analytically distinct from the rest of society makes it logical to see government regulation of business or government provision of welfare as an external interference with a market economy. While economists may disagree as to whether particular types of interference are benign or malignant, they share the view that they are *external*. In contrast, in Polanyi's analysis of the substantive economy of capitalism, these forms of "interference" are seen, not as external, but as very much part of the economy. Polanyi insisted that nineteenth-century capitalism was formed by two opposing movements. The first was the movement of laissez-faire, which sought to free economic activity from government regulation. The second was the protective countermovement that sought to protect society from the market through the formation of labor unions and through new forms of government regulation, including the Factory Acts and the development of central banking. The point is that the capitalist economy was constituted by these two movements together. The protective countermovement was not external; rather, it was essential for the vitality of a capitalist order.

The point can be seen most clearly by contrasting the two oppos-

ing accounts of the rise of market society. The neoclassical economists believe that in the first third of the nineteenth century,
political leaders in Great Britain came to recognize that letting
market forces operate without interference would produce greater
prosperity. The result was the progressive elimination of a host of
state interferences with market processes, which helped create a
free market in labor, land, and capital. With an economy free to
regulate itself, the gains in efficiency were enormous, and economic
growth accelerated. The results were so impressive that many other
countries quickly followed England's lead in granting market
freedom.

The Polanyian view is that the creation of industrial capitalism in
Great Britain was the result of a series of interacting changes in
markets, politics, and culture, and it was all of these changes together that created a historically new economy. In the labor market, for example, it was not a question of simply allowing market
forces to work; rather, the Poor Law Reforms were necessary to
force workers into the Satanic Mills of early industrial capitalism.
And once the Poor Law Reforms were in place, the Factory Acts
were also needed to place a limit on the length of the working day,
or else market competition would have led to the destruction of the
working class. As Marx shows in *Capital,* the limits on the length of
the working day had the critical effect of channeling market competition toward technological innovation rather than the dead end of
extending the hours of work.

Just as important as these political measures for the creation of
industrial capitalism was the resolution of the cultural question—
who should be the industrial proletariat and how should family life
be structured. Women and children in large part staffed the early
factories, an arrangement that was problematic for the long-term
reproduction of the working class. But the ultimate solution—a
primarily male working class that struggled for a family wage—did
not emerge overnight. Nor was it the only possible solution. It
required intense struggles, waged at the workplace, in the community, and through the state, for this new pattern to emerge.[36] Yet,
this new pattern was clearly a critical ingredient in the success of
this new economic order.

36. John Holley, "The Two Family Economies of Industrialism: Factory Workers in Victorian Scotland," *Journal of Family History* 6, no. 1 (Spring 1981): 57–69.

In short, the Polanyian approach brings the factors that are relegated to the background in neoclassical analysis into the foreground and treats them as critical for the effective functioning of a capitalist economy. Polanyi also offers a second critical contribution to economic sociology—the understanding of the interrelationship between markets, state action, and forms of social regulation.

Although Polanyi wrote powerful polemics against the idea of self-regulating markets, he understood that markets play an extremely positive role in economic life. In fact, Polanyi carved out a unique theoretical position that overcame the weaknesses of the tradition of economic liberalism and of Marxism. Ironically, these two traditions represent mirror images of each other in their beliefs about how economically rational results can be achieved.

Advocates of market self-regulation believe that if individuals have maximal freedom in the making of their microeconomic choices, the aggregate result will be rational; there is no need for any centralized mechanism for making choices. Advocates of central planning have historically believed that microeconomic choices can be eliminated and that economic rationality can be achieved through the working out of a series of centralized choices embodied in a plan. The former ignore the inevitability of institutional arrangements that will structure microeconomic choices, while the latter forget that individuals will retain some latitude of microeconomic choice under any planning regime. Hence, the claims of both about rational outcomes are inherently flawed.

The reality is that any economy involves three distinct levels. At the first level are the microeconomic choices that are available to individuals. These choices can be structured by markets, but they do not have to be; even where markets do not exist, individuals still retain some capacity to choose. While Soviet-style planning assumes, for example, that plant managers will simply follow the plan, the system of planning always leaves choices open and managers will respond to both overt and covert incentives in making their choices. Hence, much scholarship on Soviet-style planning shows that managers choose to hoard resources of labor and capital to make it easier to meet planning goals.[37]

37. See, for example, Charles F. Sabel and David Stark, "Planning, Politics and Shop-Floor Power: Hidden Forms of Bargaining in Soviet-Imposed State-Socialist Societies," *Politics & Society* 11, no. 4 (1982): 439–75.

At the second level are the state actions that structure an economy. As we have already argued, one of the problems with the idea of market self-regulation is that laws defining contract and property are a precondition for market transactions. Hence, the idea that one can completely dispense with the role of government is as great an illusion as the idea that one can eliminate microeconomic choices. But the extent of state action can vary from establishing economic ground rules to directing vast segments of the economy.

The third level, which both theorists of the free market and theorists of government planning ignore, is the vast area of social regulation—the social arrangements that condition and shape microeconomic choices. For example, Polanyi cites the complex system of rules governing market transactions in medieval society that placed limits on price competition. Social regulation encompasses all of the diverse ways in which individual economic behavior is embedded in a broader social framework. The immediate work group often exercises great influence over the choices individuals make as to the intensity with which they work. Moreover, most people work in large organizational settings in which formal and informal mechanisms regulate the behavior of their members. And even transactions between people in different organizations are governed by a variety of social mechanisms.

While the theory of market self-regulation and the theory of planning assume that rational and efficient results can be produced by the operation of only one of these three levels, the reality is that the efficiency of a particular economy will depend on how the three fit together. This means that there is no royal road that automatically leads to greater efficiency. Neither greater market freedom nor more government planning is a universal panacea; the value of either in a given historical situation can only be established through a careful and detailed analysis of the interrelation of microeconomic choices, social regulation, and governmental actions.

Economic Sociology and Postindustrial Development

This perspective that links microeconomic choice, social regulation, and state action helps to highlight the connection between the method of economic sociology and the analysis of postindustrial developments. Just as postindustrial trends have undermined established sociological categories, so too have they undermined previous economic understandings and the efficacy of established economic policy prescriptions. In fact, Western governments have moved back and forth between "free market" and "*dirigiste*" policies in an effort to solve the economy's problems through greater reliance either on markets or on planning. Yet neither policy direction has been terribly successful in restoring the macroeconomic stability of the 1950s and 1960s.

The problem is that the institutional arrangements—the particular mix of market freedom, government intervention, and social regulation—that stabilized the Western economies in the aftermath of World War II are no longer adequate for the tasks of managing either the U.S. domestic economy or the world economy. New institutional arrangements have to be devised, but the problem is far more complex than simply increasing or decreasing the amount of market freedom or government planning. Complexity has increased because some of the background factors that are left out of conventional economic analysis are changing. Preferences are shifting—for example, over who should be in the workforce and over the relative value of different economic goods. Moreover, new technologies are changing both markets and techniques of production so radically as to undermine earlier understandings of what is productive and efficient.

The perspective of economic sociology is indispensable for understanding a period of discontinuity in which the gap between economic theory and actual economic practices has widened. While a naturalizing framework leads many neoclassical economists to search for one or two variables that might explain why the economy is not able to achieve equilibrium, economic sociology seeks a more complex explanation that focuses on the historically specific fit between microeconomic choice, social regulation, and state action.

Economic sociology also illuminates postindustrial trends by revealing the problems with economists' use of the "production function." Conventional economic analysis understands production by analogy to chemical processes; inputs of labor and capital are combined in certain proportions with raw materials and energy to produce outputs. The resulting recipe or formula, the production function, ignores the particular social relations that structure this production process. As we have seen, those social relations are relegated to the category of background factors, which are assumed to remain constant over time. While this analogy has always represented a radical simplification of the more complex reality of production, it has become particularly problematic in recent years.

The problem is that postindustrial trends, particularly the growing importance of services and computer-based production, push the social relations of production to the foreground. In analyzing the production process in a hospital, for example, it seems obvious that the output is not a simple function of the inputs of labor and capital. On the contrary, social relations are absolutely central in determining the efficiency with which health care is produced. The forms of coordination between physicians, nurses, and other parts of the hospital staff; the systems of organizing and managing physicians, residents, and interns; and the network of relations between the hospital and external health providers all loom very large in determining both the quality and the efficiency of the health care that is delivered.

A similar story can be told of the contemporary computerized factory setting. Efficient production cannot be assumed to result automatically from mixing labor and capital; on the contrary, stories are legion of firms that have invested in expensive technologies that turned out to be total failures. The social relations of production—the way tasks are organized, procedures for training employees, and the whole system of labor-management relations—have a major impact on determining how effectively new technologies are used. Similarly, state-of-the-art management techniques such as just-in-time systems of inventory control also highlight the importance of the social relation between producers and supplier firms and the importance of the coordination across divisions of the factory.[38]

Since economic sociology places these social or organizational factors at the center of its analysis, it is a powerful tool for under-

38. Just-in-time techniques have been of critical importance for Japanese manufacturing. The central idea is to reduce inventories of parts by getting deliveries just in time for their incorporation into the finished product. This technique reduces inventory costs and increases the flexibility of production. It also contributes to a tightening of the production process that forces both workers and management to be more conscious of quality control.

standing an increasingly postindustrial economy. To be sure, some economists have recognized that these social factors require some modification of the chemical analogy of production. In his pioneering work in growth accounting, Edward Denison found that changes in labor and capital inputs explained a relatively small portion of postwar economic growth in the United States. He attributed the rest of the growth to a "residual" that included advances in technology and improvements in the organization of the production process.[39] Harvey Leibenstein went a step further in developing the concept of X-efficiency to convey the idea that there are social sources of efficiency that are independent of the quantitative inputs of capital and labor.[40] Yet economists tend to introduce these ideas as ways of saving the basic framework of neoclassical economics. My intention is to show that the increasing centrality of the social dimension of production in a postindustrial economy requires a new framework of analysis.

39. Denison, *The Sources of Economic Growth in the United States* (New York: Committee for Economic Development, 1962).

40. Leibenstein, *Beyond Economic Man: A New Foundation for Microeconomics* (Cambridge, Mass.: Harvard University Press, 1976).

Chapter Three

The Market

The central category of economic discourse is the market; it is the market that is supposed to produce a harmonious result out of the clash of competing interests. It is the market's capacity to perform this feat that sustains the idea of a self-regulating market society in which "external" interventions in the market are to be kept to a minimum. Yet economists almost always discuss the market at a high level of abstraction; there is remarkably little discussion in the literature of the workings of actual markets.[1] When one examines the actual markets in which commodities are bought and sold, it quickly becomes apparent that markets of the kind exalted in theory are rare.

Economists tend to respond to this observation by acknowledging its truth, but insisting that we are worse off as a result. They insist that whatever gains in economic efficiency have occurred over the past two centuries are the result of an institutional framework that has increased market freedom, and that had we moved even closer to full market freedom, the gains would have been even greater. It is argued here instead that the successes of capitalist development are a product of limitations on market freedom. The

---

1. Bernard Barber discusses the failure of most economists to analyze the market concept in a systematic fashion in "The Absolutization of the Market: Some Notes on How We Got from There to Here," in G. Dworkin, G. Bermant, and P. Brown, eds., *Markets and Morals* (Washington, D.C.: Hemisphere, 1977), 15–31. For an important exception to the neglect of actual markets, see Harrison White, "Where Do Markets Come From?" *American Journal of Sociology* 87, no. 3 (1981): 517–47.

vitality of capitalism has always rested on a particular mix of markets and limitations on markets and the abandonment of the limitations reduces the vigor of a capitalist economy. In short, the contemporary policy discourse of deregulation and greater reliance on the market is mistaken on its own terms.

Defining Terms

The idea of the self-regulating market dates back to Adam Smith, but it was not systematized until the late nineteenth century, when the marginalists developed an integrated economic theory of product, labor, and capital markets. In this model, all commodities—including labor and capital—are bought and sold on competitive markets, so that price changes bring supply and demand into balance. The result of the millions of transactions mediated by the price mechanism is a general economic equilibrium in which all resources are utilized in the most efficient way possible.

The appeal of this model rests on the promise of optimal use of resources and on the system's capacity to respond to change. When a shock occurs such as a technological innovation that makes it possible to produce widgets with half the labor, the market mechanism works to restore order. For example, because of the combination of the fall in the price of the displaced labor and the reinvestment of the increased profits earned by widget producers, some entrepreneurs will put the displaced workers back to work producing a different product. Yet it should also be recognized that the integration of this model of the economy is both a strength and a weakness. Self-regulation makes the economy a seamless web; any deviation from market principles in one part of the economy will have repercussions elsewhere. The equilibrating mechanism will be damaged if transactions are not solely determined by the price mechanism. Some economists, for example, argue that trade unions and minimum-wage legislation have led to rigidity in wage levels; these interferences with the price mechanism may result in workers being paid more than a market-determined wage. The result is that the artificially high price of labor will discourage certain investments, with the result that the economy may continue at a level of economic activity well below the full utilization of labor and capital. It is precisely the seamless nature of this self-regulating economy that makes some theorists so adamant in opposing any state action that might interfere with the price mechanism.

Most contemporary economists are somewhat more relaxed about these issues, however, because for them the model of market self-regulation is a kind of Platonic ideal that can never be realized in reality. Recent efforts to work out the mathematics of general equilibrium have made clear that it is possible to construct an economic model in which the price mechanism will actually produce a general equilibrium only by making a number of highly restrictive assumptions.[2] In short, it is difficult to imagine that market self-regulation works in reality as it does in theory. Moreover, contemporary economists are well aware of the need for government action to produce public goods that are vitally necessary for the private economy.

Nevertheless, the ideal of market self-regulation still has a powerful hold on the imagination of economists. Lester Thurow argues that most contemporary economists agree that microeconomics is fundamentally sound, and that the problems in the discipline come from the weakness of macroeconomic theory.[3] But microeconomic theory is basically the idea of market self-regulation applied to particular markets, supply and demand being equilibrated through the price mechanism. Although economists may have doubts about how all of these diverse markets contribute to a macroeconomic whole, they still understand these markets within the framework inherited from the marginalists. There is a contradiction in this perspective because there is no guarantee that an equilibrium in a particular market will contribute to the efficiency of the economy as a whole unless it is assumed that all of the markets are connected together in a seamless web that produces the rational allocation of resources between different product markets. Yet this contradiction is often ignored; microeconomic analysis of particular markets is often carried out on the implicit assumption that the larger structure of interlocking markets is functioning optimally.

It is useful to look more closely at the nature of the markets that

2. Frank Hahn, "General Equilibrium Theory," in Daniel Bell and Irving Kristol, eds., *The Crisis in Economic Theory* (New York: Basic Books, 1981), 123–38.

3. Thurow, *Dangerous Currents: The State of Economics* (New York: Random House, 1983), 3.

are assumed in the marginalist tradition. These are markets in which there are multiple buyers or sellers, and where no particular buyer or seller has enough power to unilaterally influence the price. This is essential because the price of a product is supposed to equal its marginal utility, just as the price of the worker is supposed to equal his or her marginal product. If market participants were able to influence prices by withholding products, then the equilibrium prices would not be reached.

It is also a critical assumption that the preferences of the market participants are stable and formed outside of the transactions. Equilibration requires some fixedness in preferences; were individual preferences to jump around, there is no reason supply and demand should balance. Finally, the model requires that buyers and sellers have rough equality of information. This is necessary to assure that people get what they pay for; if misrepresentations become endemic, prices will be thrown off and the effective balancing of supply and demand will be impaired.

The elements of this model suggest that the type of market being described is a spot market in which transactions occur on a one-time basis among relative strangers where there are multiple buyers and sellers. The actual markets that are closest to this description are contemporary stock markets, commodity markets, and foreign-exchange markets in which traders on the market floor represent a multitude of different buyers and sellers and engage in very rapid transactions that are driven almost entirely by price considerations.

It is striking, however, that most economic transactions are not handled on spot markets that resemble a stock or commodity exchange. Consumer purchases are generally made in retail outlets where a single seller has attached relatively fixed prices to different products. While some consumers may act as if they were confronting multiple sellers by carefully comparing prices across multiple stores, this is still different from the theory in that sellers do not receive instant information on the prices governing other transactions. Moreover, there are many purchases—both by consumers and by producers—that could not possibly be organized on a spot-market basis because they cannot be organized instantaneously. Where a service is to be provided over a period of time or a good is to be delivered at a later date, buyer and seller must agree on more than price; they must establish a relationship that is reflected in the existence of a contract. As we shall see, contractual relationships move buyer and seller some distance from the markets of economic theory.

Moreover, even those financial markets that appear to resemble pure spot markets are actually more complex in their actual operations. Those who do the actual trading—often as agents for others—develop complex sets of rules and systems of mutual regulation.[4] For example, the October 1987 stock market crash drew attention to the central role of small specialist firms in the New York Stock Exchange. These specialist firms are supposed to assure that trading in each stock is orderly by buying or selling the stock to even out price changes. In the crash, some of the specialists ceased to carry out their function and some stocks fell precipitously in value. The stock market has developed this special institutional system of market regulation precisely because a pure spot market is enormously volatile.[5] This fact alone would seem to shed doubt on the practicality of a system of purely self-regulating markets.

It is at this point that some precision in terminology is necessary. One problem is that the issue of what is or is not a market has become very confused. When a person is promoted by a firm, this is now seen as a transaction on the firm's internal labor market. Similarly, a choice of spouses can be seen as part of the operation of a marriage market. Yet if markets are simply situations in which individuals make choices, then all of social life is a market and the term has no specificity. The problem is the confusion between metaphor and reality. It is illuminating to think that the internal system of promotion within a firm is *like* an internal labor market, but to say that it is an internal labor market is merely confusing. The term *market* should be reserved for situations in which relatively

4. There is a growing body of work on this point. See, for example, Wayne Baker, "The Social Structure of a National Securities Market," *American Journal of Sociology* 89, no. 4 (January 1984): 775–811; Peter Adler and Patricia Adler, eds., *The Social Dynamics of Financial Markets* (Greenwich, Conn.: JAI Press, 1984).

5. The system of specialist firms represents a departure from pure market self-regulation. The firms are expected to accept large short-term losses as a quid pro quo for the generally lucrative privilege of organizing the market. For accounts, see "How the Stock Market Almost Disintegrated a Day after the Crash," *Wall Street Journal*, November 20, 1987, and "Panel Cites Roles of Market Makers and Institutions in Crash," *Wall Street Journal*, January 11, 1988.

independent actors come together to make economic transactions of limited duration.[6]

But an even more serious problem is that we lack a convenient means of comparing different types of arrangements for organizing economic transactions. Economic theory provides a clue as to how to do this through its central emphasis on the price mechanism as the means of equilibrating transactions. The whole idea of the pure market of economic theory is that actors are responding entirely to price signals. This means that we can construct a continuum of the "marketness" of economic transactions, with spot markets at the high end of the scale and transactions organized through organizational hierarchies at the low end. High marketness means that there is nothing to interfere with the dominance of price considerations, but as one moves down the continuum to lower levels of marketness, nonprice considerations take on greater importance. It is not as though prices are irrelevant under conditions of low marketness, it is just that they compete with other variables, so that one would expect price differences to be much larger before they led actors to respond.[7]

In this framework, the existence of an ongoing relationship and a contract represents a departure from the highest level of marketness. At the high end, for example, a stock trader's choice as to whether to buy shares from A or B will depend only on the price

6. There have been some recent efforts to develop a typology of different types of markets. Paula England and George Farkas identify three different types of markets—spot markets, markets based on contingent-claim contracts, and markets based on implicit contracts. Contingent-claim contracts are long-term contracts that are contingent on certain specified developments, such as changes in the prices of key inputs. By agreeing to adjust the terms of the contract to changes in certain key variables, the parties to the contract retain some of the same flexibility that they would have if they had resorted instead to a series of spot-market transactions. The concept of implicit contracts has been applied most typically to the labor market, where there is an ongoing economic relationship without a formal contingent-claims contract. Theorists of implicit contracts argue that employees are implicitly offered job security in exchange for high levels of work effort. The problem with this typology is that it combines two dimensions—the duration of the contract and its explicitness—that are better treated separately. See England and Farkas, *Households, Employment, and Gender: A Social, Economic, and Demographic View* (New York: Aldine Publishing, 1986), 43–51.

7. According to economic theory, all relevant aspects of a commodity are expressed in its price, so that one can, for example, pay a little more and get higher quality, quicker delivery, or virtually any other desired characteristic. The prob-

that they are asking. However, when a businessperson enters into a contract to have some quantity of chemicals delivered in six months, price differences are weighed against other variables, such as the likelihood that the firm will still be in business and that it will make the delivery on time. In general, the longer the term of the contract, the lower the level of marketness. If, for example, a firm has signed a long-term contract with a particular supplier, the contract interferes with the capacity of both firms to respond to price changes in the market. In theory, it is possible to write long-term contracts that will cover all market contingencies—contingent-claim contracts—so that the price being paid at any particular moment would be the same as if there were a sequence of spot transactions. But in reality, it is not possible to anticipate all contingencies, and it is extremely costly to construct such an elaborate contract.[8] Hence, even if such a long-term contract makes provision for adjusting prices under some contingencies, the results will be very different from a sequence of spot transactions. This is intentional, since the parties generally sign such a long-term contract precisely to protect themselves from the flux of spot markets.

However, length of the contract is not the only factor associated with lowered marketness. There are many market situations in which the information available to buyers and sellers is quite different, and the costs of correcting the information imbalance are con-

---

lem is that in actual transactions, there are considerable uncertainties about many of these relevant characteristics. One might pay a higher price to get quicker delivery, but there is no guarantee that the seller will meet this obligation. Buyers have the option of specifying relevant characteristics in advance through a contingent-claims contract that might include monetary penalties for each day of lateness. However, it is impossible to anticipate every relevant contingency; that is the meaning of uncertainty. Hence, buyers tend to respond to uncertainty by reducing the marketness of the transaction—diminishing the importance of price as compared to their level of trust in a particular supplier. This issue has been addressed in the literature on agency theory, on contested exchange, and on the Japanese model of contracting; see John W. Pratt and Richard J. Zeckhauser, eds., *Principals and Agents: The Structure of Business* (Boston: Harvard Business School Press, 1985); Samuel Bowles and Herbert Gintis, "Contested Exchange: The Political Structure of Competitive Markets," *Politics & Society,* forthcoming; Ronald Dore, *Flexible Rigidities: Industrial Policy and Structural Adjustment in the Japanese Economy, 1970–1980* (London: Athlone Press, 1986).

8. Oliver E. Williamson, *Markets and Hierarchies, Analysis and Antitrust Implications: A Study in the Economics of Internal Organization* (New York: Free Press, 1975), 65–67.

siderable. In such circumstances, the participant with less information faces considerable risk. A number of institutional forms have emerged to handle these situations. The most familiar is the development of organizational hierarchies. A number of diverse analysts have speculated that one reason that the employment relation replaced short-term contracting was that it provided entrepreneurs with a superior means of monitoring performance—a way of overcoming information asymmetries.[9] There are also a variety of agency relations in which a person is hired to carry out a task and given considerable autonomy in the methods to be used. In such situations, bonds of personal loyalty or other noneconomic motivations often play a critical role in the agent's performance of his or her duties.[10] These and other means for handling differences in information represent reductions in the marketness of the transaction, since price considerations decline in relative importance.

It is useful to supplement the marketness continuum for evaluating transactions with another continuum for evaluating the motives of economic actors. This second continuum concerns the degree of instrumentalism of individual behavior.[11] The marginalist framework assumes that individuals act on the basis of their rational economic self-interest. When one sees a commodity trader in the pit, there is supposed to be nothing at work beyond this kind of instrumental behavior. However, as the marketness of transactions diminishes, economic behavior tends to become embedded in a more complex web of social relations.[12] Hence, a purchasing manager in a firm gets to know his or her counterparts in supplying firms, and these personal ties shape his or her actions. This personal relationship might well contribute to the reliability of the supplier

9. Stephen Marglin, "What Do Bosses Do? The Origins and Functions of Hierarchy in Capitalist Production," *Review of Radical Political Economy* 6, no. 2 (Summer 1974): 60–112; Armen A. Alchian and Harold Demsetz, "Production, Information Costs, and Economic Organization," *American Economic Review* 62 (December 1972): 777–95.

10. Harrison C. White, "Agency as Control," in Pratt and Zeckhauser, eds., *Principals and Agents*, 187–209.

11. There is often a close fit between the nature of the transaction and the nature of the individual motivations. However, it is still useful to distinguish them analytically.

12. Mark Granovetter, "Economic Action and Social Structure: The Problem of Embeddedness," *American Journal of Sociology* 91, no. 3 (November 1985): 481–510.

in terms both of product quality and on-time delivery. Yet the very fact of embeddedness diminishes the relative importance of price signals; it may take quite a large price difference before a purchaser is willing to break off a relationship with a supplier of proven reliability. In this example, the purchaser is still behaving instrumentally, although not with the purely price-driven instrumentalism of the spot trader. However, it is easy to imagine situations where embeddedness leads actors to move even further away from instrumentalism, as when a purchasing agent continues doing business with someone at another firm simply out of friendship.

In other words, the continuum from instrumental to embedded combines two dimensions. The first is the degree to which behavior is price-driven, since individuals can pursue their economic self-interest in ways that have nothing to do with price. The second is the degree to which self-interest places economic goals ahead of friendship, family ties, spiritual considerations, or morality.[13] To be sure, all of the latter can be explained in terms of the pursuit of self-interest, but that is not the relevant issue.[14] The important point for examining the market model is the extent to which individual behavior is oriented to economic goals and is responsive to price changes.

Much economic analysis assumes instrumental behavior, but it is built into the model that actors obey the rules of the economic game. "Economic models . . . [treat] individuals as playing a game with fixed rules which they obey. They do not buy more than they

13. Amitai Etzioni groups all of these noninstrumental motivations under the heading of morality in *The Moral Dimension: Toward a New Economics* (New York: Free Press, 1988).

14. To demonstrate the power of their framework, economists sometimes rely on the fact that any form of behavior can be interpreted as self-interested, including the suffering of religious martyrs in search of spiritual rewards. But the reality is that the market model rests not on the axiom of self-interest, but on economic self-interest. Those things that human beings aspire to that are not directly bought and sold on a market actually interfere with the market's capacity to equilibrate all transactions through the price mechanism. For example, someone who wants to buy a firm not primarily because of the economic returns but to achieve an increase in power and status might well pay considerably more than would be justified by strictly economic criteria. And if there are others with similar preferences, the result may be a significant misallocation of capital across the whole economy.

know they can pay for, they do not embezzle funds, they do not rob banks."[15] This kind of argument is logically inconsistent; the pursuit of self-interest is not—as Weber said of historical materialism—a streetcar that one can get on and off as one pleases; once one boards, one must proceed to the final destination. If purely instrumental behavior is assumed, the analyst has to expect opportunistic actions in which individuals violate the formal or informal rules of the game by making representations they know to be false in order to take advantage of others.[16]

To be sure, a calculus of self-interest can explain why people follow the rules when there is a reasonable chance that they will be caught and penalized. But if people do not behave opportunistically when the chances of detection and punishment are slight, their behavior is not purely instrumental. In short, the existence of nonopportunistic behavior is evidence of embeddedness, of the power of noneconomic variables, such as the norms of a particular community or the strength of their personal ties to others.

These ideal types of marketness and instrumental behavior are not a caricature of the assumptions of the marginalist market model. The idea that the price mechanism can equilibrate markets effectively assumes a level of marketness near the high end of the continuum represented by pure spot markets. If, for example, a high percentage of all economic transactions for a given commodity are organized through long-term contracts, there will be a long delay before price changes can equilibrate supply and demand. Similarly, instrumental behavior is required for individuals to be able to respond quickly even to small changes in price signals. If, for example, personal ties to a supplier create loyalty, small price changes will have little effect. Finally, the argument that instrumental behavior includes opportunism follows logically from the rational pursuit of self-interest; the failure to build the likelihood of opportunism into economic models has been a logical inconsistency of analysts who have no viable explanation for why actors should not pursue their self-interest through rule violations.

15. P. Diamond, quoted in Williamson, *Markets and Hierarchies,* 7.
16. Williamson, *Markets and Hierarchies,* 26–28.

Marketness and
Instrumentalism in the Economy

If the marketness continuum is turned into an actual scale, it would theoretically be possible to rate the level of marketness of any particular economic transaction and then, by aggregating, rate the overall level of marketness of a particular economy at a particular point of time. One could also carry out a similar evaluation of the aggregate instrumentalism of individual behavior. While carrying out such an exercise would be enormously difficult, it is of considerable interest to pose the question of whether the level of marketness and instrumentalism, measured in that way, has been increasing, decreasing, or has remained the same in the hundred years from 1850 to 1950.[17] Even pursuing this question at a much more descriptive level will tell us a great deal about the actual workings of markets in capitalist societies. While it might not be possible to figure out the actual direction of change, it will become clear that the level of marketness and instrumentalism has never been as high as economic theory would suggest.

In 1850 the American economy was still dominated by agricultural production; it is estimated that in 1849 agriculture accounted for 60 percent of all value added in commodity output.[18] Yet farming represents a mixed case for the market model. Many agricultural products are sold under conditions close to those of a spot market, with prices fluctuating with supply and demand. However, the farmer is not able to respond effectively to those market signals because of the length of the production cycle. A decline in the price of wheat might lead farmers to shift to another commodity, but by the time that product comes to market, it is a whole new year and a whole new product cycle, and the market signals may be entirely different. Moreover, the urgency of getting perishable goods to market robs most farmers of any flexibility in their marketing strategies.

17. The choice of these years is meant only to be illustrative. However, a more recent endpoint for the comparison would complicate the picture by drawing in postindustrial trends.

18. Bureau of the Census, *Historical Statistics of the United States, Colonial Times to 1957* (Washington, D.C.: GPO, 1960), 139.

To be sure, this dependence on the market sometimes induces farmers to economize resources so that they can maximize returns at the market price, but agricultural markets are capricious masters. Precisely when farmers are most successful in transforming labor, capital, and raw materials into an ample supply of final products, overproduction could lead to a disastrous collapse in prices that might make it difficult even to hold on to the farm.

It is because of this capriciousness that farmers have always struggled to insulate themselves from the effects of the market for agricultural commodities. They have done this historically by raising food for family needs, by developing complex networks of reciprocal obligation with neighbors and merchants, by forcing the political authorities to grant them relief from economic distress, and by family members' earning income outside of the farm economy. Above all, farming has almost always depended on a complex family economy in which the pursuit of individual self-interest is generally subordinated to the needs of the family as defined by a male head of household. Farmers, in sum, could not afford to be purely instrumental in their behavior precisely because of their inability to respond effectively to market signals.

To be sure, since 1850 is our benchmark, it must also be emphasized that a significant segment of American agriculture was then based on slavery. Such systems of coerced labor represent another important way in which farmholders have sought to insulate themselves from the effects of the market. In a situation in which market returns are highly uncertain, planters engaging in labor-intensive agriculture search for an alternative to hiring laborers on a short-term, wage-labor basis. Slavery was one solution to this problem, and sharecropping is another.[19] But all of these solutions have the same effect; they reduce the marketness of the economy.

In sum, while agricultural commodities were often sold on spot markets in the nineteenth century, agriculture as a whole tended to have relatively low marketness because producers' ability to re-

19. For discussions of sharecropping, see Jay Mandle, *The Roots of Black Poverty* (Durham, N.C.: Duke University Press, 1978); Jeffery Paige, *Agrarian Revolution: Social Movements and Export Agriculture in the Underdeveloped World* (New York: Free Press, 1975).

spond effectively to market signals was limited. Moreover, in this period, a very high percentage of economic transactions took place within the household economy. Many families raised their own food, baked their own bread, and sewed their own clothes. The unpaid labor of women, children, and other family members was of great material importance in this period, and this further diminished the marketness of the overall economy.

Manufacturing, which accounted for 30 percent of value added in commodity output in the United States around 1850,[20] was generally organized in small units. Often this took the form of contracting systems in which merchants provided raw material to household units (putting out)[21] or subcontracting systems in which skilled laborers organized the production process within the factory.[22] Such arrangements might appear to have more marketness than pure factory arrangements, but the key question is how the contracting prices were established. For the market model to be relevant, those who wanted to perform the labor would have to have been in direct competition with one another, and the same for the contractors, so that the contract price would be the result of a competitive bidding process. But all the evidence that we have points in the opposite direction; that both contractors and contractees colluded among themselves to set price levels. Laborers struggled to defend what they considered customary and fair price levels, while employers often banded together to resist those demands and to impose wage reductions. There was competition, to be sure, but it was competition of workers against employers, not the competition of economic theory.[23] Moreover, there is considerable evidence that many manufactured goods were sold under conditions where prices were not particularly flexible. Many goods were sold locally through stable supply networks where the embeddedness of both buyers and sellers interfered with price competi-

20. Bureau of the Census, *Historical Statistics,* 139.

21. Alan Dawley, *Class and Community: The Industrial Revolution in Lynn* (Cambridge, Mass.: Harvard University Press, 1976), chs. 1–2.

22. Dan Clawson, *Bureaucracy and the Labor Process* (New York: Monthly Review Press, 1980).

23. For a discussion of this in the European context, see William Reddy, *Money and Liberty in Modern Europe* (Cambridge: Cambridge University Press, 1987), ch. 3.

tion. Textile goods, which were often sold under commodity conditions, were the major exception to this pattern, but in that case as well, the reality fell short of pure marketness. The normal arrangement was for manufacturing firms to sell their entire output to particular selling agents, who then marketed the products.[24]

In sum, we have a picture of an economy where high marketness is the exception to the rule; it is extremely difficult to imagine the market operating to equilibrate the economy under these conditions. A high percentage of what was consumed was produced directly in the household economy. While the agricultural economy was governed by market prices, farmers could not be purely economic actors—they had to find ways to insulate themselves from the market. The labor market was underdeveloped because most people were self-employed, and those who were employees, such as skilled artisans in manufacturing, tended to be hired on a long-term basis at wage levels that were shaped by nonmarket considerations such as custom and union power. Finally, at the level of individual behavior, embeddedness was high because most people carried out their work activity within a religious framework that emphasized mutual obligation, the sanctity of toil, and the importance of moral behavior.

The relatively low rates of marketness revealed in this impressionistic portrait of the American economy of 1850 can easily be explained in terms of the immaturity of market capitalism. The enormous growth of manufacturing and the creation of an integrated national market still lay in the future, so it is hardly a surprise that the society was not yet fully organized around market institutions and market behavior. However, when we jump ahead by one hundred years, there is a surprise. Many of the features that reduced the marketness of society in 1850 have disappeared or faded in importance, but they have been replaced by new features that reduce marketness in different ways.

By 1950 agriculture had declined dramatically in its contribution to overall output, and the importance of household production had diminished significantly as most families came to purchase goods and services that were previously produced in the home. These two

24. Alfred D. Chandler, Jr., *The Visible Hand: The Managerial Revolution in American Business* (Cambridge, Mass.: Harvard University Press, 1977), 71.

changes probably are the most significant in reinforcing the collective perception of the growing domination of the market over all of social life. But this very real decline in the economic self-sufficiency of families and communities is not the same thing as increased exposure to the self-regulating markets of economic theory. Moreover, the decline of the household economy was by no means total; calculations of the value of services produced in the home by unpaid family labor were still quite large relative to total GNP.[25] William Nordhaus and James Tobin estimated that in 1947 the value of nonmarket work was $159.6 billion as compared to total national income of $227.9 billion.[26]

But during the same one-hundred-year period in which agriculture dropped from 60 to 6.9 percent[27] of value added in the economy, there was very substantial growth of sectors of the economy that are not subject even to the market discipline of agricultural commodities. First, there was the dramatic expansion of the public sector, which played a negligible role in terms of employment and production in 1850. By 1950 the public sector accounted for some 11.7 percent of all paid person-hours in the economy and the addition of the nonprofit sector brings the total closer to 14 percent.[28] Second, there was another significant component of total output,

25. GNP calculations do not include the value of services produced in the home that are not sold to others. Moreover, there is no obvious way to measure the value of these services because no price is paid for the service or for the labor that went into it. However, estimates can be made by assuming that the value of the labor is equal to what the same kind of labor would earn on the market. For a recent review of these studies, see Ann Chadeau, "Measuring Household Activities: Some International Comparisons," *Review of Income and Wealth* 31, no. 3 (September 1985): 237–53.

26. Nordhaus and Tobin, "Is Growth Obsolete?" in Milton Moss, ed., *The Measurement of Economic and Social Performance* (New York: National Bureau of Economic Research, 1973), 508–64.

27. Bureau of the Census, *Historical Statistics*, 140.

28. The shift to employment data is necessary because the contribution of government and nonprofit entities to total output is measured primarily by the size of the wage bill. This is done because there is, in contrast to the private sector, no market value of the goods and services produced. The resulting asymmetry in the treatment of public and private output means that the GNP data are a problematic measure. Employment data are from Department of Commerce, *The National Income and Product Accounts of the United States, 1929–74* (Washington, D.C.: GPO, 1977), 216. Data on nonprofit person-hours are estimated from unpublished data on persons engaged in production in nonprofit institutions provided by the Bureau of Economic Analysis.

made up of private firms selling military goods only to the government. Such firms are not in a real market situation, since they cannot turn around and sell their output to someone else. Close to 10 percent of all manufacturing output was generated by defense spending in the 1950s.[29]

Another critical change in the hundred-year period has been the rise of the modern corporation, which must be understood as another means for reducing the marketness of the economy.[30] The great irony of capitalist development is that market competition leads to the growth of progressively larger firms, which use their resources to reduce the price competition of economic theory. One way in which they do this is by substituting internal procurement for market transactions. The process of vertical integration means that millions of transactions that would otherwise have occurred in a market are carried out between units of a single corporate entity. This happens not only when Ford creates its own steel mill, but also when firms create their own legal units or financial units, since these are also services that could be purchased on the market.

Corporations are also able to use their resources to reduce the marketness of final product transactions. Techniques such as predatory pricing can be used to weaken potential competitors. By accepting short-term losses as a means of driving potential competitors out of the market, corporations are often able to reduce price competition significantly.[31] They can also use political power to gain government policies that establish barriers to entry by competitors. But the most frequently used measure has been the development of the apparatus of modern advertising and brand names.[32]

The effectiveness of brand names rests on the imperfections of

29. Michael Reich, "Military Spending and Production for Profit," in Richard C. Edwards, Michael Reich, and Thomas E. Weisskopf, *The Capitalist System: A Radical Analysis of American Society* (Englewood Cliffs, N.J.: Prentice-Hall, 1978), 409–17. See also Wassily W. Leontief and Marvin Hoffenberg, "The Economic Effects of Disarmament," *Scientific American,* April 1961, 47–55.

30. Williamson, *Markets and Hierarchies*. See also Gabriel Kolko, *The Triumph of Conservatism* (New York: Free Press, 1963).

31. The importance of this and parallel tactics are emphasized in Richard B. DuBoff and Edward S. Herman, "Alfred Chandler's New Business History: A Review," *Politics & Society* 10, no. 1 (1980): 87–110.

32. John Kenneth Galbraith, *The New Industrial State* (Boston: Houghton Mifflin, 1967), 204–10.

markets; consumers often lack the information to judge the merits of competing products. A familiar brand name gives the customer the promise of reliability, which is often valued more than lower price. It has often been argued, for example, that the great success of the major fast-food franchises rests on the fact that the traveler has a higher assurance of quality control than if he or she were to enter a local restaurant without a familiar name.

However, the advantage of investing in recognizable brand names biases the economy toward large producers. First, the advertising to establish the visibility of a brand name is very expensive and creates significant barriers to entry for new competitors, particularly since strong brand names are often national in scope.[33] Second, it is particularly advantageous to place multiple product lines under the same brand-name umbrella, so that the effects of advertising are multiplied across products.

The most striking recent illustration of the importance of these considerations has been IBM's success in the market for personal computers. It is well known that when IBM finally entered this market, its products were neither technically superior nor cheaper than competitive ones. Nevertheless, IBM was able to gain a major market share and establish a standard for the industry based on the power of its reputation; its brand name provided consumers with a promise of reliability in a situation characterized by high uncertainty.[34]

If we return, however, to 1950, it is clear that even by that point, the economy was dominated by a number of huge corporations that were able to reduce the role of price competition in a wide range of markets significantly.[35]

A final important mechanism for reducing the marketness of the economy has been the growth of professional employment. Although the rise of professionalism can fruitfully be understood as an

---

33. The huge apparatus of modern advertising can also be seen as a reduction in marketness in another way. By attempting to shift the preferences of consumers, advertising violates the assumption that preferences are formed exogenously—outside of the terrain of economic transactions.

34. Pratt and Zeckhauser, *Principals and Agents*, 13–14.

35. Data on concentration by industries are provided in John M. Blair, *Economic Concentration: Structure, Behavior, and Public Policy* (New York: Harcourt Brace Jovanovich, 1972), ch. 1.

attempt to create monopolies in certain labor markets,[36] there is another aspect of professionalization that is important here. Professionalism can be understood as a social means to reduce opportunism in markets where information inequalities are particularly significant. If, for example, doctors were simply people who sold health services, the number of unnecessary procedures would be much higher than current rates. Professionalism is a means of embedding the action of an individual by socializing him or her into a code of professional ethics, and its result is supposed to be a significant reduction in the marketness of the resulting transactions.[37]

The economic importance of this aspect of professionalism is much greater than the number of professional employees would suggest. Modern capitalism relies to an increasing extent on occupational groups who are expected to be insulated from purely instrumental activity. If accountants simply "cooked the books" in the way their clients told them to, the basic data necessary for the investment process would be unreliable. If lawyers were unconstrained from selling their services and the information that they have gathered to the highest bidder, contracts would be useless. If bankers were not at all constrained by a professional commitment to prudence, and were free to maximize their returns, there would be little financial stability. These examples can readily be multiplied: the qualities of the services produced by other groups, such as engineers, journalists, stockbrokers, and university professors, would also be radically undermined were purely instrumental behavior the rule.[38]

In addition to the expansion of the public and nonprofit sectors, the growth of the giant corporation, and the rise of professions, there are other ways in which the marketness of transactions in goods and services is reduced in contemporary economies. As in

36. See Magali Sarfatti Larson, *The Rise of Professionalism* (Berkeley: University of California Press, 1977).

37. This argument has similarities to Talcott Parsons's account of the sacred dimension of the professions ("The Professions in Social Structure," in *Essays in Sociological Theory* [New York: Free Press, 1964], 33–49).

38. These examples suggest the folly of ideas of deregulating such professional services. The idea that the market, by itself, can organize such services is nonsensical, since the whole idea of such professions is to insulate their members from pure market behavior.

1850, many purchases of supplies by firms continue to be carried out on the basis of long-standing relationships or involve such small numbers of providers that genuine price competition cannot occur.[39] As for the labor market, its scope has expanded enormously with the dramatic decline in self-employment. Yet the marketness of these transactions remains relatively low. As of 1950, relatively little labor was hired under spot-market conditions. Outside of migrant labor, most blue-collar and white-collar employees worked on the basis of implicit contracts and internal labor markets that promised continuity of employment.

Implicit contracts and internal labor markets are means of responding to the problem of opportunism.[40] If an employee thinks of himself or herself as working in a particular place for only one day or one week, he or she is likely to work at a minimal level of effort. Since even an elaborate monitoring system represents only a partial solution to this problem,[41] employers tend to trade the promise of employment continuity and job mobility for higher levels of effort. To be sure, problems remain in the willingness of employees to work as hard as employers might want, but they are less severe than the problems encountered with employees hired on a spot-market basis.

Finally, if the analysis is shifted to the level of individual action, it seems clear that the religious motivations that tended to surround economic action have declined in salience over time.[42] Secularization has meant that religious beliefs have become ever more private, and the tensions between religious beliefs and the pursuit of

39. "In response, most business is conducted within the context of long-term relationships. Subtle mechanisms involving reputation, promises of future promotions, and the surplus gained from less than fully competitive long-term contracts help an economy in which information is not costlessly shared to struggle to second-best solutions" (Pratt and Zeckhauser, *Principals and Agents*, 14).

40. See Williamson, *Markets and Hierarchies*, 57–81.

41. The classic form of such monitoring is a piece-rate system, but piece rates are clearly not practical in all employment situations. Moreover, since a new employee who does not expect to stay long is unlikely to be able to "make out"—achieve the rate of production required for a bonus—he or she has no incentive to produce anything more than the minimal rate. See Michael Burawoy, *Manufacturing Consent: Changes in the Labor Process under Monopoly Capitalism* (Chicago: University of Chicago Press, 1979).

42. Fred Hirsch, *Social Limits to Growth* (Cambridge, Mass.: Harvard University Press, 1976). 137–51.

economic self-interest are less acute. Nevertheless, it would be a mistake to deny that moral considerations rooted in religious belief continue to constrain individuals from purely instrumental behavior. Moreover, new ways of embedding individual actions emerge to take up the slack. The growing importance of commitment to professional ideals has already been discussed. It is also clear that the rise of the corporation serves to embed individual action. Price-driven behavior is much less important in a corporate setting, where opportunities for mobility have much more to do with the evaluations of superiors and relatively abstract performance measures. Also, it is clear that in 1950 the individual's loyalty to the firm still militated against a singular concern with individual self-interest. The implicit promise of employment security and the possibility of mobility within the firm were reciprocated by the employees' sense of commitment to the organization, and this further reduced the appeal of instrumental behavior.

The nature of this comparison between the economy in 1850 and 1950 does not allow for any definitive judgment on whether the aggregate level of marketness and instrumentalism rose or fell. In both years, it is striking, however, that despite enormous changes in the structure of the economy, the deviations from high marketness and high instrumentalism were so great. It would seem that at both points in time, the market model of prices equilibrating supply and demand through their impact on decisions at the margins applied to only a small proportion of all economic transactions.

The historical comparison is also meant to suggest that there was not a moment in time when the level of overall marketness was significantly higher than it was in either 1850 or 1950. The forms of insulation from the market that existed in 1850—the importance of household production, the centrality of agriculture, the embeddedness of individual action in family and religious motivations—did not disappear overnight. They continued to be important well into the twentieth century. At the same time, the new forms of insulation that were salient in 1950—the rise of the corporation, the growth of the public sector, and the growing role of the professions—can be traced back to the late nineteenth century. The most that can be said is that there might have been a small increase of marketness in the last decades of the nineteenth century as older forms of insulation declined more quickly than the development of new forms of insulation, but any change was quickly counteracted by the consolidation of the modern corporation.

This argument has stressed the relative stability of the level of marketness, but the point is not to suggest that there is some equilibrium level of marketness that the society manages to maintain through a homeostatic mechanism. The point is to show that the high levels of economic efficiency that capitalism has produced have come *with* relatively low levels of marketness.[43] The next question to address is why the society has not pursued the promised benefits of substantially higher levels of marketness and greater instrumentalism of behavior.

Problems with the Market Model

There is a long tradition of argument that emphasizes the unrealistic nature of the assumptions behind the framework of market equilibration by making explicit all of the conditions that must apply for market self-regulation to occur, such as perfectly competitive markets, preferences formed exogenously, and so on. Yet this type of critique still makes it possible to hold on to the model of market self-regulation as an ideal that is ultimately unachievable but remains a goal to which society should aspire.

The argument here, in contrast, is that an effort to create an economy close to the ideal type of high marketness and high instrumentalism of behavior would have disastrous consequences.[44] Relatively low levels of marketness can be understood as the result of rational choices to avoid the high costs of high marketness. In fact, the economic benefits that capitalism has produced are a consequence of lower levels of marketness and greater embeddedness of behavior. Some of the economic defects of high marketness have

43. For similar arguments, see the discussion of the impurity principle in Geoffrey M. Hodgson, *Economics and Institutions: A Manifesto for a Modern Institutional Economics* (Philadelphia: University of Pennsylvania Press, 1988), 167–71. He writes: "A 'pure' market or exchange system, on purely contractarian lines, could not work in practice and is unacceptable in theory" (167). See also Etzioni, *Moral Dimension*, ch. 5.

44. The classical source of this argument is Karl Polanyi, *The Great Transformation* (1944; reprint, Boston: Beacon Press, 1957).

already been touched upon, but problems of information and time commitments require further discussion.[45]

Information and Transaction Costs

The market's capacity to reach equilibrium through price changes rests on enough equality of information between buyers and sellers to prevent widespread fraud. When some sizable percentage of purchasers are not getting what they think they are paying for, for example, there cannot be an effective balancing of preferences and utility. Moreover, since the costs of making up the information deficit are often considerable, societies have developed a rich variety of techniques to overcome the information problem and reduce the marketness of transactions. These devices can be understood as ways to overcome the inefficiencies built into market transactions that occur in the real world of information inequalities.

One example of such inefficiencies occurred in the American silk industry when silk manufacturers discovered that they could increase the volume of their silk output by loading the product with extra chemicals. This adulteration was not at all visible or detectable with the technologies available at the time, but the result was a significant decline in the durability of garments made from this adulterated silk. A woman might open her closet to find that her recently purchased light-colored silk dress had turned black. Since silk was sold on a commodity market and none of the producers were strong enough to create a visible brand name, competitive pressure forced everyone to engage in adulteration. Over time, the market worked, in the sense that consumers grew wise and shifted to other fabrics, but the macroeconomic consequence was the wasteful decline of what had been an extremely vital and productive

45. Some of the defects of high marketness are too familiar to belabor. It is well known that markets alone will underproduce public goods and will overproduce negative externalities such as environmental pollution. The distributional consequences of high marketness are also extremely negative; systems of public welfare can be understood as efforts to reduce the marketness of transactions in human labor. On the latter point, see Frances Fox Piven and Richard A. Cloward, "The Historical Sources of the Contemporary Relief Debate," in Fred Block, Richard A. Cloward, Barbara Ehrenreich, and Frances Fox Piven, *The Mean Season: The Attack on the Welfare State* (New York: Pantheon Books, 1987), 3–44.

industry.[46] Even in less extreme cases, the efficiency costs of such information inequalities can be great, since producers lose the incentive to produce the best-quality product with the given resources.

In cases where products are more vital for human survival, the usual consequence of the vulnerability of consumers to product adulteration has been government regulation. Professionalism is also a means to overcome information inequalities in markets for services and usually involves some government regulatory structure. As argued earlier, brand names provide consumers with some additional assurance that sellers will not take too much advantage of information inequalities. Moreover, corporations that substitute internal production for outside purchases sometimes do so to overcome their vulnerability to outside sellers.

In labor markets, high marketness reduces efficiency in three different ways. First, as I argued above, workers hired on a short-term basis have little incentive to produce at high levels. Second, if all workers are hired on the basis of spot contracts, it becomes extremely difficult to organize the on-the-job training that is part of many work settings. Employees who have already gained certain types of vital information about the production process have little incentive to share this information with other employees; such sharing would undermine their own improved bargaining position.[47] Third, such a system of contracting discourages the voicing of employees' opinions—a mechanism by which employees are able to provide more information to employers. Albert Hirschman has argued that the mechanism of voice within organizations can contribute significantly to efficiency by making managers aware of problems in the functioning of the organization.[48] However, if employees who see problems either do not care enough about the organization or simply exercise the option of leaving, voice will not be exercised, and the situation can deteriorate for some time before market signals are strong enough to highlight a problem.

46. Philip Scranton, "An Exceedingly Irregular Business" (paper presented to a seminar on "Technology and Culture," University of Pennsylvania, 1985).
47. Williamson, *Markets and Hierarchies*, 63.
48. Hirschman, *Exit, Voice and Loyalty* (Cambridge, Mass.: Harvard University Press, 1970).

Opportunism and Time Commitments

Many of the problems of information inequality can be understood as problems of opportunism, since someone is taking advantage of the inequality to pursue his or her own interests. However, there is another type of opportunism that has to do with questions of time.[49] In a commodity market, the capacity of a trader to recalculate his or her interest at lightning speed is obviously a virtue; the quicker those calculations, the more rapidly prices will reach their proper level. However, when this same rapid recalculation of self-interest occurs outside of commodity markets, the results are not as benign. The problem is that production generally depends on some degree of stability in the relations among a group of people,[50] and it is this stability that is undermined by rapid recalculations of self-interest.

A simple example is the disruptions that occur in an organizational setting when an individual is continually exploring outside employment opportunities that might prove more lucrative than present arrangements. First, such a job search consumes time and energy, and it is likely that the job performance of the individual involved will suffer. Second, the possibility that the individual may leave is likely to disrupt relations within the group. Individuals may be less likely to share important information with the potential leaver, especially if the departure might be to another firm in the same industry. Moreover, there is likely to be increased anxiety, as the potential departure forces a reconsideration of existing alliances and stimulates competition to fill the possible vacancy. Finally, the departure itself creates transition costs, as the organization must replace the individual and train a new incumbent in the specifics of the job.

To be sure, there are also benefits to an organization from a certain amount of turnover; it opens up mobility routes, and there is always the possibility that the new set of relationships will work better than the old. But the more frequent these episodes and the larger the number of individuals involved, the more difficult it is to

49. The argument here is a variant of the argument in Hirsch, *Social Limits to Growth*, that the viability of capitalism depends on the persistence of precapitalist values that tend to be undermined by economic progress.

50. Production has, in the language of economics, an intertemporal dimension.

get any work done. If all of the one hundred top managers of a firm are seriously considering outside offers every day, the level of uncertainty will become unbearable. There is nothing that anyone can count on, since there is no certainty as to who will be holding top positions in six months' time. The result is abandonment of any kind of long-term thinking and a reduction in initiatives at the lower levels of the organization.

Similar problems have been noted with organizations that cycle people through internal jobs very quickly.[51] If someone knows that they are likely to be in a particular position for only six months, they have little incentive to master the particular job and concern themselves with the long-term viability of the unit. Instead, they are likely to concentrate on results that can be quickly achieved and that are highly visible. At best, this means a reorganization of the unit that serves no genuine purpose; at worst, it can mean an effort to improve short-term results at the expense of long-term considerations. The classic instance is the plant manager who defers major maintenance expenditures to improve the bottom line in the hope that he or she will have moved to a higher position before the consequences of deferred maintenance become clear.

The rapid recalculation of self-interest that comes with a more intense pursuit of internal or external mobility possibilities also undermines the effectiveness of the networks of personal links that operate to protect people from the exploitation of information inequalities. As Granovetter argues, personal ties are often extremely important in managing market relationships such as that between a supplier and a purchaser.[52] The personal link reduces the likelihood of a shipment of inferior parts or increases the reliability of promises of prompt delivery. But when the incumbents in these two positions are highly mobile, the picture changes. If the supply manager knows that he or she will never have to deal with that purchaser again after this week because of movement to another job, then there is no reason not to send a substandard shipment or put that customer at the bottom of the delivery queue.

The importance of these arguments is clear in light of recent

---

51. Rosabeth Kanter, *Men and Women of the Corporation* (New York: Basic Books, 1977), 163, 272–74.
52. Granovetter, "Economic Action and Social Structure," 496.

developments in which corporations and units of corporations are increasingly bought and sold like commodities on a market. Although corporate mergers and takeovers have long been a feature of the landscape, these acquisitions are now often seen as temporary. One corporation will buy up another one only to reorganize its components and sell them off again for a profit. The quintessence of this process has been the phenomenon of corporate raiders who buy up firms to sell their different parts, on the theory that the separate assets are worth more than the value of the shares of the integrated firm.

All of this has been justified in the name of the market. If firms and units of firms can be bought and sold like wheat, then top managers who are not making adequate use of their productive assets can be more readily replaced by more effective managers, and capital will be more effectively allocated to the more efficient firms. What this line of argument neglects, however, is that the efficiency of the corporation rests on a relatively stable set of social relationships, which are radically disrupted by these financial dealings. The reason that the corporation replaced arrangements of high marketness in the first place was because of the inefficiencies of purely market relations; turning the firm into a commodity threatens to undermine those efficiency gains.

There is reason to believe that these corporate takeovers have high costs.[53] Some reports indicate that in firms subject to prolonged takeover battles, very little work unrelated to the takeover bid goes on in managerial circles. Those managers who are not involved in the immediate task of fighting the takeover are worrying about their employment prospects.[54] Moreover, these worries are justified, because many managers are replaced in the post-takeover period, and many others begin to look around more intensively for

---

53. See Edward Herman and Louis Lowenstein, "The Efficiency Effects of Hostile Takeovers," in John C. Coffee, Jr., Louis Lowenstein, and Susan Rose-Ackerman, eds., *Knights, Raiders, and Targets: The Impact of the Hostile Takeover* (New York: Oxford University Press, 1988), 211–40; David Ravenscraft and F. M. Scherer, *Mergers, Sell-Offs and Economic Efficiency* (Washington, D.C.: Brookings Institution, 1987).

54. Paul Hirsch reports that 52 percent of top managers jump ship within three years of their firm being taken over (*Pack Your Own Parachute: How to Survive Mergers, Takeovers, and Other Corporate Disasters* [Reading, Mass.: Addison-Wesley, 1987], 52).

other opportunities. It is difficult to imagine that such a prolonged period of uncertainty and massive turnover in the managerial ranks would not have adverse effects on a firm's efficiency. And it is often the case that once the affected firm has begun to stabilize, it is sold again and experiences another period of managerial turmoil.

The most serious danger in all of this is that financial activity—including the buying and selling of whole firms—becomes the central economic activity of the society.[55] The problem is that one can make huge amounts of money in a relatively short period of time in financial markets, while making a fortune through producing a product or managing a firm takes much longer. Hence, if individuals begin to recalculate their interests more frequently, more of them are likely to end up working around the financial markets. It is already the case that the young lawyers and investment bankers—many of them only a few years out of law school—who put together mergers and acquisition deals for New York investment banks often make tens of millions a year, more than the much older CEOs of the giant corporations involved in the deals.[56]

The result is a growing instrumentalism in the way that these top managers relate to their firms. One sign of this is the phenomenon of the "golden parachute"—the arrangements by which top managers assure themselves of extremely generous severance pay if the firm should be the object of a successful takeover effort. In one case, a single executive received a payout of $35 million as part of a golden parachute settlement.[57] These arrangements are justified as a means of assuring the loyalty of the firms' chief executives, but this only reinforces the point that with the rapid recalculation of

55. "We are throwing more and more of our resources, including the cream of our youth, into financial activities remote from the production of goods and services, into activities that generate high private rewards disproportionate to their social productivity," James Tobin has been quoted as saying (Warren A. Law, "Comment," in Coffee, Lowenstein, and Rose-Ackerman, eds., *Knights, Raiders, and Targets*, 262).

56. The outlandish financial rewards to those involved in selling junk bonds for corporate buyouts are discussed in Connie Bruck, *The Predators' Ball: The Junk-Bond Raiders and the Man Who Staked Them* (New York: Simon & Schuster, 1988).

57. John C. Coffee, Jr., "Shareholders versus Managers: The Strain in the Corporate Web," in Coffee, Lowenstein, and Rose-Ackerman, eds., *Knights, Raiders, and Targets*, 134.

interests, loyalty becomes problematic. It is easy, for example, to imagine circumstances where a firm's CEO could make much more money from trading in insider information than he or she could from managing the company properly. In light of the recent insider-trading scandals, the idea of a CEO deliberately producing bad results for a firm as a means of making big gains by selling short in the stock market does not strain credibility.[58]

In sum, loyalty and trust are essential for an economy to operate effectively, or else the very mechanisms developed to compensate for the information inequalities in markets will fail. However, when individuals act on the basis of the continuous recalculation of self-interest, the bases of loyalty and trust are destroyed. The results are economically costly levels of uncertainty and the spread of opportunistic behavior that diminishes economic efficiency.

Conclusion

This chapter began with the argument that it is theoretically possible to systematically compare the degree of marketness of different economies at different points in time as a way of evaluating how near or far those economies are from the economists' model of self-regulating markets. The point of this argument is to show that actual economies represent an extremely complex mix of micro-economic choices, social regulation, and state action. Given the complexity of these arrangements, the kinds of sweeping claims that are made by both defenders and critics of the market appear intellectually suspect. The idea that allowing greater market free-dom will invariably increase economic efficiency is a purely ideo-logical one. By the same token, claims that increases in the planning of the economy will necessarily produce greater rationality are equally problematic. One cannot know in advance the effects of increasing or decreasing the marketness of a particular economy; the outcomes depend on complex social processes.

This skepticism about the ordinary slogans of economic debate

---

58. One recent case comes close to this—KaiserTech's management sued the firm's chairman for violating the securities laws in connection with short-term transactions in the company's stock ("KaiserTech Sues Its Chairman, Clore, for Alleged Securities Law Violations," *Wall Street Journal*, March 2, 1988).

need not lead to paralysis and despair. The purpose here, on the contrary, is to clear away the underbrush of unnecessary assumptions in order to examine more concretely the actual institutional arrangements of an increasingly postindustrial economy. Such an examination will show that the concepts of neoclassical economics have increasingly diverged from reality.

Chapter Four

Labor

The concept of labor is both the most fundamental and the most inherently problematic of all economic categories. It is the category through which economists understand most of the human input into the production process. Yet in treating the major inputs into production—labor, capital, and raw materials—in a parallel fashion, economists tend to analyze labor in isolation from the social relations in which individuals are embedded. It is not actual human beings who are an input into the production process, but one of their characteristics—their capacity to do work. But this is an inherently paradoxical strategy since the individual's capacity to do work is not innate; it is socially created and sustained.

This paradox means that in analyzing the efficient use of labor, economists must have a theory about the social arrangements that will maximize the capacity of individuals to work. Such a theory need not be explicit; on the contrary, it has often been an implicit or subterranean dimension of economic analysis. Conventional neoclassical economics, in fact, tends to treat these social relations as a nonissue, while simultaneously assuming that the unquestioned authority of employers over workers is both natural and necessary. More recently, labor economists have begun to develop explicit arguments about the kinds of social relations that optimize the use of labor, and these more recent formulations often depart from neoclassical assumptions.

The argument of this chapter is that even the newer, more explicit theories developed by economists do not go far enough in analyzing the social dimension of contemporary production. The argument is developed in three parts. The first part is largely theoretical, analyzing different theories—both implicit and explicit—of the efficient use of labor. The second part is empirical, examining actual trends in skill level in the contemporary U.S. economy. The third part attempts to provide an alternative view of the efficient use of labor in light of the empirical trends.

The Theory of Efficient Labor

In neoclassical economics, the labor market is basically similar to any other commodity market. Individuals compete to sell their labor on an impersonal market where prices equilibrate supply and demand. When the system of interlocking markets for labor, capital, and commodities is working properly, the price or wage of each additional entrant into the labor market will equal his or her marginal product—the amount of added output that he or she will produce when hired by an entrepreneur. As we have seen, analysts operating within this framework sometimes argue that it does not really matter whether the capitalist hires the laborer or the laborer hires the capitalist, because labor and capital are both factors of production that at equilibrium are rewarded with their marginal product.[1]

In the purest version of this framework, the efficient use of labor means simply allowing the market mechanism to operate by itself. Interferences with the market, such as union efforts to bid wages up above market levels, are seen as inherently inefficient because they lead to a less than optimal allocation of labor. Similarly, the principle of seniority in replacing workers is also unacceptable because employers need to be free to pursue the option of hiring younger, more energetic workers if they are available. Moreover, external regulation of the market is unnecessary because economic competition places maximal pressure on each employer to make the most efficient possible use of his or her labor force.

This simplified model is most compatible with an economy in

1. Paul Samuelson has written that "in the competitive model it makes no difference whether capital hires labor or the other way around" (quoted in Samuel Bowles, "The Production Process in a Competitive Economy: Walrasian, Neo-Hobbesian, and Marxian Models," *American Economic Review* 75, no. 1 [March 1985]: 16–36).

which employees' skill levels are relatively low. Otherwise, it would be difficult to assume the rapid adjustment of the labor market to various kinds of disruptions. For example, it is assumed that if a particular industry were to go into decline for one reason or another, the displaced employees would be able to find work in another sector of the economy relatively quickly. It is implicit in such a formulation that there are relatively few industry-specific skills that would prevent unemployed auto workers from adapting quickly to the computer industry.

Much work in labor economics in recent years has concentrated on going beyond these formulations. In particular, economists have stressed two critical ways in which the simple neoclassical framework is flawed. The first has been the discovery of "internal labor markets"—the complex administrative mechanisms that firms use to allocate labor.[2] Firms tend to hire from the outside mostly for entry-level positions, from which they then promote individuals step by step. As a result, many of the hiring decisions made by a firm are relatively insulated from the external labor market. This insulation, in turn, means that there are really a multiplicity of different, partially insulated, labor markets, rather than one unified labor market that incorporates all individuals.[3]

Along with this insight has come the argument that it might well be efficient for firms to pay their employees more than the market-determined wage. This argument also grows out of the recognition that most employee-employer relationships are not on a spot-market basis; rather there appears to be an implicit contract in which the employer is offering employment security and a prospect of job mobility in exchange for higher levels of effort by employees.[4] In

2. Peter B. Doeringer and Michael J. Piore, *Internal Labor Markets and Manpower Analysis* (Lexington, Mass.: D.C. Heath, 1971).

3. For one of the most systematic critiques of the neoclassical view based on the existence of internal labor markets, see Aage B. Sorensen and Arne L. Kalleberg, "An Outline of a Theory of the Matching of Persons to Jobs," in Ivar Berg, ed., *Sociological Perspectives on Labor Markets* (New York: Academic Press, 1981), 52–74.

4. The idea of implicit contracts emphasizing wage stability is elaborated in Costas Azariadis, "Implicit Contracts and Underemployment Equilibria," *Journal of Political Economy* 83, no. 6 (December 1975): 1183–1202. Subsequent use of the idea has emphasized both income and employment security; see Paula England and George Farkas, *Households, Employment, and Gender: A Social, Economic, and Demographic View* (New York: Aldine Publishing, 1986), 132–36.

other words, employers voluntarily restrict their own ability to replace existing employees with younger, cheaper ones. "Efficiency-wage" theory has sought to provide an explanation for this choice by managers.[5]

These efficiency-wage arguments stress that labor is different from other commodities because the purchaser's capacity to obtain the full value of what he or she has purchased requires the cooperation of the laborer. Hence, wages that are higher than market wages, promises of job security, and the use of internal job ladders to motivate employees can all be seen as devices to elicit the cooperation of employees. One of the leading theorists of this school, George Akerlof, has suggested that the relationship between employer and employee should be seen as a partial gift exchange in which the employee offers more work effort than necessary and the employer reciprocates with a wage that is higher than what might otherwise be expected.[6]

This vision of the efficient use of labor is quite different from the simplified neoclassical conception. Once management is seen as acting within a web of reciprocal understandings, despotic managerial strategies in which employees are arbitrarily fired appear counterproductive. However, the avoidance of arbitrary and capricious hiring actions and of wage-cutting as a general managerial strategy are virtually the only limitations on management authority that are implicit in efficiency-wage arguments;[7] it is still assumed that efficient management of an enterprise depends on minimal interference with management authority.

Although the efficiency-wage position represents a significant advance in addressing the efficient organization of labor, its usefulness is limited by its failure to examine more closely the relationships of coercion and cooperation that lie buried beneath the surface of the employment relationship.

5. See, particularly, George A. Akerlof and Janet L. Yellen, eds., *Efficiency Wage Models of the Labor Market* (Cambridge: Cambridge University Press, 1986).

6. George A. Akerlof, "Labor Contracts as Partial Gift Exchange," in Akerlof and Yellen, eds., *Efficiency Wage Models*, 66–101.

7. Efficiency-wage theorists might well defend wage-cutting as a strategy in a specific situation in which a firm had allowed its wage level to drift higher than those of its competitors.

The Problem of Coercion and Cooperation

The explicit side of the neoclassical analysis of the labor market emphasizes unconstrained freedom of choice; the labor contract is an exchange of equivalents in which the wage is fair recompense for the worker's effort. However, Karl Marx devoted considerable effort to showing the coercion implicit in these mechanisms. The potential worker has the freedom to choose among a wide variety of employers offering different wages and working conditions, but this choice is very different from the consumer choice as to whether to buy brown pants or black. Whereas the latter decision is discretionary, the potential worker *must* sign on with an employer or risk impoverishment and possible starvation.[8] Moreover, the coercion does not end there; in signing a contract to work for a particular employer, the potential employee is agreeing to submit to the authority of the employer. Defiance of that authority is tantamount to ending the contract; the worker is likely to find him or herself unemployed for failing to obey the employer. The first form of coercion clearly reinforces the second.[9] The worker is more likely to accept the authority of the employer when he or she realizes that the only alternatives are hunger or a potentially even more despotic employer.[10]

This analysis of labor market and employer coercion has not simply been the invention of radical critics of capitalism; it has also been implicit in much economic analysis, including neoclassical formulations. The implicit belief in the necessity of these forms of coercion becomes most visible when alternatives to existing institutional patterns are debated.[11]

8. For a recent discussion, see Paola Villa, *The Structuring of Labor Markets: A Comparative Analysis of the Steel and Construction Industries in Italy* (Oxford: Clarendon Press, 1986), 6–7.

9. These forms of coercion can be seen as simply the result of biological necessity, since historically the lack of sufficient work effort by the bulk of a population might easily lead to mass starvation. In developed societies, however, where a single farmer can produce enough to feed hundreds of families, biological necessity is not sufficient to explain the existence of a particular set of social arrangements.

10. Historically, the choice was even starker, since defiant employees were often likely to find themselves blacklisted and unable to find any work in their trade.

11. To be sure, these forms of coercion have sometime been softened. Systems of unemployment insurance and welfare payments protect workers—for a time—

For example, debates over welfare policies have repeatedly re-vealed the coercive side of the labor market. There have been repeated episodes in U.S. history in which economic problems have been blamed on the existence of an overly generous welfare system, which is presumed to interfere with the proper operation of the labor market.[12] Forms of support for the needy from outdoor relief to unemployment insurance to Aid for Families with Depend-ent Children have been blamed for providing the unemployed with an alternative to taking the first job offered. The usual policy pre-scription is a dramatic cutback in the availability of welfare, de-signed to reinforce the discipline of the labor market and bolster employers in their exercise of authority at the workplace.

Even in between these campaigns for severe restrictions on wel-fare, economists and businesspeople argue that welfare programs should be market-conforming—that is, they should interfere as little as possible with the pressure of the labor market on individu-als to work and acquiesce in management authority. Hence, for example, when government tests of guaranteed income in the 1970s found that recipients of grants had some tendency to reduce their work effort, this result was enough to discredit the negative income tax as insufficiently conforming to the market.[13]

It is somewhat less common for economists and businesspeople to write about the necessity of managerial coercion, probably be-cause such coercion tends to conflict with democratic and egalitar-ian values. Defense of managerial coercion is usually implicit in arguments about "the right to manage" that emphasize the eco-nomic costs of any interference with managerial freedom of ac-tion.[14] However, the defense of such coercion becomes explicit in

---

from accepting whatever wages are offered. Moreover, family and community ties have also provided protection from the discipline of the labor market. The emer-gence of trade unions and various forms of governmental protection of employees have also placed some limits on the authority of employers.

12. See Frances Fox Piven and Richard A. Cloward, "The Historical Sources of the Contemporary Relief Debate," in Fred Block, Richard A. Cloward, Barbara Ehrenreich, and Frances Fox Piven, *The Mean Season: The Attack on the Welfare State* (New York: Pantheon Books, 1987), 3–43.

13. See Leland Neuberg, *Conceptual Anomalies in Economics and Statistics: Lessons from the Social Experiment* (New York: Cambridge University Press, 1988).

14. Howell Harris, *The Right to Manage: Industrial Relations Policies of Amer-ican Business in the 1940s* (Madison: University of Wisconsin Press, 1982).

a critical place—in the jurisprudence governing the employment contract. In deciding cases bearing on employees' rights, the courts have repeatedly upheld the sanctity of managerial authority, even where the intent of legislators was to curtail that authority. Writing about the Supreme Court's interpretation of the Wagner Act, James Atleson writes,

The restrictions on the scope of Section 7 do not arise from constitutional considerations or from concern with potential conflict with other portions of the act. Rather, the Court has created limits that are not justified by statutory language or legislative history. Courts have "balanced" broad statutory protections with considerations based upon the Court's own views of the necessities of the economic system.[15]

Foremost among these "necessities of the economic system" is that there be minimal interference with managerial authority over employees. In treating this managerial coercion as necessary, the Supreme Court has turned a background assumption of economic analysis into a legal principle.

Moreover, both labor-market and employer coercion figure prominently in arguments about the difficulty of constructing efficient alternatives to capitalist arrangements. It has frequently been argued that if socialism guarantees everyone a reasonable livelihood independent of work effort, it will have a chronic problem with slackers—those who prefer to "free ride" on other people's efforts. Without the coercion of the labor market, people will be free to be lazy, and production will suffer. Critics of socialism also argue that the combination of social ownership of the means of production and the availability of income unrelated to work will undermine managerial authority at the workplace, with the result that people simply will not work hard enough to match the productivity of capitalist societies.[16] In other words, managerial coercion is treated as an essential prerequisite for economic growth.

15. James B. Atleson, *Values and Assumptions in American Labor Law* (Amherst: University of Massachusetts Press, 1983), 82–83.

16. The experience of actual socialist societies gives some credence to these critiques. The guarantee of a job is part of a set of employment relations that contribute to relatively low levels of work effort. See Charles F. Sabel and David Stark, "Planning, Politics and Shop-Floor Power: Hidden Forms of Bargaining in Soviet-Imposed State-Socialist Societies," *Politics & Society* 11, no. 4 (1982): 439–75.

The Missing Face of the Labor Process

Although employer and labor-market coercion have loomed large in the history of market society, it is a mistake to imagine that they provide a complete picture of capitalist labor relations. On the contrary, the resulting model is far too limited in the range of human motivations it allows; it suggests that individuals can act either on the basis of economic self-interest, narrowly conceived, or in deference to authority. In actuality, there is another important set of motivations—the desire of employees to engage cooperatively with other employees and with management to complete work tasks. This cooperative impulse can ebb and flow in its intensity, just as labor-market coercion can be stronger or weaker at different times. However, the existence of this cooperative impulse is critical for understanding why the labor relation has worked even in those circumstances where coercion has proven to be relatively ineffective.

This cooperative impulse has played a critical, but neglected, role in the history of market economies as a kind of "functional substitute" for managerial coercion. In a much discussed article, Charles F. Sabel and Jonathan Zeitlin have argued that specialized manufacturing production based on high levels of worker skill represented a dynamic and important part of the capitalist economy far into the twentieth century.[17] They insist that mass production based on relatively unskilled labor was not the only route to a modern economy; there was an alternative route based on specialized manufacturing and craft skills. Even if one is skeptical about their strongest claim, Sabel and Zeitlin do provide powerful evidence for the importance and persistence of manufacturing industries based on craft skills.

This evidence, however, creates an anomaly for those who would emphasize the necessity of managerial coercion in a market economy. In craft-based industries, such as Lyonese silk or Sheffield cutlery, workers were characteristically able to exercise a good deal of power at the workplace because of their possession of craft knowl-

17. Charles F. Sabel and Jonathan Zeitlin, "Historical Alternatives to Mass Production: Politics, Markets and Technology in Nineteenth-Century Industrialization," *Past and Present* 108 (August 1985): 133–76. See also Michael J. Piore and Charles F. Sabel, *The Second Industrial Divide: Possibilities for Prosperity* (New York: Basic Books, 1984).

edge and their strong ties of collective solidarity. Moreover, the fact that they had craft knowledge made their position quite different from that of other workers. Although these craft workers sometimes had to endure bouts of unemployment brought about by the business cycle, they were much less likely to have to take whatever work happened to be offered. Their skill provided protection from market and employer coercion. Yet despite this relative absence of coercion, Sabel and Zeitlin show, many of these industries remained economically vital for long periods of time.

According to theory, the weakening of coercion should mean that workers would either significantly reduce their work effort or use their power to demand too large a share of the industry's product. Either way, profits should decline, and the industry should lose its vitality. The persistence that Sabel and Zeitlin document suggests that neither of these dynamics operated. On the contrary, the cooperative impulse—taking the form of an ethic of craft work— assured that these workers applied themselves seriously to the tasks of production. Deciding the relative income shares of employers and workers was never simple, but in those specialized industries that survived over long periods, these issues were apparently negotiated within a framework of cooperation in which each side recognized the validity of the other's claims. We can presume that on one side workers were constrained by their commitment to the preservation of the industry, while on the other employers were constrained by the need for the cooperation of their employees.

The evidence of the persistence of craft-based industries can be supplemented by other examples in which the weakening of coercive mechanisms has not interfered with the efficient working of market institutions. The contemporary equivalent of craft knowledge is professional knowledge, and there are many examples of private firms that are quite successful despite the fact that most of their employees are professionals who are well insulated from the normal forms of coercion. Again, the cooperative impulse—this time mobilized through an ethic of professionalism—can explain the viability of these forms.

This cooperative dimension of the labor contract has been recognized in various strands of thought. The Human Relations analysis of labor-management relations pioneered by Elton Mayo was based on the insight that workers have impulses to cooperate with one another and with management if only employers treat them like human beings. Much of the theory underlying the contemporary concern with quality of working life, particularly the pioneering work on socio-technical systems done at the Tavistock Institute in London, has emphasized the psychological need of individuals to complete tasks and the critical motivating importance of work groups.[18]

Most of the cited examples of the cooperative face of employment relations involve workers with higher skill levels than those generally assumed in neoclassical analysis. To be sure, the cooperative impulse can be important even with relatively unskilled workers. However, it could well be that the value of cooperation as a functional substitute for managerial coercion rises with skill level.

Once the importance of the cooperative face of the employment relationship is recognized, it seems unnecessary to conceptualize labor relations as a partial gift exchange. There is no need to draw analytic inspiration from the gift exchanges of Trobriand Islanders when analyzing a phenomenon that has a long and rich history within Western societies. The key point, however, is that if cooperation can be a functional substitute for coercion in employment relations, the traditional arguments for uncontested managerial authority must be reevaluated. A blanket defense of managerial authority is no longer justified if the same objectives can be achieved through a cooperative relationship between employer and employees.

Finally, it follows from this discussion of the different faces of the employment relationship that it is impossible to determine the most efficient way to organize labor without considering the actual skills involved in the jobs people have. There is no single answer available for all times and places, but rather multiple answers de-

18. See Larry Hirschhorn, *Beyond Mechanization: Work and Technology in a Postindustrial Age* (Cambridge, Mass.: MIT Press), 117–19. For more on Tavistock, see F. E. Emery and E. L. Trist, *Towards a Social Ecology* (New York: Plenum, 1975), ch. 9. In *Manufacturing Consent: Changes in the Labor Process under Monopoly Capitalism* (Chicago: University of Chicago Press, 1979) Michael Burawoy discovers not cooperation but workers consenting in their own exploitation through participation in a game. Yet what he actually describes is a workplace that combines elements of cooperation and coercion. For another important study of cooperation and trust in the workplace, see Alan Fox, *Beyond Contract: Work, Power and Trust Relations* (London: Faber & Faber, 1974).

pending upon the skill requirements of particular jobs. Unfortunately, assessing the skill levels that a particular economy requires is not a simple undertaking.

Empirical Trends in Skill Levels

Some commentators have suggested that there are powerful trends in the organization of work that change the skill levels of almost all jobs in the same direction in a particular historical period.[19] But the reality is that there are contradictory trends in different occupations at any given time; some occupations are being deskilled while others are being upgraded. Moreover, the same occupation might be subject to contradictory patterns at different work sites. Furthermore, determining the skills required for a particular job is very much a strategic decision, in which both managers and employees will adopt different tactics depending upon specific circumstances. Managers might resort to a strategy of deskilling as a response to worker militancy, or they might choose to upgrade skills to overcome a negative legacy of labor-management conflict. Similarly, one group of workers might struggle to resist deskilling, while another group might oppose the additional responsibilities of higher levels of skill. The point, quite simply, is that attempts to argue directly from the nature of technology or the logic of capitalism to conclusions about the level of skills will always miss the actual complexity of the empirical world, in which many variables, including conflicts on the shop floor, shape the skill content of particular jobs.[20]

The problem is further complicated by the lack of good data. The reduced funding for large-scale social science projects in the Reagan years has interfered with the kind of data collection that might provide an indication of recent changes in skill levels in the economy, particularly those associated with the massive diffusion of

19. This kind of argument is suggested by Harry Braverman, *Labor and Monopoly Capital* (New York: Monthly Review Press, 1974).

20. Studies that emphasize the contingency of work organization include Thomas Kochan, Harry C. Katz, and Robert B. McKersie, *The Transformation of American Industrial Relations* (New York: Basic Books, 1986), Barry Wilkinson, *The Shopfloor Politics of New Technology* (London: Heinemann, 1983); and David F. Noble, *Forces of Production: A Social History of Industrial Automation* (New York: Knopf, 1984).

computerization. Broad national surveys of these issues were carried out in 1969 and 1977, but no comparable study has been done in the 1980s.

Fortunately, these theoretical and empirical difficulties are not insurmountable. It is possible to piece together evidence from various sources to provide an assessment of current skill levels and likely future tendencies. This assessment leads to two conclusions. First, the majority of American employees are currently in work settings where the skill demands of their jobs are quite substantial—sufficiently high for the cost of replacing them to be considerable. Second, a review of the literature on technological change suggests that automation in blue-collar and white-collar settings is generally associated with rising levels of skill.

Before presenting the evidence for these two claims, some attention must be paid to the problem of defining skill. The problem is complicated because skill has multiple dimensions; a job can be upgraded on one dimension while being downgraded on another.[21] The issue is further complicated because some of the literature tends to confuse the skill level of a job with its attractiveness. There are, however, many situations where more highly skilled jobs—all else being equal—will be widely perceived as less desirable because they have higher levels of pressure and responsibility.[22] Also the relationship between skill level and job satisfaction is certainly not simple; even some jobs that require extensive initial training can become largely routine with the passage of time. Still another problem is that notions of skill have also been seriously affected by gender bias. The skills required for predominantly female occupations have often not been given appropriate recognition or compensation in comparison to the skills in predominantly male occupations.[23]

Despite these complexities, it is useful to define the concept of skill in terms of the amount of time it takes an average person to

21. William Form, "On the Degradation of Skills," *Annual Review of Sociology* 13 (1987): 29–47; Paul Adler, "New Technology, New Skills," *California Management Review* 29, no. 1 (Fall 1986): 9–28.

22. Moreover, everything else is often not equal. Pay levels do not exactly mirror skill levels, as much of the work on comparable worth has demonstrated.

23. Roslyn Feldberg, "Comparable Worth: Toward Theory and Practice in the United States," *Signs* 10, no. 2 (Winter 1984): 311–28.

master the responsibilities of a particular job.[24] This is the most relevant dimension for the efficient use of labor because training time determines the costs to managers of replacing an employee. Where these costs are high, managerial coercion tends to be weakened because of the need to maintain continuity of production. At the same time, the greater complexity of work requiring longer training periods usually makes it harder for management to monitor performance levels; the costs of establishing a sound monitoring system can be considerable. Finally, supervision itself can become problematic at high levels of skill; management acting unilaterally might simply not be able to figure out the most efficient way to organize the labor force and the distribution of tasks.[25]

There are circumstances under which managers might choose to replace competent employees even when their skill levels are quite high. For example, in the PATCO strike in 1981, a monopoly of an unusual skill did not suffice to protect the air traffic controllers from being fired. Nevertheless, it seems reasonable to hypothesize that the willingness of managers to replace workers varies inversely with the length of training time; as long as an employee is competent and effective, the employer is reluctant to incur the considerable costs of training a replacement. A rough operationalization is that a rational employer would be particularly reluctant to replace an employee after investing at least a quarter of a year's wages on him or

24. For a useful discussion of the stages of mastery, see Hubert L. Dreyfus and Stuart E. Dreyfus, *Mind over Machine: The Power of Human Intuition and Expertise in the Era of the Computer* (New York: Free Pres, 1986), ch. 1.

25. It complicates the story to distinguish between skills learned on the job and those learned elsewhere. If firm-specific skills are minimal, then the costs to the firm of replacing a person who has specialized training would seem relatively low. Yet it is often the case that when people with specialized training are hired, they are still required to learn many firm-specific procedures and techniques. Moreover, it is often the case that groups with high levels of specialized training— whether professionals or craftworkers—are able to restrict access to the training to maintain relative scarcity of their particular skills and to bid up wage levels. Finally, even if the particular specialized skill is in abundant supply on the market, the costs of assessing and monitoring performance for these workers with specialized skills tend to be high, so it is costly to replace a skilled employee of known competence because of uncertainty as to whether the replacement will prove competent. While there is obviously a range of variation, it seems reasonable to conclude that whether the skills are learned on or off the job, higher levels of employee skill make the replacement of employees more complex and costly.

her without compensating output.[26] If it is also assumed that employees average only 50 percent of standard productivity during their training periods, then it follows that six months' training time is the rough dividing line between jobs defined as low skill and jobs defined as high skill.

Data on Training Times

There are some systematic data on the length of training periods for the labor force and for particular occupations. The data are available from the *Dictionary of Occupational Titles (DOT),* a reference source developed by the Department of Labor to evaluate various occupations on a variety of dimensions.[27] One of these dimensions is called "Specific Vocational Preparation" (SVP), which consists of a scale from 1 to 9 (see table 1).[28] SVP includes both on-the-job training time and formal preparation, such as apprenticeship programs or graduate degrees that are above and beyond the standard high school or college education. Hence, individuals in categories 1–3 are easily replaceable at relatively little cost, while the costs of replacing individuals rated 5–9 are quite substantial. Category 4 lies on the borderline.

There are some problems with this data source. The most recent *Dictionary of Occupational Titles* was produced in 1977, so it is possible that some specific occupations have changed markedly in

26. There is little empirical evidence that most U.S. employers are, in fact, rational in their calculations concerning employee turnover. This is not surprising, in that they tend to operate within a neoclassical economic paradigm that has systematically neglected replacement costs. There is, however, a growing management literature that seeks to make employers conscious of the immediate costs of turnover. See, for example, Thomas E. Hall, "How to Estimate Employee Turnover Costs," *Personnel* 58, no. 4 (July–August 1981): 43–52; G. Spencer Blakeslee, Edward L. Suntrup, and John A. Kernaghan, "How Much Is Turnover Costing You?" *Personnel Journal* 64, no. 11 (November 1985): 99–103.

27. For discussion of the *DOT,* see Ann R. Miller et al., *Work, Jobs, and Occupations: A Critical Review of the "Dictionary of Occupational Titles"* (Washington, D.C.: National Academy Press, 1980), and Pamela S. Cain and Donald J. Treiman, "The *Dictionary of Occupational Titles* as a Source of Occupational Data," *American Sociological Review* 46 (June 1981): 253–78.

28. These ratings are published in Department of Labor, *Selected Characteristics of Occupations Defined in the Dictionary of Occupational Titles* (Washington, D.C.: GPO, 1981).

TABLE 1.
Specific Vocational Preparation

9	Over 10 years
8	4–10 years
7	2–4 years
6	1–2 years
5	6 months–1 year
4	3–6 months
3	30 days–3 months
2	Short demonstration–30 days
1	Short demonstration only

the intervening years.[29] Some sense of the impact on training times of these recent changes can, however, be gathered by looking in greater detail at some of the most widely used new technologies, such as numerically controlled machine tools and office automation. Another possible problem is that of subjectivity in the way Department of Labor evaluators decide how much preparation is required for a particular occupation. However, detailed analyses of the data show that evaluator bias plays a relatively minor role.[30] In sum, the *DOT* data do provide a plausible approximation of training times across the whole economy.[31]

29. As Cain and Treiman point out, too, much of the 1977 edition of the *DOT* carries over descriptions of occupations from previous editions, so the problem of time lag can be substantial (*DOT* as a Source of Occupational Data," 272–73).

30. Miller et al., *Work, Jobs, and Occupations*, 168–73, show that the reliability of the SVP rating is fairly high. They also argue (188–91) that gender bias in rating skills has been reduced in the fourth edition of the *DOT*.

31. There have been a number of studies that have used the *Dictionary of Occupational Titles* to address the issue of aggregate changes in skill levels, but most of them have focused on the *DOT*'s assessment of how much formal education is required for each particular occupation. However, it seems that the SVP measure comes closer to the costs incurred by employers. See Kenneth Spenner, "Deciphering Prometheus: Temporal Change in the Skill Level of Work," *American Sociological Review* 48 (December): 824–37, and the studies cited in Paul Attewell, "The Deskilling Controversy," *Work and Occupations* 14, no. 3 (August 1987): 323–46.

TABLE 2. *SVP Scores for Selected Occupational Categories*

Occupations	SVP
Electrical and electronic engineers	7.9
Tool programmers, numerical control	7.3
Accountants	7.3
Supervisors, auto	7.2
Managers and administrators, finance, insurance and real estate	7.2
Computer programmers	7.1
Secondary school teachers	7.0
Machinists	7.0
Registered nurses	6.9
Carpenters	6.9
Office machine mechanics and repair personnel	6.9
Automobile mechanics	6.8
Farmers	6.6
Buyers, wholesale and retail	6.2
Elementary school teachers	6.1
Clinical laboratory technologists and technicians	6.0
Secretaries	6.0
Cooks	5.9
Computer and peripheral equipment operators	5.9
Technicians	5.4
Sales representatives, manufacturing	5.1
Bank tellers	5.0
Bookkeepers	4.8
Police and detectives	4.6
Checkers, examiners, and inspectors, manufacturing	4.1
Stock clerks	4.0
Nursing aides, orderlies	3.9
Typists	3.8
Sales clerks, retail trade	3.6
Janitors and sextons	3.6
Sewers and stitchers	3.5
Truck drivers	3.5

TABLE 2. *SVP Scores for Selected Occupational Categories (cont.)*

Occupations	SVP
Metalworking machinery operators	3.4
Assemblers	3.3
Cashiers	3.0
Waiters	3.0
Laborers	2.8

SOURCE: Patricia Roos and Donald J. Treiman, "DOT Scales for the 1970 Census Classification," in Ann R. Miller et al., *Work, Jobs, and Occupations: A Critical Review of the Dictionary of Occupational Titles* (Washington, D.C.: National Academy Press, 1980), 336–89.

Table 2 provides average SVP scores for a range of different detailed occupations within the 1970 Census categories. These scores were compiled on the basis of a Current Population Survey that coded individuals' occupations both in terms of census categories and the more detailed categories of the *Dictionary of Occupational Titles*.[32] Moreover, using the source for table 2, it is possible to give an approximate sense of trends for the occupational structure as a whole. Table 3 divides the occupational structure into four categories by SVP scores.[33] The highest category are the elite occupations rated between 6.3 and 9. Then comes a group of highly skilled occupations that rank between 5 and 6.3. The intermediate category have SVP scores between 3.5 and 5, and the low-skill occupations have skill levels between 1 and 3.5.[34]

Table 3 shows a significant pattern of increasing skill, as the two highest skilled categories have grown from 51.9 percent of all em-

32. The data in table 2 were compiled by Patricia Roos and Donald Treiman for Miller et al., *Work, Jobs, and Occupations*, 336–64. They used a Current Population Survey coded in terms of census occupational categories and *DOT* categories as a means to aggregate the extremely specific *DOT* occupations.

33. Not every occupation grouped within these categories will have that particular SVP score, but it represents an average for the broad category.

34. There is a problem in constructing a continuous time series on the occupational composition of the labor force because the 1980 Census introduced a system of occupational classification different from that used in 1970. See Gloria Peterson Green et al., "Revisions in the Current Population Survey Beginning in January 1983," *Employment and Earnings* 30, no. 2 (February 1983): 7–15. However, it is possible to generate a continuous series by constructing a third scheme

TABLE 3. *Occupational Categories by SVP Scores*

Year	1970	1979	1982	1983	1987
	(thousands of people)				
Elite occupations	28,533	38,122	40,183	40,328	46,199
SVP 6.3–9 (% of total)	(37.6)	(39.3)	(40.4)	(40.0)	(41.1)
Professionals	10,133	13,280	14,966	12,820	14,426
Managers and administrators	6,371	10,516	11,493	13,730	16,888
Craft	10,610	12,880	12,272	12,328	13,568
Farmers	1,419	1,446	1,452	1,450	1,317
High-skilled occupations	10,848	15,903	16,985	18,457	21,562
SVP 5–6.3 (% of total)	(14.3)	(16.4)	(17.1)	(18.3)	(19.2)
High-level sales personnel	1,572	2,574	2,582	3,295	3,874
Technicians	1,218	1,770	1,985	3,053	3,346
High-level administrative support personnel	5,409	7,806	8,327	8,297	10,009
Others[a]	2,649	3,753	4,091	3,812	4,333
Intermediate Occupations	26,621	29,323	28,469	27,280	28,894
SVP 3.5–5 (% of total)	(35.1)	(30.2)	(28.6)	(27.1)	(25.7)
Operatives	10,499	10,909	9,429	7,744	7,994
Transportation equipment operatives	2,958	3,612	3,377	4,201	4,712
Other administrative support personnel	8,339	9,807	10,119	8,098	8,247
Protective services	952	1,406	1,546	1,672	1,907
Retail sales workers	3,873	3,589	3,998	5,565	6,034
Low-Skilled Occupations	9,848	13,597	13,877	14,770	15,787
SVP 1–3.5 (% of total)	(13.0)	(14.0)	(13.9)	(14.6)	(14.0)
Handlers, laborers, and farm workers	4,380	5,922	5,789	6,397	6,969
Private household workers	1,146	1,088	1,042	980	939
Cleaning and janitorial personnel	1,862	2,450	2,515	2,736	2,886
Others[b]	2,460	4,137	4,541	4,657	4,993

SOURCES: Bureau of the Census, 1970 Census of Population: Occupation by Industry (Washington, D.C.: GPO, 1972): 241–48; *Employment and Earnings*, various issues; Patricia Roos and Donald J. Treiman, "DOT Scales for the 1970 Census Classification," in Ann R. Miller et al., *Work, Jobs, and Occupations: A Critical Review of the "Dictionary of Occupational Titles"* (Washington, D.C.: National Academy Press, 1980): 336–89. DOT scales for the 1980 census classification were made available by Paula England.

NOTE: This classification is only approximate. Within the more aggregated occupational categories, there are some detailed occupations that do not fit in terms of their SVP scores. However, the larger anomalies were eliminated by shifting the detailed occupations to the more appropriate level. Since the remaining anomalies operate in both directions, it seems unlikely that they would substantially affect these results.

[a] Includes barbers, hairdressers, cooks, and health-service workers.

[b] Includes personal services and selected food workers, including fast-food workers.

ployment in 1970 to 60.3 percent in 1987.[35] The dynamic behind this change has been the rapid growth of managerial employment and higher-level clerical jobs simultaneously with a decline in operative positions. Since some of those in the next category—intermediate occupations—also have training times of six months, it would appear that fully two-thirds of current employees require at least six months of training time.

This pattern of rising skill might be less pronounced if there were significant downward shifts in skill within occupational groups. This could happen in either of two ways. First, it might be that a growing percentage of employees within a category, such as managers, were less skilled—in terms of training time—than in 1970. Second, it could be that updating of the *Dictionary of Occupational Titles* would detect a lowering of the average SVP score for some of the larger occupational categories, such as secretaries. However, there is no strong evidence for either of these patterns, and it is clear that both of these tendencies would have to be quite pronounced in order to offset the upgrading pattern indicated in table 3.

In terms of recent changes that the DOT would have missed and future changes, the issue centers on the impact of different types of automation on the distribution of jobs across categories. Does factory automation deskill craft workers, who comprise an important portion of those in elite occupations, or does it reduce the number of relatively low-skilled operatives? Does office automation downgrade secretaries, who are in the high-skilled category, and expand

that reaggregates the data differently from both the 1970 and 1980 classifications. To show the plausibility of this new scheme, table 3 juxtaposes the 1982 data collected within the 1970 scheme with the 1983 data that used the 1980 Census scheme. There are only a few places where the year-to-year difference is large, and the differences at the aggregate level are small.

35. Some corroboration for this data is provided by the 1977 Quality of Employment Survey. The survey asked a random sample of employed people to assess how long it would take an average person with the right amount of formal education to learn their particular job. Four weeks or less was the response of 29.8 percent of the sample; five weeks to three months of 11.1 percent of the sample; four to six months, of another 11.5 percent; seven months to one year, of 15.8 percent; and two years or more, of 31.8 percent. These figures suggest that the median training period for the labor force was then about six months, with almost a third of all employees at very high levels of skill. Robert P. Quinn and Graham L. Staines, *The 1977 Quality of Employment Survey: Descriptive Statistics with Comparison Data from the 1969–70 and the 1972–73 Surveys* (Ann Arbor: Institute for Social Research, 1979), 203.

the number of clerical workers in the intermediate category, or does it do the opposite? To answer these questions requires a survey of the literature on factory and office automation.

Craft Workers, Operatives, and the Impact of Factory Automation

The category of craft workers is roughly divided three ways—into mechanics and repairers; construction trades; and precision production workers. Many of the detailed mechanical and repair occupations have SVP scores of 7 (auto mechanics, maintenance mechanics, and office-machine servicers), and although some deskilling is possible in these occupations through the development of self-diagnosing machinery, the growing complexity of the technologies that need to be repaired creates a powerful countertendency. Someone needs to be able to fix the equipment when the self-diagnosing capacity has failed. Moreover, the rapid expansion in the use of sophisticated equipment such as robotics will mean continued increases in the numbers of skilled repair people.[36]

Similarly, most construction trades have SVP ratings of 7 or 8. While there are ongoing efforts to weaken construction craft unions and modernize the technological base of construction, there are also countertendencies rooted in the greater complexity of more advanced construction technologies. The general point, however, is that it would take a great deal of very rapid deskilling in construction to lower average skill levels to the range of SVP 4 or 5.

The final component of the craft-worker category consists of production workers such as machinists (SVP 7), whose fate depends directly on trends in factory automation. It is now generally understood that there is a sharp contrast between what was called automation in the late 1950s and early 1960s and the current phase of automation, which is characterized by increasing flexibility.[37] Earlier systems, such as the transfer machines introduced into the automobile industry in the 1950s, involved substantial fixed investment and were highly rigid. Today's automation is generally built

36. The growing importance of skilled repair work in manufacturing is emphasized by Harley Shaiken, *Work Transformed: Automation and Labor in the Computer Age* (New York: Holt, Rinehart & Winston, 1984), 185–86.

37. Hirschhorn, *Beyond Mechanization;* Office of Technology Assessment, *Computerized Manufacturing Automation* (Washington, D.C.: GPO, 1984).

around computer technologies that make possible the flexible re-programming of the production process. This flexibility makes auto-mation economically feasible for small-batch production and for products that will have relatively short production runs.

Flexible automation tends to shift manufacturing in the direc-tion of continuous-process production. Continuous-process tech-nologies have been used for years in the chemical industry; they make possible the transformation of raw materials into finished products without human beings actually touching the product. The role of workers is to supervise and maintain the production appar-atus rather than to engage directly in the transformation of raw materials.[38] These new technologies also tend to reduce the de-mand for labor in the immediate production process. In fact, in advanced manufacturing, direct labor costs have fallen to less than 10 percent of the total costs of production.[39] As technology displaces human labor from the tasks of directly transforming materials, the size of the factory labor force shrinks. The tasks that are left center on supervising the production process and maintaining the equip-ment, and computerization can also reduce the amount of labor devoted to process-control operations.[40]

The impact of this new wave of factory automation has been highly uneven; the diffusion of the new technologies through indus-try will take many years. However, there is already a considerable body of work on the impact of these technologies, which reminds us that the same technology can be used quite differently in different settings. These variations in use make it difficult to generalize about

38. Moreover, the new types of automation can also play a central role in making continuous-process operations more efficient. Computerized process con-trols can carry out certain operations automatically, such as adjusting the heat level in a particular chamber, and they can also provide the workers who are managing the production process with increased information on all phases of production. Here again the result is increased flexibility within continuous process, since process controls can be reprogrammed for different kinds of products. See David A. Buchanan and David Boddy, *Organizations in the Computer Age* (Aldershot, U.K.: Gower, 1983).

39. Christopher Fuselier, "The Executive Dilemma: New Industrial Automa-tion Systems," in Paul Kleindorfer, ed., *The Management of Productivity and Technology in Manufacturing* (New York: Plenum, 1985), 189–95. The decline in the size of the operative category in table 3 reflects this reduction in the role of direct labor in manufacturing despite the fact that manufacturing output has been increasing.

40. Buchanan and Boddy, *Organizations in the Computer Age*, 203–31.

the impact on skill levels. Still, there are enough common findings in the literature for some conclusions to be drawn.

Three themes emerge repeatedly from the literature on flexible automation. The first is the distinction between skill depth and skill breadth.[41] Skill depth refers to the time it takes to learn a particular task, such as machining a complex job. Skill breadth refers to the range of different types of knowledge that employees must have to carry out their jobs. Flexible technologies tend to reduce skill depth precisely because the relationship of worker to materials is now mediated by technology. The kind of hands-on knowledge that production workers often accumulated over a long period of time can become obsolete.[42] For example, with the shift from ordinary machine tools to numerically controlled machine tools of increasing sophistication, the tacit knowledge of the skilled machinist becomes less essential to the production process. Experience gave the skilled machinist the capacity to adjust for some factors that the inexperienced machinist barely understood, such as the sharpness of the tool. However, the newer machines can make these adjustments automatically. Yet the same technologies also tend to increase skill breadth because jobs become interdependent and different types of knowledge become essential. For example, David Noble reports the case of machinists who taught themselves to read the mylar tape containing the program for a numerically controlled machine tool so as to be able to catch programming errors and prevent the machine from acting unpredictably.[43]

A second theme that emerges from the literature is that flexible automation tends to make errors more costly.[44] The more production resembles a continuous process, the greater the likelihood that if something goes wrong, it will ruin the entire batch of product currently being worked on. Automatic machines can stamp out hundreds of incorrectly machined parts before anybody even no-

41. Office of Technology Assessment, *Computerized Manufacturing Automation*, 110–12.

42. This is a central theme of Shoshana Zuboff's *In the Age of the Smart Machine: The Future of Work and Power* (New York: Basic Books, 1988), chs. 1 and 2.

43. David Noble, "Social Choice in Machine Design: The Case of Automatically Controlled Machine Tools, and a Challenge for Labor," *Politics & Society* 8, no. 3–4 (1978): 313–47.

44. The issue of error is one of the central themes of Hirschhorn's *Beyond Mechanization*.

tices the error. Similarly, since the capital goods are more complex and interdependent, errors can lead to considerable damage to expensive machinery. Harley Shaiken quotes one executive as saying, "If you have a $500,000 machining center, you don't want some clown pressing the wrong button, even if the machine has all the fail-safe devices in the world built into it. I don't see us getting to the level where the untrained worker can step up and run the equipment by pushing a button."[45]

The third theme is the tension between different managerial objectives in utilizing these new technologies. On the one hand, flexible automation is often sold to executives as a way to bring down labor costs and significantly reduce their dependence on skilled workers. David Noble has documented the fact that this was a central concern not just in the marketing but in the development of numerically controlled machine tools as the technology of choice for automating machining.[46] On the other hand, flexible automation can also be used to enhance a firm's performance on other dimensions. Specifically, flexible automation can be useful in facilitating high-quality production, since it is theoretically possible to stay closer to product specifications with computerized machinery. Furthermore, firms can use the technology to improve their flexibility—to make changes from one product line to another more quickly or to maintain continuous output of a wide variety of different products. In a word, flexibility means allowing the manufacturing operation to be far more responsive to marketing considerations.

Although flexible automation can usually reduce direct labor costs through the elimination of many repetitive tasks, there is often a profound conflict between the goal of reducing a firm's dependence on skilled workers and that of increasing quality and flexibility. Workers with limited skill breadth will be unable to cope with unanticipated machine errors, so that quality goals may prove elusive. Even more critically, the lack of skill breadth will interfere with flexibility. A change in the production process with deskilled workers requires creating a new set of narrowly defined job tasks

45. Shaiken, *Work Transformed*, 92. See also National Research Council, Committee on the Effective Implementation of Advanced Manufacturing Technology, *Human Resource Practices for Implementing Advanced Manufacturing Technology* (Washington, D.C.: National Academy Press, 1986).
46. Noble, *Forces of Production*, ch. 11.

and reallocating the tasks among the workforce. This is likely to be a difficult process that stirs up worker resentment because it disrupts an established routine without providing any compensations; all that the workers receive is a somewhat different boring task.[47] In contrast, when management emphasizes skill breadth, such changes in the production process can be organized far more smoothly.

With these three themes in mind, it is useful to examine three of the most important of these technologies in greater detail.

Numerically Controlled Machine Tools. Numerically controlled machine tools have been in use for twenty-five years or more, but the current generation of machines are numerically controlled by computer. They can be programmed either by microcomputers attached to the machine or through a central computer, which may be attached to several different machines. As with earlier innovations in the industry, these newer machines reduce the need for the skill depth of the experienced machinist; it is possible to produce parts to precise tolerances without years of experience. The result is that highly skilled machinists often complain of boredom and dissatisfaction when working with these new machines.[48]

However, these complaints should not be taken as evidence of a systematic decline in skill levels. On the contrary, David Noble's discussion of the experience of GE workers with an earlier generation of numerically controlled machine tools makes it clear that new machines can require more skill rather than less. "The local argued that N/C demanded greater attention while the machine was in operation, in order to anticipate and correct for, or avoid, foul-ups and that this required skill and experience and resulted in more tension and fatigue."[49] The problem for the employees is that the application of skill is far more intermittent than it was earlier, and it is broken by long periods of tedium.

This intermittent demand for skill explains two otherwise puzzling findings. First, it often still makes sense to use highly skilled

47. The difficulty of achieving flexibility when job tasks are deskilled and narrowly defined is developed at length in Harry C. Katz, *Shifting Gears: Changing Labor Relations in the U.S. Automobile Industry* (Cambridge, Mass.: MIT Press, 1985), and in Piore and Sabel, *Second Industrial Divide*.
48. Shaiken, *Work Transformed*, 128–32; Office of Technology Assessment, *Computerized Manufacturing Automation*, 185.
49. Noble, *Forces of Production*, 270.

workers to run these machines.[50] Highly skilled machinists remain invaluable for troubleshooting difficult problems and for machining highly complex parts. Second, an Office of Technology Assessment study found that "less experienced workers and those whose previous work experience was largely on NC preferred NC, while workers with high levels of skill and extensive backgrounds on conventional equipment did not like NC machines unless they had become involved in programming."[51] This suggests that the work of operating these machines continued to be challenging, but that the shift to the intermittent exercise of skill was extremely frustrating for those with years of experience.

Since not all machinists have this considerable amount of experience, there is reason to doubt that deskilling is general. In fact, new workers hired to run these machines must go through a long period of training and require considerable conceptual skills.[52] At the same time, new occupational positions have opened up that require significantly higher skill levels.

The most important of these positions is that of programmer. In a minority of factories, the machine operators are taught to do their own programming—a significant increase in skill breadth. A recent study of small machine shops reported that in more than 20 percent of the shops, the machinists were doing their own programming.[53] In another 33 percent of the shops, the jobs were done by full-time programmers, but this is a job category that recruits many of its members from the ranks of skilled machinists, since such programmers are required to understand both computer languages and the complexity of machine cutting. But even when programmers are recruited from outside the ranks of machinists, the growth of this task increases management dependence on highly skilled workers.

Finally, the new machines require more sophisticated maintenance.[54] If the same labor force of mechanics and electricians are to

50. Office of Technology Assessment, *Computerized Manufacturing Automation*, 195.

51. Ibid., 185.

52. Bureau of Labor Statistics, *Technology and Labor in Four Industries* (Washington, D.C.: GPO, 1982), 31.

53. Donald Hicks, *Automation Technology and Industrial Renewal* (Washington, D.C.: American Enterprise Institute, 1986), 125. See also Maryellen Kelley, "Programmable Automation and the Skill Question: A Reinterpretation of the Cross-National Evidence," *Human Systems Management* 6 (1986): 223–41.

54. Bureau of Labor Statistics, *Technology and Labor*, 31; Peter Senker, "Training for Automation," in Malcolm Warner, ed., *Microprocessors, Manpower*

repair and maintain the new machines, they need extensive additional training. Alternatively, the hiring of new technicians to carry out these jobs also raises the skill level of the workforce.

In sum, the shift to machine tools numerically controlled by computer might very well be accompanied by increases in boredom and dissatisfaction among some categories of workers, but the general tendency is to an increase in the aggregate level of skill among those engaged in production. Moreover, the more weight a particular firm places on quality and flexibility, the greater the emphasis on expanding worker skills.

Flexible Manufacturing Systems. The step beyond computer-controlled machine tools is flexible manufacturing systems—an integrated apparatus of machine tools and automatic shuttles for moving parts that is under the control of a central computer. These systems move machining further in the direction of a continuous-process technology, since a complex part can be made from start to finish without being touched by human hands. As with numerically controlled machine tools, managers are drawn to FMS by the dream of a production process without skilled workers. Some of the FMS systems in the United States have been designed and operated to minimize the skill level of the workforce. However, there is a mounting body of evidence that this has proven to be a costly mistake; performance levels are very poor when worker knowledge is not integrated into the operation of the FMS. In one study, Seymour Melman has contrasted the performance of an FMS organized with poorly skilled workers with that of one organized around a labor process emphasizing learning and mastery of the technology by workers.[55] The first system experienced dramatically higher down time than the second, whose knowledgeable workers were able to anticipate some problems and correct others to keep the system working. Moreover, with this kind of expensive technology, the percentage of down time is probably the major element in determining the profitability of the operation.

In a more recent study, Ramchandran Jaikumar compares the

and Society: A Comparative Cross-National Approach (New York: St. Martin's Press, 1984), 134–46.

55. Seymour Melman, "Alternatives for the Organization of Work in Computer-Assisted-Manufacturing," *Annals of the New York Academy of Science* 426 (November 1984): 83–90.

use of FMS in Japan and the United States.[56] He found that in all dimensions, the Japanese have been far more successful in its use: shorter development times for their systems, much higher utilization rates, and higher rates of output. Most important, the Japanese utilized the flexibility of the technology to produce dozens of different parts in relatively small runs, whereas American firms employed long production runs for a relatively small number of parts. In short, the Japanese have been able to use the technology to create fully automated factories with extremely high productivity rates, while the United States is still far from this goal.

Not surprisingly, the differences in skill levels between the Japanese and American employees were very substantial. In describing the Japanese plants, Jaikumar writes: "Operators on the shop floor make continual programming changes and are responsible for writing new programs for parts and systems as a whole. They are highly skilled engineers with multifunctional responsibilities."[57] In Japan 40 percent of the FMS workforce were college-educated engineers, compared to 8 percent in the United States. Jaikumar also found that the Japanese spent three times as much time as U.S. firms upgrading the skills of their employees.

It is possible to challenge Jaikumar's findings by arguing that there are multiple ways to utilize any particular technology. U.S. firms may ultimately find effective ways to use FMS technologies that are quite different from the Japanese patterns. Yet the dramatic size of the differences Jaikumar found and the press of international competition make it quite likely that American firms will ultimately copy the Japanese example. There is ample evidence that many U.S. firms are already moving in this direction, placing greater emphasis on flexibility and workers learning to master the technology.[58] In this case, the Japanese use of FMS represents the wave of the future for manufacturing.

Robotics. The quantitative impact of robotization is already much greater than that of flexible manufacturing systems, since

---

56. Ramchandran Jaikumar, "Postindustrial Manufacturing," *Harvard Business Review* 64, no. 6 (November–December 1986): 69–76.

57. Ibid., 72.

58. See National Research Council, *Human Resource Practices;* and Richard J. Schonberger, *World Class Manufacturing: The Lessons of Simplicity Applied* (New York: Free Press, 1986).

robots can be introduced into assembly tasks on a modular basis. Whereas FMS calls for a major investment that reorganizes the whole production process, robots can be introduced incrementally, and the cost of robots has dropped very rapidly.

The studies that have been done to date show that robotization can dramatically reduce the size of the manufacturing labor force. An often-cited study at Carnegie-Mellon University found that in theory first- and second-generation robots (second-generation robots have rudimentary sensory capabilities) could replace 40 percent of all the metalworking craft workers, operatives, and laborers in U.S. manufacturing.[59] The figure would be much higher if it were based on subsequent generations of robots with more sophisticated sensory capacities. Another study, which extrapolated from actual displacement, predicted that between 1980 and 1990, 6–11 percent of all operatives and laborers in the automobile industry would be replaced by robots.[60]

Moreover, the evidence also points to robots increasing workers' skill levels. According to a survey of robot users, 60 percent of firms stated that operators' jobs required greater skill after the introduction of robots.[61] Moreover, it is indisputable that skill levels for support personnel rise, as mechanics and electricians must learn how to maintain the robots. There has been considerable discussion of training robot technicians in two-year community college programs.[62] At one GM facility, a training program for skilled trades personnel has been developed that provides 1,000 hours of training in robotics and related materials; the students in the program divide their time equally between work and training.[63]

One study that attempts to predict the structure of employment within the robotics industry itself anticipates that most of the new jobs created in the industry will be highly skilled, and that over half will require two or more years of college education.[64] This finding has important implications for the entire manufacturing sector.

59. Robert U. Ayres and Steven M. Miller, *Robotics: Applications and Social Implications* (Cambridge, Mass.: Ballinger, 1983), 204–5.

60. H. Allan Hunt and Timothy L. Hunt, *Human Resource Implications of Robotics* (Kalamazoo, Mich.: Upjohn, 1983), 78.

61. Ayres and Miller, *Robotics*, 95.

62. Hunt and Hunt, *Human Resource Implications*, 154–58.

63. Ellen Kehoe, "The Industrial Side of Robotics Training," *Robotics Today* 6, no. 5 (October 1984): 31–33.

64. Hunt and Hunt, *Human Resource Implications*, 140.

In sum, operatives with low skill levels are diminishing in number, but there is increasing need for employees with broad conceptual skills, including technicians and programmers. Similar trends can be seen with the introduction of computerized controls in continuous-process plants.[65] Moreover, the more employers emphasize product quality and the exploitation of the flexibility of these new technologies, the stronger the drive to broaden workers' skills will be. The rate at which the new technologies will diffuse through the economy depends on many variables, and there will be significant variations across industries. However, it seems probable that there will be continuing shrinkage in the number of operatives, and that the general tendency in manufacturing will be toward higher skill levels.

Clerical Occupations

The future of clerical occupations depends on trends in office automation where there is also a tension between the impulse to reduce workers' skill and the need for improved quality and flexibility. The tension between these conflicting goals results in divergent empirical findings, with some analysts emphasizing the reduction in workers' skill and others emphasizing the broadening of skill and the upgrading of clerical tasks. These different findings reflect radically divergent managerial strategies in using these new technologies.

However, there are two other factors that complicate any effort to evaluate trends in the skill level of clerical work. First, secretarial work has historically been devalued precisely because it tends to be done by women. The complexity of the tasks carried out by a secretary has to be denied in situations where male managers are paid many times the salaries of their female secretaries. Yet secretaries routinely carry out managerial tasks, often without receiving appropriate rewards or recognition.[66] In this respect, the *Dictionary of Occupational Titles* is a useful corrective—the category of secretary—as distinguished from typist or clerk typist—is given an SVP score of 6.

Second, as in manufacturing, there are different stages in the

---

65. Buchanan and Boddy, *Organizations in the Computer Age*, 24–26.
66. Rosabeth Kanter, *Men and Women of the Corporation* (New York: Basic Books, 1977), ch. 4.

process of automation. The initial period of computerization, for example, created large numbers of low-skilled data-entry jobs—many of which have subsequently been eliminated with more sophisticated data-entry systems. Similarly, in the early phase of the development of word processing, it was common for firms to establish a central word-processing pool. Secretaries would be transferred from assignment as a personal secretary to the word-processing pool, where they would be full-time typists.[67] More recently, however, the trend appears to be toward a more decentralized use of computers and word processing, with more positive consequences for clerical skills.[68]

The confusion created by issues of secretarial status and by differing stages of technology can be largely bypassed by examining trends in specific industries such as insurance and banking. These are both industries that have used large numbers of clerical workers outside of the traditional secretarial role and that are also making use of more advanced forms of office automation. Since these two industries account for close to 20 percent of all clerical employees, it seems reasonable to see them as indicative of trends in clerical employment as a whole.[69]

In the case of the insurance industry, there have been a number

67. For studies rooted in this early period that report significant deskilling, see Diane Werneke, *Microelectronics and Office Jobs* (Geneva: ILO, 1983); Anne Machung, "Word Processing: Forward for Business, Backward for Women," in Karen Brodkin Sacks and Dorothy Remy, eds., *My Troubles Are Going to Have Trouble with Me: Everyday Trials and Triumphs of Women Workers* (New Brunswick: Rutgers University Press, 1984), 124–39; Rosemary Crompton and Gareth Jones, *White Collar Proletariat: Deskilling and Gender in Clerical Work* (Philadelphia: Temple University Press, 1984). Barbara Garson, *The Electronic Sweatshop: How Computers Are Transforming the Office of the Future into the Factory of the Past* (New York: Simon & Schuster, 1988), bases her account of recent trends in the organization of office work on the creation of word processing pools; see ch. 7.

68. Studies rooted in this more recent phase include Eli Ginzberg, Thierry J. Noyelle, and Thomas M. Stanback, Jr., *Technology and Employment: Concepts and Clarifications* (Boulder, Colo.: Westview Press, 1986): Thomas M. Stanback, Jr., *Computerization and the Transformation of Employment: Government, Hospitals and Universities* (Boulder, Colo.: Westview Press, 1987); Juliet Webster, "Word Processing and the Secretarial Labour Process," in Kate Purcess et al., eds, *The Changing Experience of Employment* (London: Macmillan, 1986), 114–31.

69. J. David Roessner et al., *The Impact of Office Automation in Clerical Employment, 1985–2000: Forecasting Techniques and Plausible Futures in Banking and Insurance* (Westport, Conn.: Quorum Books, 1985), 5.

of careful studies that have focused on the impact of the most recent waves of office automation. As with blue-collar workers, the major finding is a significant decline in the number of clerical jobs. Barbara Baran found that by 1981 there had already been a decline in clericals as a percentage of the insurance labor force, and J. David Roessner anticipates another 30 percent decline in clerical employment in insurance between 1985 and the year 2000.[70]

Even more important, Baran found a dramatic shift in the nature of clerical work. In the traditional factory office, each clerical worker is responsible for carrying out a narrow operation on the assembly-linelike flow of paper. The logic of the new office is to integrate tasks, with each clerical employee working directly at a computer terminal. Instead of processing one piece of information on hundreds of different policies, the employee is able to use the computer to make an overall assessment of an entire policy. The result is what Baran calls "highly computer-linked, multi-activity jobs" that combine clerical and professional tasks.[71] The result is a significant upgrading of clerical work, including increased training times.[72]

Similar developments are also visible in banking. Earlier phases of computerization in banking separated a back-office operation from the work the tellers did with the customer. The result was that the back office required many clericals to enter paper accounts into the computer. The further development of computerization makes it possible and desirable for tellers to enter information directly into the computer, eliminating the need for a large back-office staff. Roessner's projections are that clerical employment in banking will also decline by 30 percent from 1985 to 2000. At the same time, the trend is to increase the responsibility of each of the clerical employees who now works directly with a computer terminal. As Paul Adler shows in his study of French banking automation, the need for greater accuracy on the part of these clerical employees requires

70. Barbara Baran, "Office Automation and Women's Work: The Technological Transformation of the Insurance Industry," in Manuel Castells, ed., *High Technology, Space, and Society* (Beverly Hills, Calif.: Sage, 1985), 143–71; Roessner, *Impact of Office Automation,* 149.

71. Ibid., 152.

72. For further evidence on the insurance industry, see Attewell, "Deskilling Controversy," 336–40, and Eileen Applebaum, "The Impact of Technology on Skill Requirements and Occupational Structure in the Insurance Industry, 1960–1990" (Department of Economics, Temple University, 1984).

that they develop a conceptual understanding of what they are doing. Adler's conclusions are bolstered by interviews that Roessner did with bank managers, who also predicted increases in the skills of clerical workers in banking.[73]

In short, office automation dramatically reduces the need for labor for such routine tasks as typing and filing, and by making large amounts of information readily available to clerical employees, it allows them to carry out more complex functions. One analyst predicts:

Twenty to thirty years from now . . . there will be more than 20 million jobs in clerical categories. But these jobs will be totally different from what we understand as "clerical" today. Instead of performing support functions, with scantly discernible economic value added, these jobs will include many of the specialist tasks now performed by professional and technical workers. We already have sufficient experience to know that clerical personnel can deliver superb results in such positions, provided that their organizations make the necessary investments to make such work possible.[74]

Although there are clear indications of this direction of change for clerical work, there are still many examples of clerical work organized on the basis of extremely limited skills. Computer-based technologies are being used to reduce skill levels, so that labor will be cheaper and more easily replaced.[75] In extreme cases, firms are using new communication technologies to export certain types of clerical work to low-wage countries in the Third World.[76] However, these could simply be transitional measures. Entering information with an optical scanner is already cheaper than hiring keypunchers in the Third World,[77] and other types of routine clerical work will also gradually be automated.

73. Roessner, *Impact of Office Automation*, 149; Paul Adler, "Automatisation et Travail: Le Cas des Banques" (thèse de doctorat de troisième cycle, Université de Picardie, France); "Does Automation Raise Skill Requirements? What Again?" (paper prepared for Conference on Microelectronics in Transition: Industrial Transformation and Social Change, University of California, Santa Cruz, May 1983).

74. Paul Strassman, *Information Payoff: The Transformation of Work in the Electronic Age* (New York: Free Press, 1985), 198.

75. Garson, *Electronic Sweatshop*.

76. Office of Technology Assessment, *Automation of America's Offices, 1985–2000* (Wasington, D.C.: GPO, 1985), 218.

77. Strassman, *Information Payoff*, 216.

There remains, however, serious resistance to the upgrading of clerical work that appears to be based not so much on economic grounds as on status considerations. Women clerical workers are often the lowest status group in an organization, and managers who invest their energies in working to reorganize the clerical labor process risk a decline in their status.[78] Training and development personnel, for example, seem to prefer to work with managerial employees rather than with secretaries. In industries, such as insurance, where clericals constitute a large percentage of the labor force, these status considerations are overcome by economic pressures. But in many other organizations, the role of clericals is less obvious and the pressure to challenge status considerations is less great.

One indication of the reluctance of firms to invest in upgrading their clerical workers is the growing use of temporary agencies as centers for training. Although agencies that provide temporary workers are generally associated with low-skilled, easily replaced workers, the recent trend has been for these temporary agencies to carry out the training that firms are reluctant to do themselves. Hence, temporary agencies are providing people with sophisticated word-processing skills that are in substantial demand in the labor market.[79]

Yet this also appears to be a transitional phenomenon. If the upgrading of clerical employees increases organizational effectiveness, firms will gradually be pressured to overcome status considerations and devote resources to the training and development of their clerical workers. In fact, it is already the case that increasing office productivity through automation and upgrading of the skills of clericals has become a central concern of business consultants and planners.

78. The neglect of training in efforts at office automation is discussed in Alan F. Westin et al., *The Changing Workplace* (White Plains, N.Y.: Knowledge Industry Publications, 1985). It is a sociological truism that the status of professionals varies directly with the status of their clients. Hence, human-resource personnel who work with clericals will have lower status than those who work with most other categories of employees.

79. Eileen Applebaum, "Restructuring Work: Temporary, Part-Time, and At-Home Employment," in Heidi Hartmann, ed., *Computer Chips and Paper Clips: Technology and Women's Employment* (Washington, D.C.: National Academy Press, 1987), 2:281.

Nevertheless, it must be reemphasized that in both white-collar and blue-collar settings, there is no necessary correlation between upgrading of skills and improved levels of job satisfaction. Increased training time is often matched by increased stress and a loss of autonomy in carrying out tasks. Moreover, even a job that takes five years to learn can become mind-numbingly boring as the work becomes routine. Finally, even if it is rational for employers to improve their treatment of employees with higher levels of skill, there is no guarantee that they will.

The Problems of Dualism and Structural Unemployment

The argument to this point is that automation in factories and offices tends to raise the average skill levels of both manufacturing and clerical workers. These tendencies, combined with the continued growth of professional and managerial employment, mean that a large majority of the labor force continue to be in occupations that require substantial training periods.

However, these trends also suggest countertendencies. Since factory automation and office automation can be labor-displacing, the percentage of the total labor force made up of clerical and manufacturing workers can be expected to contract. One possibility is that the proportion of the total labor force made up of low-wage, low-skill employees will expand as employers accelerate the pace at which they create low-technology service-sector jobs. Another is that unemployment rates will tend to rise and that a growing percentage of the labor force will face greater economic insecurity.

In recent years, there has been considerable debate as to whether such countertendencies are actually operating in the United States. Theorists of the "declining middle" have argued that a disproportionate share of new jobs are low-wage and that the traditional middle-income jobs have been shrinking in number. The most influential of these studies, done by Barry Bluestone and Bennett Harrison, found that fully 58 percent of the new jobs created by the U.S. economy between 1979 and 1984 were low-wage jobs.[80] A parallel body of work has emerged to show that a

80. Barry Bluestone and Bennett Harrison, "The Great American Jobs Machine: The Proliferation of Low-Wage Employment in the U.S. Economy" (paper

growing number of people are marginal to the labor force—either suffering from unemployment or underemployment or forced to accept "contingent employment"—jobs that provide few benefits and no promise of employment security.[81]

The most recent statement of Bluestone and Harrison's position has focused on trends in compensation for full-time year-round employees. They found that the percentage of these workers who earned less than $11,103 in 1986 dollars had risen from 14 percent in 1979 to 17 percent in 1986.[82] This occurred after a sharp drop from over 21 percent to under 13 percent during the 1960s.

The trend toward increasing polarization in the 1979–86 period is not reflected in table 3 above, however, which shows the low-skill percentage of the labor force remaining at around 14 percent.[83] Bluestone and Harrison are strictly concerned with wage levels rather than skill. It could be that an increasing number of the intermediate-skill jobs have been compensated at lower wage levels in this recent period. Such a development would explain their findings and would be consistent with the recent decline in the bargaining power of organized labor. In fact, the two-tier wage contracts that were very popular in the Reagan years represent a pure case of lowering the wage levels for new entrants to jobs that

---

prepared for the U.S. Congress, Joint Economic Committee, December 1986). See also Bennett Harrison and Barry Bluestone, *The Great U-Turn: Corporate Restructuring and the Polarizing of America* (New York: Basic Books, 1988).

81. Robert Kuttner reports a growing divergence between the official unemployment rate and an alternative indicator that adjusts the data for part-time and discouraged workers. Between 1979 and 1988, the official rate went from 5.8 to 5.5 percent, while the unofficial rate rose from 9.7 to 10.3 percent. "The Labor Market Is a Lot Looser Than It Looks," *Business Week*, March 27, 1989. See also Ward Morehouse and David Dembo, *The Underbelly of the Current "Recovery": Joblessness and Pauperization of Work in America,"* Special Report no. 1, Council on International and Public Affairs, October 1984; On contingent employment, see Jeffrey Pfeffer and James N. Baron, "Taking the Workers Back Out: Recent Trends in the Structuring of Employment," *Research in Organizational Behavior* 10 (1988): 257–303.

82. Since they are comparing real wages over time, the quality of the deflator—the adjustment for price changes—will have a significant bearing on their results. Problems with these measures are addressed in chapter 6 below.

83. Table 3 includes both full-time and part-time employees. Yet that would make it seem more likely that a trend to increased polarization would be visible here, since low-wage part-time work has been expanding more quickly than low-wage full-time work.

were earlier compensated at higher levels. However, there is reason to question whether such efforts to reduce the compensation of
employees with intermediate levels of skills will be successful over
the long term.[84]

Actually, the polarization argument is more convincing when it is
broadened to encompass the experience of those who are not full-
time, year-round employees. Bluestone and Harrison's figure of 58
percent reflects the fact that a disproportionate share of the new
jobs created in the 1980s were part-time and low-wage and often
held by women. Moreover, many firms have resorted to a strategy
of covering fluctuations in demand with contingent employees—
often hired from temporary agencies—who are usually unlikely to
work for the entire year.[85] These employer strategies have created
an expanded group of employees with relatively limited bargaining
power.

It is not easy to evaluate the weight of these tendencies relative
to the whole economy and it is difficult to know whether the 1979–
86 period was typical of future trends or atypical. There are, however, two important points that can be made. First, it is not necessary for the argument developed here that the theorists of growing
dualism be proved wrong. On the contrary, dramatic growth in
low-wage, low-skill employment is perfectly consistent with the
observation that most jobs in the economy have and will continue to
have relatively high levels of skill. It would take a very great
expansion of low-skill work—much stronger than any tendency
documented to date—for the percentage of jobs in the low-skill
category in table 3 to rise from 14 percent of total employment in

84. In fact, there is already evidence of considerable management disillusion-
ment with some of the two-tier arrangements. The creation of two classes of
employees working side by side creates a variety of tensions. See Aaron Bernstein,
"Why Two-Tier Wage Scales Are Starting to Self-Destruct," *Business Week*,
March 16, 1987. One study suggests that a central problem is diminished job
security for the more highly paid workers since management has a substantial
incentive to replace them with workers paid at the lower rate. Peter Capelli and
Peter D. Sherer, "Assessing Worker Attitudes under a Two-Tier Wage Plan"
(Department of Management, University of Pennsylvania, Working Paper no.
726, July 1988), 24–25, 39. Note, however, that Capelli and Sherer stress the
continuing willingness of management and labor to enter into these two-tier
contracts (44–45).

85. Applebaum, "Restructuring Work," in Hartmann, ed., *Computer Chips
and Paper Clips*, 2:268–310.

1986 to the 20 percent level by 1995. That would represent a stunning expansion of low-skill employment. Such a shift would have a very significant economic impact in expanding the total number of people living at or near the poverty level. Yet it could easily be that in 1995, jobs with SVP scores of 5 or higher will constitute 60 to 70 percent of all employment. Under those circumstances, the average skill level in the economy would remain relatively high, and most employers would have to struggle with the difficult problems of managing high-skill employees.

The second point is that the rate at which the number of low-skill jobs expands or contracts is not the result of inexorable economic laws. Social policies play a central role in shaping these trends, and different countries have had radically different experiences, particularly in terms of the skill content of newly created service jobs.[86] Regulations governing wages and benefits and the extent and form of government provision of social services can have a particularly strong impact on the growth of low-wage employment.

The same thing can be said for employment trends in general. Although it seems likely that advanced technologies will diminish the size of such important employment sectors as manufacturing and clerical work, it is hardly inevitable that there will be growing structural unemployment. Service-sector employment seems likely to continue to expand, with government policies playing a critical role in determining the relative weight of fast-food clerks and child-care workers. But the most important long-term determinants of the rate of unemployment will be those factors that shape labor supply—the length of the average work week and work year, the mix between part-time and full-time work, and the labor-force participation rates of different demographic groups.[87] In the United States, labor-force participation rates have been rising steadily from 60 percent of the population sixteen and over in the early 1960s to 65 percent in 1986. This increase has helped to fuel substantial

86. Swedish service-sector job creation has been public and relatively high-skill in contrast to the trend in the United States where service-sector employment growth has been private and often low-skill. See Goran Therborn, *Why Some Peoples Are More Unemployed Than Others: The Strange Paradox of Growth and Unemployment* (London: Verso, 1986), 83–88.

87. Ibid. is also valuable in demonstrating the substantial differences among nations with respect to these variables.

employment growth, but it could well be that these historically high participation rates are undesirable from a macroeconomic perspective.[88]

Reconceptualizing the
Efficient Use of Labor

The above discussion makes possible a reconceptualization of what is necessary for the efficient use of labor in an increasingly postindustrial economy. The idea here is simply to specify some of the minimal prerequisites for efficiency; specific institutional reforms addressing these prerequisites are discussed in a later chapter. Two sets of prerequisites will be discussed; those that operate at the level of the firm and those that operate in the process of matching individuals to jobs across the whole economy.

The Level of the Firm

The problem of motivating employees becomes even more central in workplaces where skill levels are high. Management needs employees to work hard and to work well even when close supervision is impractical or too expensive, and it also needs employees to contribute ideas about the most efficient ways to organize the flow of work.

The problem of motivation is often conceptualized narrowly as simply discouraging employees from slacking. Yet in high-skill settings, managers often need employees to work with high levels of attention and intellectual creativity. The problem of attention is acute in a variety of computerized settings where the consequences of error can be severe.[89] Mental lapses by a machinist in charge of an expensive automated system or by a bank teller entering information directly into the computer are very costly in their conse-

---

88. For an argument to this effect, see Fred Block, "Rethinking the Political Economy of the Welfare State," in Block et al, *Mean Season*, 128–34.

89. In contrast to the Marxist view of industrial management as centering on the extraction of surplus value, Hirschhorn has usefully conceptualized the problem of postindustrial management as the extraction of attention. The formulation is deliberately paradoxical, in that attention cannot easily be coerced. Personal communication.

quences. The reduction of these types of errors can be a critical ingredient in a firm's economic success or failure.

Intellectual creativity is required whenever problem-solving becomes a routine part of a job, and this emphasis on problem-solving is characteristic of many computer-based jobs. Since routine tasks are done by automatic machinery, the human beings are left with nonroutine tasks, which generally involve some intellectual creativity. Debugging a program or effectively troubleshooting a broken piece of machinery calls for something other than working through a preestablished protocol of steps. Quite often, problem-solving tasks will also involve developing more effective coordination with other individuals or units in the organization.

In labor economics, the issue of employees' collective contribution to problem-solving has been usefully conceptualized in terms of Albert Hirschman's concept of "voice." In *Exit, Voice and Loyalty*, he poses the example of a firm whose product quality is declining and argues that complaints by employees about the deterioration—the exercise of voice—might be a quicker and more efficient route to reversing the decline than waiting for signals from the marketplace.[90] But voice need not simply be a vague cry for help; it can also be a central mechanism for moving the firm toward the efficient use of resources. In complex computer-based production systems, for example, it is not at all obvious which way of organizing the work will be better than others. In this context, the exercise of employee voice can play a key role in helping a firm find ways to improve the organization of production.

In fact, many firms have sought to systematize the exercise of worker voice by establishing institutions for collective problem-solving.[91] Whether these are called quality circles or something else, they rest on the insight that collective and individual problem-solving are closely linked. First, collective efforts can be important in facilitating individual problem-solving. Individuals can easily become stuck on a problem, and input from others can contribute new insights that make it possible to solve it. Second, individual efforts are usually interdependent; if one is trying to improve a

90. Cambridge, Mass.: Harvard University Press, 1970.
91. Thomas Kochan et al., *The Transformation of American Industrial Relations* (New York: Basic Books, 1986), ch. 4.

particular part of an apparatus or program, it is likely to have implications for someone else who is in charge of a neighboring part of the machinery or software. Third, there are usually a whole range of important issues relating to the work that are not the exclusive jurisdiction of any one person, but can fruitfully be thought about by the entire group.

While the mobilization of employee voice through institutions for collective problem-solving can be extremely useful for an organization, it is not a simple matter to persuade people to exercise their voice in a group setting. There are risks to the individual of participation, such as the possibility of humiliation and the danger of revealing information that others may use to their advantage. Moreover, the benefits to the individual of participation are far from certain; his or her valuable ideas may be ignored, or he or she may be excluded from any benefits arising from the use of those ideas.

The problem for management is that it is difficult to coerce people to be effective at these different types of problem-solving. Participation in groups will often be pro forma when employees feel the group to be an imposition from above. When stress levels are too high, even individual problem-solving capacities are impaired.[92] Hence, an atmosphere in which individuals are punished for a failure to solve problems is likely to be counterproductive.

It is certainly true that the factors efficiency-wage theorists have emphasized—higher wages, employment security, and the promise of mobility up the job ladder—can contribute to these dimensions of employee motivation. But what is really called for in these situations is the mobilization of the cooperative impulse of employees. The cooperative face of employment relations is indispensable for sustaining high levels of attention and problem-solving capacity.

How then does management go about strengthening the cooperative impulse to assure high levels of employee motivation? There would seem to be two basic requisites for fostering cooperation; the weakening of management and labor-market coercion and an equitable system for employees and employers to share both the risks and the rewards of doing business.

92. "A large body of research shows that under stress people's decision-making becomes less rational" (Amitai Etzioni, *The Moral Dimension: Toward A New Economics* [New York: Free Press, 1988], 73).

If cooperation can substitute for coercion, it also follows that one cannot increase the one without decreasing the other. The more employees feel they are subject to the arbitrary exercise of managerial authority, the less they may be expected to commit themselves to the goals of the firm. Moreover, since problem-solving often involves taking risks, a climate in which unsuccessful choices routinely lead to firings will discourage any exercises in employee creativity. Hence, measures that attenuate managerial and labor-market coercion, such as procedural safeguards against arbitrary employer action and measures to ensure income security even in the event of job loss, are likely to foster cooperation.

In the contemporary context, a serious threat to cooperation comes from the ease with which an existing management team can be replaced by new management as the result of a corporate takeover. Even if the old management was highly successful in fostering cooperation, employees have no assurance that the new managers will respect the previous employee-employer understandings. In a word, the existence of a market for corporate management inhibits the cooperative impulse of employees, since they cannot rely on continuity over time. This suggests that maximizing cooperation requires providing employees with some voice in deciding who will control the firm.

Similarly, cooperation is difficult to sustain when employees have reason to believe that others are benefiting disproportionately from their labor. It is also disruptive of cooperation if the risks that would result from the firm's failure are radically different for top managers relative to other employees. Hence, various mechanisms for equitable sharing of both gains and burdens are a critical requisite for strengthening the cooperative impulse.

The Level of the Labor Market

Not all problems of efficiency can be solved at the level of the firm, since some have to do with the operation of the overall labor market that matches individuals with jobs. The discovery of "internal labor markets" has made it problematic to conceptualize a single homogeneous labor market that allocates all labor, but it is still valuable to think about the labor market in aggregate terms. This aggregate market can operate more or less effectively depending on how well individuals are slotted into appropriate jobs. For example, an aggregate labor market that channels large numbers of talented individuals into low-wage, low-skill positions is one that is contributing to the inefficient use of resources.

When we conceptualize this aggregate labor market without the preconceptions of neoclassical theory, it is apparent that it has always been structured by "background factors" that are not economic in origin. In any particular society, there are broad cultural understandings about the type of work that it is appropriate for particular population groups to perform, whether they be women, racial minorities, or younger people.[93] These cultural understandings can become contested, resulting in struggles over the types of jobs that different groups can obtain.[94] But the basic point is that these cultural understandings structure the organization of the labor market in extremely important ways.

A second set of background factors are understandings of how much work constitutes a job. Conceivably one could have a labor market in which each individual negotiated freely about how many hours he or she was willing to work, but the actuality is that jobs are generally defined in advance as involving twenty, forty, fifty, or sixty hours of work. These definitions have been shaped in the developed capitalist countries particularly by national legislation that has established limits on the length of the normal working day for certain categories of protected workers.[95] Similarly, the length of part-time jobs has often been defined in negative relationship to rules guaranteeing certain benefits to employees who work a certain total number of hours.

The relative rigidity in the number of hours associated with a particular job can create hardships for employees who need to reconcile work and family obligations. Moreover, the fact that part-

93. One could go farther and argue that these cultural understandings extend to people with different amounts of schooling. See Ivar Berg, *Education and Jobs: The Great Training Robbery* (New York: Praeger, 1970).

94. See, for example, Ruth Milkman's valuable study of women electrical and auto workers during World War II, *Gender at Work: The Dynamics of Job Segregation by Sex during World War II* (Urbana: University of Illinois Press, 1987).

95. For the United States, see Ronnie Steinberg, *Wages and Hours: Labor and Reform in Twentieth-Century America* (New Brunswick: Rutgers University Press, 1982).

time jobs are almost universally of low status and cut individuals off from promotional possibilities creates additional rigidity.[96] These features of the labor market make it difficult for individuals to construct a series of jobs over time that allow them to meet other obligations while also progressing up a career ladder.[97]

Finally, the labor market is also structured by a set of arrangements that govern how individuals receive training that can contribute to their effectiveness as employees. Corporations do use "internal labor markets" to train employees, but the vast bulk of the money they provide for formal training is directed at professional and managerial employees.[98] Firms have generally been reluctant to invest in training blue-collar and clerical employees for fear that they will use their new skills to earn more elsewhere. There are a few industries that have developed innovative programs whereby management subsidizes the pursuit of higher education by employees, but in general the burden of financing training falls on the individual. However, individuals tend to underinvest in their own skills because of uncertainty over their ability to find jobs where possession of new skills will be rewarded.

Each of these cases—discrimination, inflexibility in hours, and underinvestment in training—represents a potential failure of the labor market to match individuals effectively with jobs. In theory, if these failures are widespread, innovative firms that are particularly responsive to employees' concerns should be able to win greater loyalty at lower cost by accommodating them. The success of those innovators would then quickly be copied by other firms that see the economic advantages of different policies. However, when the aggregate labor market is divided into a series of relatively insulated internal labor markets, this self-correcting dynamic is likely to be very weak.

These labor-market imperfections can place severe limitations on the effectiveness of individual choice, as when an individual be-

96. Veronica Beechey and Tessa Perkins, *A Matter of Hours: Women, Part-Time Work and the Labour Market* (Minneapolis: University of Minnesota Press, 1987), esp. 166–69.

97. This is a central theme of Carmen Sirianni, "The Self-Management of Time in Post-Industrial Society: Towards a Democratic Alternative," *Socialist Review* 88 (October–December 1988): 5–56.

98. Lee Lillard and Henry W. Tan, *Private Sector Training: Who Gets It and What Are Its Effects* (Santa Monica, Calif.: RAND Corp., 1986), 12.

comes locked into part-time work with no advancement opportunities, or when an individual's resources are so limited that he or she cannot risk investments in learning new skills. These limitations on the effectiveness of individual choice also have economic consequences when significant numbers of people are employed in positions that do not take advantage of their potential to learn. The problem is even further exacerbated when the amount of low-skill work is expanding, further limiting mobility options.

Another prerequisite for the efficient use of labor is thus the development of social policies that can help restructure the aggregate labor market to expand the effectiveness of individual choice. One area where public policy has already had some successes is antidiscrimination legislation that outlaws job assignments based on racial, ethnic, gender, or age criteria. However, there is still considerable room for further attacks on labor-market discrimination. Policies that provide employees with greater flexibility in the structuring of their work time, including measures that give individuals the opportunity to shift back and forth between part-time and full-time employment, are another important area.

However, the most basic prerequisite is the existence of a set of social policies that give individuals the opportunity in adulthood to develop their intellectual skills, whether this means completing a liberal arts or graduate degree or pursuing specific vocational training. These opportunities could be expanded by providing both partial public subsidies for the cost of education and income supplements to allow individuals to devote extensive amounts of time to their studies for several years. Social policies could also be directed at firms to provide incentives for increased spending on education and training opportunities for their employees. With these kinds of policies in place, individuals trapped in unattractive jobs or jobs that did not tap their intellectual potential would have a realistic chance of becoming more satisfied and more productive.

Conclusions

This kind of reconceptualization of the efficient use of labor is particularly important because so much of the public debate over labor issues continues to be dominated by neoclassical assumptions.[99] Those assumptions, rooted in a theoretical framework that emerged out of the early period of industrialization in Great Britain, are still routinely used to justify one set of policy proposals or to oppose another. For example, in contemporary political debates, unions are generally seen as necessary evils at best, because their exercise of monopoly power in setting the price of labor interferes with the market's efficient allocation of resources—the same logic that underlay the Combination Acts that outlawed unions in England. The recent finding of Richard Freeman and James Medoff that unionized firms tend to be more productive than their nonunion counterparts has been almost totally ignored in public debate because it flies in the face of this conventional neoclassical wisdom.[100] However, the nature of production and, more specifically, the skills and responsibilities of the typical employee have changed dramatically from early nineteenth-century England to today. It involves an enormous leap of faith to imagine that the same theory could fully specify the efficient use of labor in both of these historical situations. Instead of making this kind of leap, it seems far preferable to follow the logic of this chapter—to develop a theory of the efficient use of labor out of the actual circumstances of the contemporary workplace.

99. It seems that the efficiency-wage theorists and other labor economists who are critical of the neoclassical perspective have so far had relatively little influence on public policy debates. This might be changing, as some analysts of labor law are now drawing on this body of work to justify changes in the legal regime governing employment practices. See, for example, Paul Weiler, "The Law at Work" (Law School, Harvard University).

100. Richard Freeman and James Medoff, *What Do Unions Do?* (New York: Basic Books, 1984).

Chapter Five

Capital

The concept of capital raises problems quite different from those encountered with the concept of labor. In the case of labor, it is possible to begin by examining the conditions for the efficient use of human labor. To pose the same question in regard to capital assumes what is most problematic—that we know what capital actually is. This has always been a problem, but postindustrial trends radically undermine the coherence of any existing definitions or measures of capital.

The argument of this chapter develops in four steps. First, it is increasingly problematic to attribute output to capital inputs as opposed to a range of organizational factors that influence how physical capital is utilized. Second, pervasive processes of capital savings—technological advances that make physical capital more powerful without commensurate increases in price—both undermine attempts to measure capital inputs and further highlight the importance of the social contexts in which machines are developed and used. Third, these developments mean that traditional forms of capital accounting are increasingly problematic for the firm and for the entire economy. Finally, these conceptual and measurement difficulties in turn raise profound questions about the privileged treatment of capital that is a central aspect of our current political-economic arrangements.

Traditional Issues in Defining Capital

The problem of defining and measuring capital precisely has plagued economists for years.[1] It is not easy to establish the boundary line between capital expenditures and other types of expenditures either theoretically or empirically. For example, while it is obvious that heavy machines and factory buildings are part of capital investment, there is disagreement as to whether "intangible expenditures" such as spending for research or training should also count as capital. Moreover, even when analysts resolve that question to their satisfaction, other problems still loom large. The capital stock of a nation consists of an extremely diverse group of goods, produced in different years. Since only a relatively small share of total capital will actually have been purchased in the most recent year, it is not satisfactory to measure all capital in terms of the original market price. There has to be some kind of adjustment for changes in price levels and procedures for assessing the value of older capital relative to newer capital in light of technological advances and depreciation. In addition, the analyst must also decide how to handle the fact that some capital goods lie idle because of excess capacity while those that are used may be operated at radically different levels of intensity, as in the difference between three daily shifts and one. Different solutions to these problems can lead to quite divergent estimates of the economy's capital stock at a particular point in time, with significant implications for estimates of productivity and economic growth.

It is also important to remember Marx's critique of the way classical economists treated capital. He argued that economists assumed that capital is a thing—an input into the production process—albeit a thing with extraordinary properties, since capital is seen as animating the production process and as earning a reward comparable to the reward of the human beings who constitute labor. Marx insisted on the contrary that capital is a social relationship. For Marx, rather than being in itself a piece of capital, the machine is inserted into a set of social arrangements that endow it with certain properties.

1. See "Introduction," in Dan Usher, ed., *The Measurement of Capital* (Chicago: University of Chicago Press, 1980), 1–21, for a concise discussion of some of the definitional problems.

What is a Negro slave? A man of the black race. The one explanation is as good as the other.

A Negro is a Negro. He only becomes a slave in certain relations. A cotton-spinning jenny is a machine for spinning cotton. It becomes *capital* only in certain relations. Torn from these relationships it is no more capital than gold in itself is money or sugar the price of sugar.[2]

It is human beings who establish the social context in which machines appear to animate the production process and earn economic returns. In sum, capital is the name of the social context into which those machines are inserted.

Ironically, Marx's elaboration of the tendency of the rate of profit to fall undercut his own insight into the nature of capital. Generations of Marxist economists who have sought to calculate the production of surplus value or the organic composition of capital have adopted a framework in which capital is nothing more than a thing that can be measured in some objective fashion.

Nevertheless, Marx's critique remains a powerful reminder that there is something deeply problematic in the conceptualization of capital as simply an input into the production process. This reminder becomes particularly pressing as postindustrial trends increase the importance of the social context within which capital goods are used. This can be seen clearly with a relatively simple thought experiment.

A Thought Experiment

It is useful to imagine two work settings that begin with the same stock of physical capital and a labor force with the same education and skills, being utilized to produce the same output.[3] For example, the two plants could be producing consumer appliances with advanced production technologies. Then it is possible to examine the ways in which the output and the profitability of these two workplaces may vary significantly.[4] Economists tend to think in

2. Karl Marx, "Wage Labor and Capital," in Robert C. Tucker, ed., *The Marx-Engels Reader* (New York: Norton, 1972), 176.

3. A classical source for this kind of comparison is Harvey Leibenstein, *Beyond Economic Man: A New Foundation for Microeconomics* (Cambridge, Mass.: Harvard University Press, 1976).

4. It would be nice if one could rely on an actual comparison between two closely matched production facilities, but such comparisons are very rare in the

terms of a production function in which output is a function of capital and labor inputs, but in this thought experiment, it is other variables that explain differences in economic performance. First, it is clear that there can be significant differences in worker productivity that can be traced to motivation and training. Plant A might be able to motivate its employees to produce more through better wages, greater employment security, and attractive career lines. Furthermore, efforts to systematize learning among the workers might make them better problem-solvers. This could show up, for example, in significant differences between the two plants in the amount of down time—time in which the automated equipment is idle—and in the amount of time devoted to preparing the machinery for production. Even with relatively simple technologies of production, differences in motivation and training may be significant, and as the technologies become more complex, the differences may become much larger.

Second, the two plants may also differ in the yield from a certain volume of output because of differences in the quality of the final product. If the product is delivered to customers despite defects, the plant might well lose customers and suffer a significant decline in profitability. On the other hand, if the defects are caught and corrected, this requires a significant expenditure of time and effort, which may erode productivity rates. Where product quality is an issue, it is clearly preferable to organize the production process to do it right the first time. Here again, the motivation and training of the workforce are key variables. However, there are also other organizational factors that are critical for optimizing quality. A number of ethnographic studies show that quality control can often be subordinated to managerial drives to maximize output.[5] If quality-control inspectors are subject to pressure to pass substandard products, then the whole effort at quality control becomes a charade.

---

literature. Part of the problem is that firms are often reluctant to pass on the relevant information to independent researchers. But even with access, it is difficult to control all of the variables that could influence the comparison. If one of the plants has a strike, a layoff, or turnover at the managerial level during the period of observation, that would be enough to upset the comparison.

5. Tom Juravich, *Chaos on the Shop Floor* (Philadelphia: Temple University Press, 1985), 117–37; Michael Burawoy, *Manufacturing Consent: Changes in the Labor Process under Monopoly Capitalism* (Chicago: University of Chicago Press, 1979): 56–57, 182–83.

This is one of the areas in which the superiority of Japanese management has often been emphasized; the Japanese have developed organizational forms in which quality control is not a separate function but is integrated into all production tasks.[6]

If we take the additional step of imagining that our identical plants are producing services rather than goods, the issue of quality becomes even more salient. In a hospital or a bank setting, for example, the quality of the interaction between customer and employees is a major part of the service. Yet just as in an industrial setting, it is easy for managers to orient themselves primarily to quantitative—and easily measurable—output goals. In such cases, the qualitative dimension of the service is likely to suffer. The result could well be sharp differences in economic performance between production units with equal initial resources of labor and capital.

Third, the two plants may also differ significantly in the efficiency with which materials and inventory are handled. Recent research indicates that American firms tend to keep poor account of the use of raw materials in the production process. However, the amount of raw material wasted in the production process can have a significant impact on the overall efficiency of the firm. One study showed that in continuous-process production, a one-point decline in the percentage of total raw materials that were wasted was associated with a 3 percent increase in total factor productivity.[7] In light of the rising costs of disposal of industrial wastes, including the social costs of hazardous wastes, the gains in organizing production to minimize waste could be considerable. Energy conservation is another important dimension of waste. Even when two plants have identical physical facilities, ways may be found to conserve energy in the production process that would have a significant impact on total energy costs.

In addition, the costs to a firm of maintaining large inventories of raw materials can be considerable. In metalworking industries, a

6. Robert E. Cole, *Work, Mobility, and Participation: A Comparative Study of American and Japanese Industry* (Berkeley: University of California Press, 1979), 135–39.

7. Robert Hayes and Kim B. Clark, "Exploring the Sources of Productivity Differences at the Factory Level," in Kim Clark, Robert H. Hayes, and Christopher Lorenz, eds., *The Uneasy Alliance: Managing the Productivity-Technology Dilemma* (Boston: Harvard Business School Press, 1985), 151–88.

part is usually being worked on only 5 percent of the total time that it is in the plant.[8] If the part is worked on for five days, there would be three months in which it is simply sitting there. By reducing the lead time—the time the part is not being worked on—the firm can significantly reduce its investment in inventory, freeing up its resources for more productive uses. Yet the way in which the firm manages its inventories is a variable that is independent of its initial stock of capital and labor.

Fourth, the two plants may also differ significantly in their capacity to respond flexibly to changing market circumstances. Differences in workers' motivation and training, as well as differences in organizational design, may make it possible for plant A to retool far more quickly and more effectively than plant B. Since firms can no longer expect demand for a given good or service to remain constant, this capacity for flexibility can prove extremely important.

The flexibility variable also has implications for the firm's capacity to be effective in using new capital goods. When the time comes for the two plants to replace obsolete machines, the more flexible firm is likely to make a better choice of appropriate technologies, manage the transition more efficiently, and, finally, derive greater output from the new capital equipment. Even if one preserves the requirement that the two plants pay the same amount for this second round of capital, the differences in output may easily become more pronounced with each additional dollar of investment.

Fifth, the productivity of labor, the quality of output, and the flexibility of the firm may all be affected by the quality of the software used with computer-based technologies.[9] Whether one is talking about mainframe computers, personal computers, or various forms of computer-assisted manufacturing, the computers need operating systems and applications software for particular tasks.

---

8. Robert U. Ayres and Steven M. Miller, *Robotics: Applications and Social Implications* (Cambridge, Mass.: Ballinger, 1983), 283–85.

9. In national-income accounting, expenditures on software are not included as investment; they are treated instead as intermediate goods that are part of the cost of production. At the level of the firm, however, some expenditures for software can be treated as capital expenditures for tax purposes, although there is considerable ambiguity about the costs associated with developing software within the firm. On this latter point, see Robert W. McGee, *Accounting for Data Processing Costs* (New York: Quorum Books, 1988), esp. ch. 6.

The codes for this software may be written with varying levels of skill, with differential consequences for the amount of machine time and human labor required to complete a particular task. Moreover, better software makes it possible to automate tasks that previously had to be done manually or could not be done at all.

Finally, the two plants may differ dramatically in their safety records in terms of fire, worker safety, customer safety, malpractice, and environmental pollution. Carol Heimer shows that for certain areas of liability, the insurance industry has encouraged the development of elaborate procedures to assure that firms take an active role in reducing these risks, but the degree of effort still varies greatly between firms.[10] But the key point is that even when a firm is protected from some of the costs of poor performance in this area by insurance or by lax public enforcement, these costs have to be carried by the society. Moreover, with modern chemical and nuclear technologies, the costs of serious accidents can be huge. Accidents on the scale of Bhopal or Chernobyl are rare, but their costs are so great as to overwhelm normal calculations of profit and loss.

Even this listing of six areas of significant difference hardly exhausts the relevant variables. If one extends the analysis beyond the level of the plant to include the steps taken before and after the production process, there are other important factors that shape the costs and benefits of production. There is the research and development effort through which a firm decides what products to produce. Even with very similar staffs and physical facilities, management at one firm may be far more successful in facilitating the generation of new product ideas or new ideas about organizing the production process. There may also be significant differences in the success of the two firms' marketing efforts, with one firm far better at shaping its products to meet consumer needs. Many products, including consumer appliances, require ongoing service and support for customers after their purchase, and these functions of repair, maintenance, information, and support may be performed more or less effectively. In some cases, these services are an additional source of revenue for the firm, while in others they may simply influence the

10. Carol Heimer, *Reactive Risk and Rational Action* (Berkeley: University of California Press, 1985).

amount of customer loyalty the firm can generate. Either way, they are important for the firm's profitability. Finally, at all stages of the process, the speed and quality of communication among different parts of the organization, and between the organization and outsiders such as suppliers and customers, will have a major bearing on efficiency. Obviously, hardware such as telephones and computer networks can facilitate communication, but there are a variety of organizational variables that may impede or accelerate the flow of information. Firms that are able to structure their organizations to facilitate communication and make maximal use of communications hardware will gain a competitive edge.

It should be clear that while many of these nontraditional factors of production have always played an economic role, they have become progressively more central to the economy. A steadily shrinking share of national output is accounted for by goods that have the characteristics of the economists' widget. Widgets are a standardized good that can be produced by unskilled labor, have no discernible differences in quality, and require no special marketing or customer support after purchase. Most services—which now account for the bulk of consumer purchases—have little resemblance to a widget.[11] Moreover, many goods—particularly consumer durables and capital goods—are produced by skilled employees under conditions where quality differences are increasingly salient, and where customers receive continuing support from producers.

Moreover, several features of contemporary technologies reinforce the importance of these nontraditional inputs into the production process. First, production increasingly depends on highly complex, tightly linked systems that are vulnerable to failures.[12] Factories have been vulnerable to fire and accidents since the start of industrialism, but the scale of potential disaster has increased. Particularly in such industries as chemicals, nuclear power, health

11. One possible exception is the fast-food hamburger for those who are unable to discern the differences in quality between a Whopper and a Big Mac. But while fast-food restaurants are often seen as emblematic of the entire service sector, they are actually quite atypical. For health and business services—two of the fastest-growing service categories—quality differences are extremely important.

12. Charles Perrow, *Normal Accidents: Living with High-Risk Technologies* (New York: Basic Books, 1984).

care, and air and rail transportation, the negative payoffs for organizational neglect of safety issues have become ever more important.

Second, computer-based technologies have combined with changes in consumer preferences to produce a significant shift toward greater differentiation of product lines.[13] In some industries, a unified mass market has been replaced by a multitude of specialized market "niches." In baked goods, for example, the dominance of homogenized white breads has been displaced by the rise of a broad variety of specialty breads. At the same time, computer-based technologies make it far easier for a single production facility to produce a range of different products. In banking, for example, the computer has made it possible to dramatically increase the range of savings instruments that can be provided for customers. But whatever the sources of this destandardization of products, the end result is the increasing importance of flexibility on the shop floor to make possible the production of a variety of outputs. And with more complex products, and in industries near the cutting edge of technological change, flexibility means, not just the capacity to use an existing technology to produce a different product, but the ability to adapt quickly to entirely new technologies.

The Problem of Conceptualizing Capital

Once we have identified many of the nontraditional factors that have an increasing bearing on a firm's effectiveness, the question is how they should be conceptualized and measured. Expanding the budget for software or safety or quality control can have positive results. When these increased expenditures take the form of purchases of physical capital, such as a new computer for the quality-control function, they are clearly classified as capital investment. But if the resources are the time and effort of employees or services purchased from outsiders, the situation becomes more complex.

Since the development of human-capital theory, some economists have made the argument that certain of these categories of expenditures should be counted as part of the economy's aggregate

13. Destandardization of product markets is a central theme in Charles F. Sabel and Michael J. Piore, *The Second Industrial Divide: Possibilities for Prosperity* (New York: Basic Books, 1984). See also Alvin Toffler, *The Third Wave* (New York: Morrow, 1980).

investment. In empirical studies, John Kendrick and Robert Eisner have attempted to measure the society's total spending on intangible capital—a category that includes expenditures on education and training and research and development.[14] Significantly, these studies show that the percentage of GNP devoted to capital investment is far higher than when capital is defined conventionally as tangible investments, and the ratio of investment to total output has been rising.[15]

Yet these efforts to measure "intangible capital" are examples of a larger measurement dilemma that economists face on a number of different fronts. The dilemma results from the tension between a long-established method of economic accounting and changes in the nature of economic activity that make that accounting system problematic. This dilemma usually gives rise to two responses—a traditionalist one and a technically innovative one. The traditionalists, who have generally dominated the Commerce Department's Bureau of Economic Analysis, argue against changing established methods on the grounds that new techniques introduce too much uncertainty into well-established statistical series. They generally argue that the creation of new measures involves too many subjective judgments that will destroy the value of the data. The technical innovators generally respond that failing to revise the data will lead to an increasingly inaccurate picture of the economy, and that techniques can be developed to reduce the subjective element of the new measures.

What is particularly interesting about these debates is that they almost never call into question the basic concepts of economic analysis. They are debates about the appropriate ways of operationalizing a particular category, whether it be capital or Gross National

14. John W. Kendrick, *The Formation and Stocks of Total Capital* (New York: National Bureau of Economic Research, 1976); Robert Eisner, "The Total Income System of Accounts," *Survey of Current Business*, January 1985, 24–47.

15. National-income accounting treats business capital expenditures and business current expenditures differently; the former are added directly into GNP while the latter are not. Hence, studies that expand the definition of capital lead to much higher GNP figures than those in the official accounts. The political implications of these measurement issues are discussed in Fred Block, "Rethinking the Political Economy of the Welfare State," in Fred Block, Richard A. Cloward, Barbara Ehrenreich, and Frances Fox Piven, *The Mean Season: The Attack on the Welfare State* (New York: Pantheon Books, 1987): 118–20.

Product or producers' durable equipment. The traditionalists simply want to hold on to an existing operationalization, while the technical innovators want to measure the category in a new way. In fact, the innovators sometimes appear to avoid theoretical issues by resorting to technical virtuosity. Both views are thus sharply different from the approach taken here, which is to call for a reconsideration of the basic concepts of economic analysis.

In the case of measuring capital, innovators like Robert Eisner and John Kendrick have problems of theoretical consistency because they redefine only some of these nontraditional variables as capital. If one defines all of a firm's costs for labor and outside services that are used in research and development as a form of capital, why not do the same for safety and pollution control or for software development? In each case, these are not simply current expenses, but expenditures designed to have a long-term impact on the organization's capacity to produce. Furthermore, business services such as management consulting are among the fastest-growing segments of the economy, and the purchase of such services can also be seen as an investment in increasing organizational effectiveness.

Expenditures on an organization's marketing capacities or its capacities to provide support and service to customers are more ambiguous. Here it is necessary to make distinctions between ongoing activities that are necessary to do the firm's business and other activities that are designed to have a long-term payoff. Hence, in marketing, one might distinguish between routine contacts with customers and major research projects to examine the future contours of the market. Similarly, in customer support, one might distinguish between the labor involved in providing the support on a day-to-day basis and efforts to provide an improved level of service, which would include research activities. This means one would logically want to measure marketing capital and customer-support capital as well.

This way of thinking about capital poses enormous empirical problems; to distinguish adequately between current expenses and this expanded concept of capital, an analyst would have to go through virtually every expenditure and every person on the payroll. Yet the results would be uncertain even if one did this, because of the enormous possible variations in the effectiveness of these kinds of expenditures. For example, the two firms could spend an identical amount on training to upgrade the human capital of the labor force, but the results of the expenditure might be radically different. And the same thing can be said about expenditures for any of these other types of "intangible capital." Hence, it seems unlikely that this procedure would end up with the empirical result that differences in outputs can be explained in terms of differences in quantitative inputs of labor and of different types of capital.

Yet these empirical problems pale in comparison to the theoretical ones. It is useful to think of the accounts of a small firm making use of the most sophisticated technologies, such as a Japanese manufacturing firm using flexible manufacturing systems.[16] In such a firm, there would be no traditional semiskilled production workers or clericals, because production and office work would be fully automated. Since most of the work to be done would consist of figuring out how to manage the production process ever more effectively, it is easy to imagine that 30 percent of labor costs might be allocated to research and development, 20 percent to software development, 20 percent to improvement of human capital, 20 percent to organizational development, and 10 percent to safety capital. In short, the firm would have no labor costs; everything except for purchases of raw materials would represent a capital expenditure. This hypothetical firm represents the logical endpoint of a dynamic that removes human beings from routine, repetitious tasks and makes them into problem-solvers who are continually upgrading their intellectual capacities. Yet the notion of all labor expenses becoming capital expenses is a reductio ad absurdum; it is a demonstration that the whole accounting scheme that focuses on labor and capital as the key inputs into the production process can no longer make sense of the firm's balance sheet or of the actual sources of economic output.

It seems far more logical to pursue an alternative conceptualization in which these various nontraditional inputs are grouped together as organizational factors recognized to be the key determinants of the society's productive capacity. Whether the society or

16. Ramchandran Jaikumar, "Postindustrial Manufacturing," *Harvard Business Review* 64, no. 6 (November–December 1986): 69–76. For the sake of simplicity, it will be assumed that marketing and customer support are not important issues for this firm.

the firm spends more or less on physical capital will never be as important in determining economic output as the strength or weakness of these organizational factors. As Marx stressed, the machine is not a productive force in and of itself, it only becomes so in a particular social context, and this is provided by the organization's strengths and weaknesses in using human beings and technology.

One obvious objection to this conceptualization is that it interferes with the kind of quantitative analysis that the discipline of economics has emphasized. If one introduces organizational variables that cannot be measured in terms of money, the traditional production function becomes highly problematic. However, the problem is not with the conceptualization but with reality. It is historical development that has increased the importance of the organizational variables and made it impossible to explain the bulk of economic growth in terms of labor and capital inputs. Moreover, the project of quantification can continue to go forward; it is just that analysts will need to take account of previously neglected variables. New ways will have to be devised to assess and measure the different components of organizational effectiveness, and these variables can then be introduced into complex econometric models. Such analyses could have valuable empirical results by narrowing the size of the residual—the share of growth that cannot be explained by changes in labor and capital inputs. But the most important payoff will be the policy insight that the key to improved economic performance comes through improving the effectiveness of organizations. The desirability of this reconceptualization is further reinforced by parallel problems in the measurement and assessment of physical capital. The process of capital savings serves to further underline the centrality of organizational factors.

The Issue of Capital Savings

Capital savings means that a more effective machine is available without a commensurate increase in price, or that a machine of the same effectiveness is available at a reduced cost. Significant capital savings will depend on scientific and technological advances that reduce the costs of producing the capital good.

It creates problems for economic measurement if capital savings occur on a significant scale, and it is entirely possible that constant dollar capital expenditures will fall for the economy as a whole. Such a decline is ordinarily treated as a danger signal—a sign of recession and of inadequate renewal of the society's capital. But if the slowdown is simply the consequence of capital savings, this would be a misinterpretation. The society's capital stock could be growing in terms of effectiveness even while real capital expenditures are declining.

Despite the importance of correct diagnoses of changes in real expenditures on physical capital, the available data do not take account of capital savings. In the National Income and Product Accounts, and in the Bureau of Labor Statistics price indexes that are used to construct deflators, almost no efforts are made to adjust for "costless quality changes"—changes in the quality of a product that are not linked to increases in production costs.[17] For example, if there is a model change for a particular type of numerically controlled machine tool that increases the cost by 5 percent while increasing the machine's capacity to produce by 25 percent, this will probably be treated simply as a 5 percent price rise. Assuming that the same number of such machines are sold in both years, this would show up as a 5 percent decline in output when there had really been a 25 percent increase in productive capacity.

Economic traditionalists have generally resisted efforts to assess the impact of this kind of capital savings. They argue that the market given price is a more valuable indicator of the utility of the product than an alternative estimate of the services a particular product provides.[18] They further insist that in the case of capital

17. Zvi Griliches, "Comment," in Murray F. Foss, ed., *The U.S. National Income and Product Accounts* (Chicago: University of Chicago Press, 1983), 143–44.

18. "In this kind of price index, the transactions unit is the product itself and not the service it provides. Thus, if an automobile tire lasts longer, the price quotation cannot be directly adjusted to take account of this increase in the store of services, even if this could be unequivocally assessed, because it is tires and not tire-miles which are priced in the market place" (Gordon J. Garston and David A. Worton, "Reply," in John Kendrick, ed., *The Industrial Composition of Income and Product* [New York: National Bureau of Economic Research, 1968], 482–85). See also Edward Denison, "Theoretical Aspects of Quality Change, Capital Consumption, and Net Capital Formation," in *Problems of Capital Formation* (Princeton: Princeton University Press, 1957), 215–60.

goods, failure to measure capital savings is relatively insignificant, because any such savings will show up elsewhere in the accounts in the form of increased and cheaper production of final products.

The problems of measuring capital savings are also severe, inasmuch as there is usually no single relevant dimension for a particular capital good. An improved machine might perform certain operations faster and be able to perform operations the previous machine could not do at all. Moreover, the size of the increase in capacity will most certainly depend upon such factors as the skill and motivation of the operators, the organization of the production process, and so on.

Nevertheless, economic innovators have developed tools to make calculations about the relationship between price changes and multiple characteristics of a product. The most important of these tools are "hedonic" price indexes. These indexes measure the costs of multiple characteristics of a particular product by using regression analysis on data on the prices of products having different measured amounts of different characteristics. Constructing a hedonic price index can, in theory, solve the problem of measuring changes in the utility of capital goods.[19]

In practice, however, there are several major problems with using hedonic techniques. First, the proper use of the technique requires a great deal of information about a particular product before one can even develop a sense of which of the characteristics of the product are actually relevant for purchasing decisions. Second, there is a need for many price observations in each year to assure information for all of the relevant characteristics. Developing good hedonic indexes becomes an expensive and time-consuming technique. Third, ongoing changes in the characteristics of products will interfere with the effectiveness of hedonic techniques. There are limits to the number of characteristics that can fruitfully be analyzed for statistical reasons, but if a previously neglected characteristic starts becoming important, prior hedonic results will be of questionable value. Fourth, it is usually impossible to develop accurate measures of durability, a product characteristic that is extremely important to purchasers; in the automobile industry, for example, reduced expenditures for maintenance and repair

19. Zvi Griliches, ed, *Price Indexes and Quality Change: Studies in New Methods of Measurement* (Cambridge, Mass.: Harvard University Press, 1971).

have been an increasingly important selling point, but one cannot even estimate such a characteristic without a five- or ten-year time lag. Finally, and most important, characteristics are generally a problematic indicator of the utility of a capital good.[20] The speed of a machine tool, for example, is not a certain indicator of the capacity of the machine to produce. In short, hedonic techniques are an indirect and imperfect way to measure changes in the worth of capital goods.

Recent Developments in Capital Savings

Issues of capital saving, costless quality change, and the use of hedonic price indexes have remained on the margins of economic analysis for some time because the problems have not seemed particularly pressing. Although technological breakthroughs that can lower the costs of particular capital goods happen from time to time, the overall effect from year to year is generally thought to be small. But this has changed with successive advances in the miniaturization and cheapening of electronic devices that are used in a wide variety of capital goods. In particular, the development in the early 1970s of the microprocessor—the computer on a chip—represented a qualitative leap forward in the process of capital savings. With the microprocessor, a broad range of devices could be produced at significantly lower costs; machines that relied on electromechanical controls with many moving parts could be redesigned around far cheaper electronic controls.

The development of the microprocessor was not a single event, and it launched a process of continuous innovation. With each successive microprocessor, engineers managed to put many times the number of logic circuits on a chip of the same size, so that the microprocessors could become progressively more powerful in processing information. Since the costs per chip decline dramatically with mass production, the result has been a tremendous increase in information-processing capacity per dollar invested. This has resulted in continuous capital savings across the full range of capital goods that incorporate electronic controls.

20. Arthur J. Alexander and Bridger M. Mitchell, "Measuring Technological Change of Heterogeneous Products," *Technological Forecasting and Social Change* 27 (1985): 161–95.

Developments have been most dramatic for the computer industry itself, where the costs of computing power have fallen by as much as 25 percent a year.[21] In fact, the whole computer industry has been transformed, inasmuch as complex operations that previously required an expensive mainframe computer can now be carried out on a small personal computer. While these developments have created many new applications for computer technology, they have also made it possible to replace previously available computer power at a fraction of prior cost.

This economic transformation was completely ignored in available government data until the end of 1985. The Bureau of Labor Statistics had not developed a price index for computers, so that in compiling the National Income and Product Accounts, government statisticians simply assumed that the price of computers had remained constant. The dollar value of computer output for each year was simply entered into the National Accounts without any adjustment for price changes. This led to two different types of distortion. First, price declines were treated as declines in output. For example, if the price of a particular model dropped 20 percent from one year to the next, but the volume of sales remained the same, the government's technique would report a 20 percent decline in output. Second, quality changes—increases in computing power per dollar—were ignored even though it is well known that today's dollar buys many times the computer power of a dollar spent five years ago.

Government economists attempted to respond to both problems in late 1985 by introducing a price index developed by economists at IBM that used hedonic techniques to measure changes in the costs of computing power. The size of the resulting adjustments to GNP and purchases of capital goods provide a preliminary indication of the scale of capital savings. With the new index, 1984 GNP (measured in 1972 dollars) was $100 billion higher than previously estimated, and the annual growth rate of producers' durable equip-

21. Different calculations produce different rates of decline. However, the consensus view is reflected by Kenneth Flamm who writes: "In real terms, this price has fallen, on average, more than 20 percent each year over the last three decades and may even have exceeded 25 percent (that is, relative to some average price for all goods and services produced in the economy.)" *Creating the Computer: Government, Industry, and High Technology* (Washington, D.C.: Brookings Institution, 1988), 1.

ment between 1972 and 1982 went from 5.6 percent to 12.6 percent. In other words, this single adjustment for computer prices led to more than a doubling in the rate of growth of spending for capital goods when measured in 1972 dollars.

However, at the same time that the government statisticians introduced the new computer price indexes, they also shifted the base year for calculating prices from 1972 to 1982. This normally routine shift counteracted the impact of the new computer price index on the national accounts. When a product drops sharply in price while sales are increasing dramatically, as happened with computers, the shift of the base year will change the weight of the product relative to the rest of the economy. In this case, the $100 billion gain that occurred in 1972 dollars disappeared with the shift to 1982 dollars.[22] The mere fact that the trends in economic growth are so sensitive to a technical matter such as the choice of a base year is ample evidence of the extraordinary difficulties of measurement created by this kind of capital savings.[23]

Yet the impact of rebasing is only one of the problems with these efforts to account for changes in computer output. In making use of

22. In current prices, it is a simple matter to calculate the weight of computers relative to the rest of the economy or the rest of the capital-goods sector. But when deflated prices are introduced for computers, how does one calculate their weight relative to the deflated weight of the rest of the economy? The technique used by the Bureau of Economic Analysis led to results that change dramatically depending upon the base year. The reason for this can be seen if we begin with the roughly accurate assumption that the real dollar output of computers grew by a factor of 30 from 1972 to 1982. When one uses 1972 as the base year, the 1972 figure for computer output would be the actual dollar value of computers produced in that year, while the 1982 figure would be 30 times that. When one switches to 1982 prices, the 1982 figure will be the current value of computers in 1982—a dollar value that will be relatively low because of the continuous price declines—while the 1972 figure will be one-thirtieth of that. When rebasing has such a radical impact, one procedure that can be used is to average out the results by combining both base periods. If this procedure had been used, the 1984 increment to GNP from the revaluation of computer output would still be on the order of $50 billion.

23. Robert Gordon develops an alternative weighting technique designed to handle these index number problems in "The Postwar Evolution of Computer Prices" (National Bureau of Economic Research Working Paper no. 2227, April 1987). A revised version of this paper has since been printed in Dale W. Jorgenson and Ralph Landau, eds., *Technology and Capital Formation* (Cambridge, Mass.: MIT Press, 1989), 77–125. While his method is an improvement over those used by the Bureau of Economic Analysis, the assumptions made about the weight of computers relative to other elements of the economy continue to be problematic, since they are based on nominal prices rather than deflated prices.

the IBM research, government economists struggled with the standard dilemma of measurement traditionalists against innovators. Government economists had previously refused to use hedonic techniques to measure changes in the utility of capital goods. Their position had been that the government data could not capture costless quality changes, but had to center on changes in prices of similar goods.[24] However, in the case of computers, qualitative changes had been so dramatic as to make it almost impossible to construct price indexes by matching similar models over years. The solution of the Bureau of Economic Analysis (BEA) was to choose the IBM hedonic index closest to the standard techniques of matching models. This showed an annual price decline for computers of 14 percent a year from 1972 to 1984—a far more conservative figure than standard estimates.[25] The BEA rejected another hedonic indicator that showed a significantly higher rate of price declines.

In the event, the BEA ended up with a price index that probably measures only a very small fraction of the quality change in computer power. Moreover, the IBM economists had relied on list prices, even though it is well known that discounting is widespread in the computer industry. Since it seems likely that discounting will be greater for an older product than a new one, it is probable that the IBM calculations significantly understated the size of the price decline even for matched models. Furthermore, the IBM data did not include personal computers and small disk drives, where price declines on matched models have been dramatic during the 1980s.[26]

24. This technique is called matched models, since one compares similar models across different years. It tends to ignore the costless quality changes that exist when models cannot be matched.

25. Gordon makes the same point about the conservatism of the Bureau of Economic Analysis index, noting that "the rate of decline of the BEA index seems implausibly slow." His index shows an annual rate of price decline for computers of 21.3 percent for the 1972–84 period ("Postwar Evolution of Computer Prices," 43–44).

26. Gordon calculates a 21.8 percent per year price decline for personal computers between 1982 and 1986 on a matched-model basis, using price data from magazines ("Postwar Evolution of Computer Prices," table 23). Another revision of the Bureau of Economic Analysis data that includes an index for personal computer prices has been introduced by David Cartwright and Scott D. Smith in "Deflators for Purchases of Computers in GNP: Revised and Extended Estimates, 1983–88," *Survey of Current Business*, November 1988, 22–23.

In short, it would seem that capital savings in computer power were significantly higher than the 14 percent per year price decline the government used. The central point, however, is that differences in the calculation of the computer price index and in the weighting schemes used to link these indexes to the larger economy can have a significant impact on key economic measures. For example, Robert Gordon's alternative computer price index and weighting scheme shows spending for producers' durable equipment rising at an annual rate of 6.5 percent between 1973 and 1979, in contrast to the BEA's data, which show an annual rise of 4.9 percent in that same period.[27] Although this increase is not as large as the one measured in 1972 dollars, it is still significant that the rise in capital spending in the United States should be almost one-third higher just because of an adjustment for computer price changes.

Even so, by late 1988, traditionalists counterattacked against the new BEA price index for computers.[28] They argued that the government data overstated the growth of manufacturing in the 1980s by exaggerating the expansion of computer output. These critics have made some valid points,[29] but the basic thrust of their argument is that estimates of the increased utility of products should not be substituted for market prices, a contention that seems highly problematic in a period of intense capital savings.

In actuality, the main problem with the government's efforts to develop improved output data is that they are confined to the computer industry itself. There are many other capital goods industries where there is a similar lack of any usable historical price indexes.[30] And for many of these goods, there have been significant

27. Calculated from Robert Gordon, "Postwar Evolution of Computer Prices," table 22, and data from the *Survey of Current Business*.

28. Lawrence Mishel, "Of Manufacturing Mismeasurement," *New York Times*, Sunday Business Section, November 27, 1988; the Bureau of Economic Analysis also responded to unnamed critics in "Gross Product by Industry: Comments on Recent Criticisms," *Survey of Current Business*, July 1988, 132–33.

29. They note, for example, that the government data do not take adequate account of the import of computer components. They also question the validity of the Commerce Department's figures on manufacturing's share of total output. On the latter point, see Fred Block, *Revising State Theory: Essays in Politics and Postindustrialism* (Temple University Press, 1987), ch. 8.

30. The Bureau of Labor Statistics has embarked on a major effort to improve the Producers' Price Index by covering many previously neglected products. However, many of these new series lack any historical data, so they cannot be used to analyze price trends over the past fifteen years.

gains in effectiveness without corresponding increases in costs. To date, there has been no systematic effort to measure the overall extent of the capital savings that have accelerated as a consequence of the development of and advances in microprocessor technology.

One indication of the magnitude of the capital savings is the shift in the nature of physical capital itself. In its data on capital investments, the BEA has begun to group together computers and office machines, communications equipment, instruments, and photocopying machines under the category of information-processing equipment. This category has increased from 16.8 percent of all purchases of producers' durable equipment in 1965 to 30.5 percent in 1985 (in current dollars).[31] However, computers and office machines accounted for only 36.4 percent of this information-processing category in 1985. Yet almost all of the capital goods within this category make substantial use of computer technologies, so one might expect costless quality changes to have been substantial.

One of the most important of these other types of information-processing equipment is communications equipment, which includes telephone and broadcasting equipment. This category was valued in 1985 at $35.9 billion, as compared to $34.3 billion for computers and office machines. Yet the elaborate switching machines used to direct telephone signals are one of the most important types of communications equipment (constituting 33.6 percent of the sales of the telecommunications equipment industry).[32] Whereas these switches used to be electromechanical, they are now electronic, and are essentially special-purpose computers that have increased dramatically in capacity with the advances in microprocessor technology. One price index estimates that the cost of a switch for a center with 60,000 trunks declined at the rate of 10 percent a year between 1974 and 1982.[33]

31. The growth is even more dramatic in constant dollars because capital savings has been most dramatic in the information-processing category.

32. Department of Commerce, *The Telecommunications Industry* (Washington, D.C.: GPO, 1983), 20.

33. Bellcore data cited in Kenneth Flamm, "Technological Advance and Costs: Computers versus Communications," in Robert W. Crandall and Kenneth Flamm, eds., *Changing the Rules: Technological Change, International Competition, and Regulation in Communications* (Washington, D.C.: Brookings Institution, 1989): 13–61. See, particularly, pp. 42–43 and Appendix B-2, p. 405.

Other examples of capital savings in information-processing equipment can easily be added. In the case of photocopying, a Xerox desktop machine introduced in 1983 was three times faster and one-seventh the size of the first generation of Xerox machines introduced in 1959 and the 1983 machine sold at a much lower price.[34] Moreover, photocopying and computer technology have come to play an increasingly important role in printing. With the development of laser printers, "desktop" publishing has become a reality. *Business Week* reports that one newspaper was on the verge of buying a $117,000 electronic composition system, but instead purchased a group of Apple Macintoshes and laser printers that cost $43,000 including the software.[35] Still another important area of innovation is medical instruments, where computerization has made possible both the cheapening of existing products and the development of entirely new products.

Moreover, the process of capital savings has not been confined to the information-processing segment of capital; the introduction of new technologies has had a major impact on the second important segment of producers' durable equipment—industrial equipment. Computer technologies have been incorporated into a broad range of industrial capital goods, with broad implications for the relationship between the cost and the effectiveness of these goods. These trends can be tracked most clearly in metalworking equipment, which represented 7 percent of all producers' durable equipment in 1980.

There have been several major changes in machine tools for metalworking. Numerically controlled machine tools—machine tools equipped with control systems capable of logically processing prescribed programs—were first introduced in 1959.[36] Their diffusion was still relatively slow through the 1960s, but during the 1970s the shift to numerical control accelerated. Also during the

---

34. Office of Technology Assessment, *Automation of America's Offices, 1985–2000* (Washington, D.C.: GPO, 1985), 324.

35. "In News Graphics, Macintosh Makes the Front Page," *Business Week*, January 19, 1987, 87.

36. The definition is from D. Kochan, ed., *CAM: Developments in Computer-Integrated Manufacturing* (New York: Springer-Verlag, 1986), 8. On the history of numerical control, see David F. Noble, *Forces of Production: A Social History of Industrial Automation* (New York: Knopf, 1984).

1970s, an increasing percentage of numerically controlled machine tools incorporated computer controls; this provided the capability not only to run a program but to write or rewrite programs as well. One study reports that of all numerically controlled machine tools shown at major international exhibitions, the percentage that were CNC rose from less than 10 percent in 1970 to more than 75 percent in 1977.[37] Hence, by the 1980s virtually all new NC machines could be classified as CNC. Finally, groups of CNC machines have been integrated together into flexible manufacturing systems that are controlled by a central computer and involve automatic transfer of components from machine to machine.

There have been few attempts to develop systematic data on the comparative effectiveness of these different technologies, since much depends on the organizational context and on what is being produced.[38] Still, there is a good deal of information that suggests very substantial capital savings. A survey of users of numerically controlled machine tools in the United States in the early 1970s asked managers to compare the performance of NC tools with that of conventional tools. For most categories of tools, the mean response was a halving of the time for actual machining of a part.[39] In addition, the study also reported significant savings of time in setting up jobs, in inspection labor, and in scrap and rework costs. A more recent source that has attempted to rate the comparative productivity of different machine tools suggests that on the average a CNC machine tool is 2.6 times as productive as a conventional

37. Arndt Sorge et al., *Microelectronics and Manpower in Manufacturing: Applications of Computer Numerical Control in Great Britain and West Germany* (Aldershot, U.K.: Gower, 1983), 20.

38. Nevertheless, the lack of systematic data comparing the efficacy of different generations of machine tools casts doubt on the rationality of the criteria used by managers in making investment decisions. If they have no available source of data on the relative efficacy of different tools, how do they maximize the effectiveness of their investment dollar? David Noble makes this point: "In reality, which is considerably less tidy than any economic model, such [capital investment] decisions are more often than not grounded upon hunches, faith, ego, delight, and deals. What economic information there is to go by, however abundant, remains vague and suspect" (*Forces of Production*, 217).

39. Wilbert Steffy, Donald N. Smith, and Donald Souter, *Economic Guidelines for Justifying Capital Purchases* (Ann Arbor: Industrial Development Division of the Institute of Science and Technology, 1973), 26.

machine tool.[40] Another source argues that a CNC machining center will replace three conventional machine tools.[41]

Moreover, the journals in the field are full of anecdotal reports of efficiency gains of a similar order of magnitude. For example, *Production Engineering* reported that CNC turning machines are 3–4 times faster than a turret lathe and 5–8 times faster than an engine lathe.[42] Another article reports that it is not uncommon to see 100 to 200 percent improvements in productivity with new computerized stamping presses.[43] Still another reports that an automatic welding machine can improve productivity of a welding operation by a factor of 2 or 3, "while capital investment costs are generally moderate."[44] It is also the case that new generations of machine tools have been able to take advantage of significant improvements in materials used for cutting tools.[45] In 1974 ceramic-coated inserts were introduced that allowed for 100 to 200 percent increases in cutting speeds without reductions in tool life.[46] Altogether, these gains in the effectiveness of the machines have been so great that one government report mentions the increasing capacity of machine tools as a reason for the slowing growth of output in the industry.[47]

Not only have the machines clearly become progressively more effective, but the difference in costs between conventional machines and CNC machines has narrowed significantly. "Whilst NC machines have traditionally been more expensive than conventional machines, this is increasingly less so," Arndt Sorge et al.

40. Lawrence and Beatrice Hackamack, *Manual for Computerized System Analysis for Machine Replacement* (De Kalb, Ill.: n.p., 1985).

41. Arthur Francis, *New Technology at Work* (Oxford: Clarendon Press, 1986), 32.

42. 27, No. 9 (September 1980): 43.

43. Ibid., 59.

44. Ibid., 91.

45. As Sorge et al. write: "CNC machines also feature highly improved machine construction, drives and tools, and make much faster cutting possible. This is not a necessary consequence of CNC, but NC and CNC is necessary to keep such fast cutting processes under control" (*Microelectronics and Manpower*, 80). In short, advances in cutting technologies have been independent of microelectronics, but they are only usable in the context of computer controls.

46. Ibid., 75.

47. Bureau of Labor Statistics, *Technology and Labor in Four Industries*, Bulletin 2104 (Washington, D.C.: GPO, 1982), 26.

wrote in 1983.[48] The reason is that the cost of the computer controls has dropped sharply with the cheapening of computer power. Hence, even though NC machines have increased dramatically in the sophistication of their controls, the cost of the controls as a share of the total value of the system has fallen from 32 percent in 1970 to 17.1 percent in 1978.[49]

Although flexible manufacturing systems are still extremely expensive, they can also involve significant capital savings, because they dramatically reduce the number of machine tools needed while expanding output, reducing labor inputs, and improving quality. Compared to stand-alone NC machines, an FMS in West Germany reduced the number of machines required by 52.6 percent, reduced production time by a similar amount, and cut capital investment costs by 10 percent.[50]

Finally, new technologies are having an impact on the other key item of capital investment—expenditures for buildings. The combination of factory automation with efforts to control inventories and shorten production lead times reduces the amount of physical space required for factories. These space savings can be quite substantial, since multipurpose computerized machine tools take up much less room than the array of standard machine tools that would have been necessary to make the same products. An IBM facility in Raleigh, North Carolina, reduced the space needed for production from 51,000 to 9,000 square feet, and a Westinghouse facility in West Mifflin, Pennsylvania, cut its floor space from 125,000 to 52,000 square feet.[51] Ramchandran Jaikumar reports that a Japanese factory that introduced a flexible manufacturing system reduced its floor space from 16,500 square meters to 6,600 square meters.[52] In short, the trend is for manufacturing firms to downsize their production facilities, with considerable potential savings in construction costs.

This list of examples could be extended, but the basic point is clear—computerization has contributed to a systematic process of

48. Sorge et al., *Microelectronics and Manpower*, 20.
49. Ibid., 21.
50. Kochan, ed., *CAM*, 37–38.
51. Cited in Richard Schonberger, *World Class Manufacturing: The Lessons of Simplicity Applied* (New York: Free Press, 1986), 231–32.
52. Jaikumar, "Postindustrial Manufacturing," 73. Similar data on space savings with FMS is provided in Kochan, ed., *CAM*, 47.

capital savings that makes the official data on capital investment highly suspect. Although these capital savings predate the emergence of the microprocessor,[53] there has been a clear acceleration since the early 1970s. Yet there is no adequate way to measure the extent of these capital savings. As the Commerce Department's problems in reevaluating the value of the computer industry's output indicate, even when one is dealing with a fairly standardized product, the measurement problems are formidable. And the capital-goods sector is made up of thousands of different products, some of which are produced on a one-of-a-kind basis.

Aside from the technical difficulties of measurement, there are theoretical reasons for not attempting to translate these quality improvements in capital into dollar values. Most of the quality improvements in capital depend on the organizational context in which the technology is used. Even with computerization, dramatic increases in the computing power of a particular machine will be meaningless if the firm does not have the software and personnel to take advantage of that power. A methodology that assumes that increases in output are inherent in the equipment itself will divert attention from the centrality of organizational factors. Furthermore, attempting to develop dollar measures of capital savings slides over the critical question of how one explains the phenomenon of capital savings itself. Costless quality changes originate in scientific and technological breakthroughs and in the organizational dynamics that make it possible to incorporate those advances into actual products. In short, the origins of capital savings are not in physical capital expenditures but in such organizational variables as the effectiveness of research operations and the flexibility of firms. But if one takes the path of adjusting capital expenditures to capture quality changes, there is a tacit denial of the extraordinary importance of these organizational variables.

The alternative approach is to see capital savings as simply another indication that organizational variables have become the key factors in shaping the economy's capacity to produce. It is organizational factors that lie behind the successes of research and development efforts that generate the breakthroughs that make capital

---

53. Robert J. Gordon, "Measurement Bias in Price Indexes for Capital Goods," *Review of Income and Wealth* 17 (June 1971): 121–74.

savings possible, and it is organizational factors that determine whether the additional capacities of the more sophisticated capital goods will actually be realized.

In sum, the arrival of systematic, large-scale capital savings is the most dramatic evidence of a new postindustrial economy in which the old rules no longer apply and the sources of value lie outside of the traditional factors of production. It is not enough simply to tinker around the edges of the existing frameworks for measuring economic output. Instead, it must be recognized that the assumptions implicit in that framework are no longer adequate to make sense of the production of value.

Organizational Accounting

Similar problems in the evaluation of capital investments exist with current accounting methods at the level of the firm. When firms consider major investments in computer-based technologies—either for office or factory automation—they encounter two intersecting difficulties. First, with standard accounting techniques, it is often difficult to justify investment in new technologies; even with capital savings, the gains in increased output often do not justify the expense. Second, the standard techniques also tend to understate the organizational costs of the process of automation; it is too often assumed that physical capital is the only important expense. Both of these problems arise from a failure to understand that these new technologies are qualitatively different from earlier technologies.

One of the central reasons that existing accounting techniques discourage investments in new technologies is that they are a product of the short-term time horizon of the American corporation. It has frequently been argued that American corporate managers are preoccupied with current returns because of the central role of the stock market as a source of corporate finance. The bias toward producing strong results in the current quarter provides a disincentive for making expenditures that will strengthen the firm over the long term.[54] As one observer writes, there is a fundamental accounting paradox because "the existing financial accounting systems

54. See, for example, Robert U. Ayres, *The Next Industrial Revolution* (Cambridge, Mass.: Ballinger, 1984), 238–43.

signal short-term increases in accounting profits when firms decrease their economic wealth by foregoing investment in their long-term information and productive capital."[55] This orientation translates into requirements that any new capital investment pay for itself in as little as two years.[56]

To make matters even worse, conventional accounting practices focus singlemindedly on direct labor costs and gross output, while ignoring indirect costs and the increasingly important organizational variables. Hence, the justification for an investment in automation often hinges not so much on increasing output or reducing direct labor costs as on its contribution to product quality, to the reduction of inventories and waste of raw materials, to the expansion of the organization's flexibility, and to the reduction of the lead time for getting new products to market. Even if a manager has a strong sense that these improvements will have a positive influence on the firm's profitability, it can be difficult to make the case within the existing accounting framework. Firms often lack any solid information on these variables, and they are not easily translated into dollar terms, so that it is difficult to insert them into the calculus of the benefits of automation.[57]

55. Robert S. Kaplan, "Accounting Lag: The Obsolescence of Cost Accounting Systems," in Kim B. Clark, Robert H. Hayes, and Christopher Lorenz, eds., *The Uneasy Alliance: Managing the Productivity-Technology Dilemma* (Boston: Harvard Business School Press, 1985): 195–226. See p. 200.

56. One study describes how the Japanese introduction of a Flexible Manufacturing System returned in the first two years only $6.9 million on an initial investment of $18 million. "Using conventional accounting principles, this scale of return on investment would be difficult, if not impossible, to justify using traditional procedures for economic justification." However, in this example, the firm was ultimately able to reduce the number of its employees from 215 to 12, space requirements from 103,000 square feet to 30,000, and so on. See John Airey and Clifford Young, "Economic Justification—Counting the Strategic Benefits," in K. Rathmill, ed., *Proceedings of the 2nd International Conference on Flexible Manufacturing Systems* (Bedford, U.K.: IFS Publications, 1983), 549–54. See also Donald Gerwin, "Innovation, Microelectronics and Manufacturing Technology," in Malcolm Warner, ed., *Microprocessors, Manpower and Society: A Comparative Cross-National Approach* (New York: St. Martin's Press, 1984), 66–83.

57. Robert S. Kaplan, "Yesterday's Accounting Undermines Production," *Harvard Business Review* 62, no. 4 (July–August 1984): 95–101; "Must CIM Be Justified by Faith Alone," *Harvard Business Review* 64, no. 2 (March–April 1986): 87–93, and "Accounting Lag." Stephen Hunter, "Cost Justification: The Overhead Dilemma" (paper presented at Robots 9 Conference, June 2–6, 1985, available through National Machine Tools Builders' Association).

Yet there is no question that the benefits of flexible automation are very substantial in these poorly measured areas. For example, the great advantage of numerically controlled machine tools is that they make it far easier to achieve much more precise tolerances. Even the Michigan survey in the early 1970s found that firms were able to cut time on inspection of parts from 32 to 44 percent, depending on the specific type of machine, and advances since then have added to the precision of production. This increased precision contributes directly to the quality of the final product. Similarly, these new technologies can be extremely important in reducing lead times, so that the firm can save on inventory and make production more responsive to demand.[58]

In white-collar settings, office automation can also contribute to quality by making the firm far more responsive to customer needs. In banking, for example, automatic teller machines and banking by phone can make services more available and reduce waiting times for other transactions. At the same time, computerization has made it possible for banks to greatly expand the range of financial instruments that they offer. In many service industries, the capacity of employees who deal with customers to call up relevant information on the computer and make corrections can significantly improve customer relations.

Moreover in both office and factory settings, automation can make it possible for workers and managers to take on entirely new responsibilities. In a factory setting, for example, automation of production might allow blue-collar employees to take over responsibility for maintaining day-to-day relations with suppliers to ensure just-in-time deliveries. While some of these gains can be anticipated in advance, others cannot; they will simply emerge in a context where motivated employees are able to take advantage of increasing information. In short, to have even a vague inkling of the gains to the organization that can come with automation, it is necessary to have some vision of how a reorganized production process

---

58. In a report on Rolls-Royce's use of an FMS: "Currently work-in-progress is valued at no less than £600 million and the company expects to cut this to £300 million reducing interest payments by around £30 million a year. So big are the savings that the company expects to be able to pay for each FMS with the savings made in work-in-progress in one year" (John Hartley, *FMS at Work* [Bedford, U.K.: IFS Publications, 1984], 156).

might work. When managers persist in thinking of workers in terms of costs that need to be minimized, it is doubtful that they will arrive at a reasonable assessment of the benefits that could come with automation.

But if some potentially beneficial capital expenditures are not made because of inadequate accounting, it is also the case that highly questionable investments are made for the same reason. This is most likely to happen when a new technology is sold to managers primarily because of its potential for reducing direct labor costs. Often such technologies are marketed with the promise that they can simply be inserted into the existing organizational structure with no significant adjustment other than to make the organization less dependent on skilled workers. As mentioned earlier, this kind of appeal has been central to the marketing of numerically controlled machine tools; managers were promised that they would be able to increase production while also dispensing with the need for highly skilled and often rebellious machinists.[59] Such promises are closely linked to the dream of the perfect machine—a dream shared by managers and industrial engineers.[60] The perfect machine is one that works so effectively that it eliminates the need for human labor and all of the problems of managing human beings.

In reality, however, there are no perfect machines and the promises of those who invoke that fantasy are rarely realized. In the real world, complex technologies sometimes fail, and they do so in unanticipated ways, so there is always a need for the human factor in maintaining, monitoring, and improving these complex systems.[61] Moreover, as was argued in the previous chapter, the general trend of advanced technologies in office and factory settings has been to raise skill levels. Although it might appear to make economic sense to cut skill levels to save on labor costs, the consequence is often a far from optimal use of the new technology's potential. As Jaikumar's observation of the Japanese use of flexible manufacturing systems makes clear, realizing the full potential of new technologies can require a radical reorganization of the production process that dramatically increases skill levels.[62]

59. Noble, *Forces of Production*, 217–19.
60. Hirschhorn, *Beyond Mechanization*, 57–58.
61. Ibid., 61–109.
62. Jaikumar, "Postindustrial Manufacturing."

Here again, it is often the poorly measured variables such as product quality and control of inventories and wastage that become most important. A particular piece of automatic equipment might be able to expand output dramatically, while also deskilling the labor force, but this can come at the cost of deteriorating product quality or increases in waste of raw materials owing to the scrapping of defective product. In the office setting, this could take the form of an automated billing system whose error rate requires a great deal of organizational effort to straighten out the mistakes.

While vendors of new technologies have an obvious interest in understating the disruption and additional expenditures that a new piece of capital equipment will entail, the reality is that these hidden expenditures can be even more substantial than the costs of the machinery. One recent analysis of office automation, for example, has sought to develop realistic figures on the first-year costs of equipping managerial and professional employees with personal computer workstations.[63] In this account, only about a quarter of the total first-year costs of $10,000 can be traced to hardware itself. Another quarter consists of software and other services, such as telecommunications, that are necessary to operate the workstations effectively. The other half of the budget is taken up by organizational costs that include training for the employees on the use of the technology, salary for support staff, and start-up expenses, particularly the loss of employees' routine services as they struggle to master the new technology.

This particular analysis centers on professional and managerial employees, but the situation is not that different when automation affects clerical or blue-collar workers. Even the relatively small step of introducing word processors into an office setting includes the cost of software, employee training, support personnel, and a considerable start-up period, when output suffers. More elaborate systems for automating clerical work tend to have even greater organizational costs.

In the factory setting as well, the hardware costs are only a fraction of the total costs of the transition to machine tools numerically controlled by computer or to robotics. Steven M. Miller ar-

---

63. Paul Strassmann, *Information Payoff: The Transformation of Work in the Electronic Age* (New York: Free Press, 1985), 82–83.

gues, for example, in robotic applications for machine loading and unloading, the basic robot comprises as little as 20–30 percent of the total costs.[64] There is also considerable evidence of the difficulties experienced in bringing high-technology plants or elaborate computerized systems on line. Even with highly effective management, it can take more than a year before everyone has learned enough to run the plant at its full production capacity.[65] This kind of extended start-up period adds considerably to the total organizational costs associated with the new investment.

It is certainly the case that if all of these associated costs were known in advance, some investments in automated technology could not be justified. Managers who envision a technological "quick fix" to their problems can easily fall victim to exaggerated claims by vendors and purchase capital goods that generate organizational and other costs that are sufficiently high to offset any resulting benefits. One obvious example are those cases where insufficient attention is paid in the investment decision to issues of software compatibility, so that the costs of developing new software cancel any potential gains from the new hardware.

The point is that the decision to invest in automation technologies requires both a broader conception of benefits and a broader conception of costs than traditional accounting procedures have used. Moreover, the calculation is further complicated by the fact that some of the most important variables, such as greater organizational flexibility or the size of start-up costs, are either not easily quantified or extremely difficult to predict with any accuracy. There is, in sum, great indeterminacy in this kind of decision-making,

64. Miller, "Industrial Robotics and Flexible Manufacturing Systems, in Paul R. Kleindorfer, ed., *The Management of Productivity and Technology in Manufacturing* (New York: Plenum, 1985), 18.

65. John B. Ettlie, "Implementation Strategy for Manufacturing Innovations," in Warner, ed., *Microprocessors*, 31–48; Robert H. Hayes, Stephen C. Wheelwright, and Kim B. Clark, *Dynamic Manufacturing: Creating the Learning Organization* (New York: Free Press, 1988), 171–73. On office settings, see James N. Danziger and Kenneth L. Kraemer, *People and Computers: The Impact of Computing on End Users in Organizations* (New York: Columbia University Press, 1986), 110–22. Moreover, reports of disastrous experiences with computer-based systems are common in business journalism. "It's Late, Costly, Incompetent—But Try Firing a Computer System," *Business Week*, November 7, 1988, 164–65; "Service Industries Find Computers Don't Always Raise Productivity," *Wall Street Journal*, April 19, 1988.

since organizational assumptions—whether conscious or unconscious—play a key role in shaping assessments of the costs and benefits of investments in new technologies.

Conclusions

The argument of this chapter is that it is increasingly problematic to view capital as a thing that can be accurately measured in dollar terms. Such a view obscures both pervasive capital savings and the growing importance of the organizational context in which physical capital is mobilized. Above all, this view diverts attention from the fact that both the efficiency and the quantity of production depend increasingly on organizational variables—the specific ways in which human beings and technology are brought together. The traditional concept of capital makes it difficult to grasp that human beings and their networks of interrelations are the society's central productive force.

The formulations of many contemporary economists acknowledge some of the difficulties with the traditional concept of capital, and much valuable work has been done to overcome these limitations. However, it is not an exaggeration to argue that public debates over economic policy continue to be dominated by what can be termed an intravenous model of capital investment. Capital is seen as the life-sustaining substance that is injected into the veins of the economy. Too slow a flow of capital makes the economy lethargic, producing slow growth and the buildup of inflationary pressures. With a faster flow, the economy becomes healthier as growth and productivity accelerate.

This intravenous model is continually invoked by business interests as a way of fighting for reduced corporate taxes and improved incentives for capital investment. Higher rates of taxation on profits and on the income of the rich are supposed to slow the flow of capital into the economy, while the opposite policies are supposed to accelerate the flow, contributing to improved economic health.

Yet the intravenous model of capital is not just a useful lobbying tool for capitalists; it serves as a justification for some of the most basic features of the existing political economy. A steady and strong flow of profits to capital holders is necessary to compensate them for their willingness to sacrifice immediate consumption in favor of investment. This necessity justifies the huge inequalities of income and wealth in the United States and provides a powerful argument against redistributive tax policies.

The same logic also contributes to the devaluation of public spending relative to private investment. Since higher public-sector spending generally requires increased taxation and the potential that those taxes will fall on wealth holders, it is often claimed that public-sector spending is inherently wasteful. Such claims help to obscure the reality that in the contemporary economy, public-sector spending on both physical capital and in such areas as education, training, research, and health care is indispensable for the effective functioning of the economy.

The intravenous model also serves to justify a hierarchical corporate form that vests ultimate power in the shareholders. The theory is that the willingness of capital holders to risk their wealth in a particular firm necessitates that they collectively be given unquestioned control over the firm.[66] Without such control, it would be impossible to assure that their capital received adequate compensation. Any steps to give the firm's employees a formal voice in the direction of the firm—independent of their possible role as shareholders—are generally resisted as interfering with the prerogatives of shareholders and the functioning of capital markets.

The fact that the intravenous model of capital is not valid serves to undermine each of these justifications of existing institutional arrangements. Pervasive capital savings mean that there is no need to mobilize ever-larger pools of money for investment in physical capital. In fact, there is reason to believe that most of those investment needs can now be met through the retirement savings of the many rather than through the accumulated wealth of the few. At the same time, the growing importance of organizational factors means that the amount of money invested is less important than how it is utilized. This destroys the logic of privileging shareholders relative to employees; it makes increasing sense to recognize employees as critical stakeholders in the firm.

66. To be sure, shareholder sovereignty is often a myth, because entrenched managements have organizational resources that the diffused shareholders lack. See Edward S. Herman, *Corporate Control, Corporate Power* (New York: Cambridge University Press, 1981). However, the recent takeover fever has made it clear that those who control the majority of the shares control the corporation.

A similar conclusion flows from the difficulties of organizational accounting that firms experience when they are assessing new investments in advanced technologies. It was argued earlier that it is remarkably easy for firms either to underinvest or to overinvest in new technologies, since managers can easily guess wrong about the magnitude of key variables, especially those most affected by the attitudes of the workforce. Precisely because of these complications, the traditional arguments for exclusive management control over investment decisions lose their persuasiveness. Since employees will have much to do with the success or failure of new capital investments, it follows that organizational decision-making can be improved by including those employees in such decisions.[67] A democratization of investment decision-making has the potential to improve organizational rationality, because broadening the number of people involved in the process decreases the likelihood that relevant variables will be neglected. Furthermore, when employees are involved from the start in decision-making about new technology, they are less likely to see it as a threat. This increases the likelihood that its full potential will be realized.[68]

In sum, the alternative to the intravenous model of capital is a view that recognizes the centrality of the organization's human resources in determining a firm's effectiveness. This recognition in turn justifies a reversal of the traditional privileging of investors' interests relative to employees' interests; it points toward a transformation of the corporate form that vests more power and responsibility in the firm's employees.

67. Hayes, Wheelwright, and Clark discuss the advantages of substantial input into investment decisions from those further down in the organization (*Dynamic Manufacturing*, 87, 94–95).

68. This insight appears occasionally in the business press; see "Management Discovers the Human Side of Automation," *Business Week*, September 29, 1986, 70–77.

Chapter Six

Output

In recent years, U.S. presidential elections have centered on the issue of whether the electorate is better off than it was four or eight years ago. While it is possible to imagine many different elements to such a comparison, the actual debate has been preoccupied with only one question—how has an individual's or a family's real income changed since the last election.[1] A broad and classical theme of politics—the effectiveness of the existing regime in terms of popular well-being—has been transformed and narrowed into a question about changes in income.

This narrowing is closely linked to changes in the way people think about economic output. The creation in the 1930s and 1940s of the technology of national-income accounting meant that economic output was no longer a vague and diffuse concept; it could be precisely operationalized through the concept of Gross National Product.[2] It has seemed unnecessary to engage in arguments about the nature of economic output when the government produces highly respected reports each quarter of the latest changes in GNP.

The argument of this chapter, however, is that GNP has become an increasingly problematic measure of economic output, and that the data have become an unreliable source of information on how well or badly the economy is doing. The argument is elaborated in

1. Republican speeches in 1988 tended to focus on trends in family income, while Democrats emphasized the trends in individual incomes, since the former showed improvement and the latter declined.
2. Gross National Product is used here to subsume a family of interrelated measures that includes Net National Product and National Income.

three parts. The first considers the dimensions of economic output that have been excluded from the GNP measure and suggests that recent changes in some of these factors would overwhelm changes in measured output. The second part focuses on problems that are internal to the GNP measure. The argument is that for both methodological and theoretical reasons, GNP is a decreasingly accurate indicator of general trends in economic output. The final part examines an additional set of factors that create a gap between trends in measured GNP and popular perceptions of changes in economic well-being.

The purpose of this critique of the GNP concept is to reopen old debates about the nature and purpose of economic output.[3] Reliance on the GNP data as *the* measure of economic output makes it difficult to raise a whole series of important questions about what is and what should be produced.

What GNP Measures

It is a commonplace among economists that the Gross National Product is not a measure of the welfare of the population.[4] It cannot be this because it lacks a distributive dimension; a given level of GNP could be linked to a highly egalitarian or a highly inegalitarian distribution of income. Moreover, there are many other elements of the population's well-being that are excluded from the GNP data—such as environmental quality and life expectancy. Defenders of the GNP measure argue that even though it does not measure welfare, it does provide the best available indicator of the rate of growth of the economy over time. Although this argument has carried the day and has contributed to the extraordinary respect for the GNP reports, it cries out for reevaluation.

3. Some of these debates are not even very old, but they seem to have been forgotten in the 1980s. In response to the social movements of the 1960s and 1970s, some mainstream economists elaborated a critique of the GNP concept. The resulting debate is well reflected in Milton Moss, ed., *The Measurement of Economic and Social Performance* (New York: National Bureau of Economic Research, 1973). Tibor Scitovsky's important book *The Joyless Economy: An Inquiry into Human Satisfaction and Consumer Dissatisfaction* (New York: Oxford University Press, 1976) is a product of the same period.

4. The discussion in this part of unmeasured aspects of economic output draws heavily on the arguments of Scitovsky, *Joyless Economy*.

From the start, the GNP concept has been closely tied to market transactions; the idea has been to measure the value of final goods sold on the market.[5] The reasoning is that market prices are the obvious indicator of the worth of purchased goods and services, and it follows that a measure of gross output should be as closely linked as possible to those market prices.[6] For example, in the case of broadcasting (still predominantly radio when the GNP measures were devised), there was no clear way to value the programs that people received over the airwaves. Hence, it was decided that broadcasting would be treated as an intermediate good—as part of the advertising expenditures of the firms that paid for air time.[7] In certain cases, this emphasis on market prices had to be suspended,

5. The distinction between final goods and intermediate goods is often problematic, since it requires a judgment as to what is an end and what is a means to an end. Simon Kuznets once suggested that a not insignificant share of GNP represented costs of modernity—items treated as final goods that are really intermediate. "Do all goods flowing to individuals and households really represent final products in the sense of being sources of satisfaction to consumers as consumers? If a person must use trolleys and buses to go to work, buy banking services because he is a member of a money economy, pay union dues, live in a city—not for any personal satisfaction but as a condition of earning his living—should these services be counted as a positive return to him from the economic system?" (*Economic Change: Selected Essays in Business Cycles, National Income, and Economic Growth* [New York: Norton, 1953], 195).

6. Part of the logic of the GNP accounting system was that it measured production rather than consumption. Yet this analytic choice is highly problematic, since economics insists that goods and services are produced to meet the needs of consumers. Hence, the distinction between a production index and a consumption index is often difficult to sustain. On this issue, see William D. Nordhaus and James Tobin, "Is Growth Obsolete?" in Moss, ed., *Measurement of Economic and Social Performance*, 508–64; Milton Moss, "Welfare Dimensions of Productivity Measurement," in Panel to Review Productivity Statistics, *Measurement and Interpretation of Productivity* (Washington, D.C.: National Academy of Sciences, 1979), 276–308; Robert Eisner, "Extended Accounts for National Income and Product," *Journal of Economic Literature* 26 (December 1988): 1611–84.

7. In light of the very high reported rates of television viewing, it is interesting to speculate on the impact of an alternative choice of measurement. It is arguable, for example, that one should impute a dollar value for each hour that an individual watches television—$1.00 per hour would seem appropriate since that is about the going price for renting an hour's worth of videotapes. The Michigan study of time use in 1975–76 found that for the average adult, television watching was the primary activity for 14.32 hours per week (Martha S. Hill, "Patterns of Time Use," in F. Thomas Juster and Frank P. Stafford, eds., *Time, Goods, and Well-Being* [Ann Arbor: Survey Research Center, University of Michigan, 1985], 173). Since children tend to watch more television than adults, using the same figure for the entire population in 1976 would result in a dollar value of $149 billion.

but this was done very gingerly. In the case of government and most nonprofit organizations, there was no price for the various services that were produced, so the architects of the GNP framework decided to measure government and nonprofit output in terms of the market price of the inputs—labor, materials, and, in the case of nonprofit organizations, interest payments. This particular solution to the conceptual dilemma has the effect of reinforcing the notion that nonmarket production is inherently inefficient, since government and nonprofit organizations are unable to show significant gains in labor productivity. As long as output is measured by the cost of labor inputs, a more efficient use of labor will only lower the recorded output.

However, the focus on market prices has an even more serious consequence. Several broad categories of output produced by the economy are excluded from the GNP measure because they do not have a market price. These include the labor done in the home by family members, leisure, nonpecuniary rewards of work, and such economic externalities as improvement or deterioration in the environment or in the health of the population. When taken together, these "satisfactions"[8] appear to overwhelm measured output.

In some of these cases, there have been efforts by economists who are technical innovators to develop ways to impute a value. However, both the theoretical and the methodological foundations for these imputations are often shaky. The dilemma is that holding on to the emphasis on market prices in GNP accounting provides a truncated view of economic output, but adding a whole series of complex imputations to GNP accounting can potentially deprive the national income accounting system of the appearance of objectivity.

Efforts to calculate output by imputations pose the problem of utility for whom. Within the marginalist framework, it is a given that individuals have different preferences and that the utility of a given product will depend on the needs of a particular customer. Hence, there can be no concept of aggregate utility other than the sum of the individual preferences expressed in the market. Within this framework, economic analysis appears to be objective; the economic valuations are being carried out by the economic actors

8. This is Scitovsky's useful term in *Joyless Economy*, 80.

themselves.[9] However, when imputations are made, economists substitute their own valuation for those of economic actors, and the seemingly objective character of economic measurement is compromised. The risk becomes great that all of the moral and political judgments implicit in a process of economic valuation will become subject to debate.

Household Production

Keynes's famous observation that the man who marries his housekeeper diminishes total GNP remains very much to the point, because services produced in the home by family members are excluded from GNP. This includes the traditional types of housework—childcare, cleaning, and meal preparation—as well as unpaid work done on maintaining and improving housing and consumer durables such as automobiles. Furthermore, this category also includes various types of volunteer labor done for charitable or community purposes. However, the massive entrance of married women into the labor force of the past thirty years and the related changes in family life make it impossible to treat this type of production as something that has remained constant over time.

One obvious consequence of the exclusion of household production from GNP is that some of the measured growth of GNP does not represent an actual increase in utility, but simply a shift of activities from household to market. In an earlier period, this meant the substitution of store-baked bread for home-baked; more recently, it has involved the shift of child care from the family to the market as the mothers of young children increase their participation in the labor force. Similarly, any reduction in the amount of volunteer labor in the society—in neighborhood and community groups—that is a consequence of the increased participation of women in the labor force could result in an entirely unmeasured fall in actual output.

One recent effort by Robert Eisner to measure the dollar value of unpaid household labor estimated that in 1981 such labor was worth

9. The claim to objectivity rests on an individualistic epistemology in which all individuals are seen as acting independently. When it is recognized that preferences are shaped by cultural understandings and differential power, "objectivity" can be seen as taking the existing social structure as a given.

$981 billion, as compared to an official GNP figure that year of $2,954 billion.[10] However, even the suggestion that unmeasured GNP is equal to a third of the official figure seems too conservative. For one thing, this estimate is confined to housework; Eisner does not attempt to calculate the time spent on home and automobile maintenance or in volunteer activities.[11] Moreover, there is also a problem in determining the appropriate hourly wage for calculating the value of this kind of output. Eisner's study uses the average wage for paid domestic workers, but this is problematic. Domestic workers are poorly paid in part because they perform labor that is socially devalued and that is usually done by wives working for nothing. Depending on the technique for assessing the hourly value of household labor, studies have estimated household production at anywhere from 20 to 50 percent of GNP.[12]

It is a particularly thorny problem to determine whether this unmeasured component of output has been rising or falling relative to GNP as a whole. It seems that the total quantity of unpaid housework has been rising, since the number of separate households has been growing more quickly than any reduction in the average hours of housework per unit. At the same time, there continues to be a marked shift of activities from the household sector to the market, particularly child care and meal preparation.[13] Any evaluation of these trends ultimately depends not simply on total hours of work, but on the productivity of this unpaid labor and on the quality of the output. If, for example, household technolo-

10. Eisner, "The Total Income System of Accounts," *Survey of Current Business*, January 1985, 30. I. A-H. Sirageldin estimated that nonmarket work provided from 42 to 48 percent of a family's money income in a 1969 study (cited in Scitovsky, *Joyless Economy*, 87).

11. Martha S. Hill argues that in 1975 unpaid labor on houses and durable goods was worth close to $60 billion ("Investments of Time in Houses and Durables," in Juster and Stafford, eds., *Time, Goods, and Well-Being*, 216–17). The same Michigan data base found that adults average 1.76 hours a week in various voluntary organizations; assuming 180 million adults, and that this work is worth an average of $4 an hour, this would add another $66 billion to GNP (Hill, "Patterns of Time Use," in id., 172).

12. Ann Chadeau, "Measuring Household Activities: Some International Comparisons," *Review of Income and Wealth* 31, no. 3 (September 1985): 237–53.

13. There is also a countertrend: the growth of what Jonathan Gershuny calls the self-service economy, where consumers are required to produce for themselves. Jonathan I. Gershuny, *After Industrial Society?: The Emerging Self-Service Economy* (Atlantic Highlands, N.J.: Humanities Press, 1978).

gies and various convenience services make it possible for parents to spend more of their housework time in "quality time" with children, there would arguably be an upward trend in this sector's contribution to total output.

Leisure Time

Utilities involving leisure itself are another type that is not measured. Within economic theory, labor is generally seen as a disutility; this is why people must be paid to work.[14] Yet the accounting scheme based on market values means that there is no measure of the value of leisure as a component of output. Hence, the fact that the amount of labor per capita has dropped sharply is not reflected in the GNP data, and neither are recent declines in the weight of paid labor on the adult life course.[15] This means, as well, that two societies might be reported as having the same GNP even though one produced the given output on the basis of an average work week of twenty hours while the other did it with a forty-hour work week. One study that sought to put a dollar value on the leisure time that the economy produced estimated that in 1965 the leisure time was worth $626.9 billion as compared to a total measured GNP of $617.8 billion (in 1958 dollars).[16] In other words, the value of the leisure time exceeded the total GNP.

Here again, analysts confront familiar problems. First, there is the issue of determining the appropriate dollar value of each hour of leisure and of calculating how those dollar values might vary among different population groups.[17] Second, there is the problem of separating out voluntary from involuntary leisure. Since some econo-

14. The pervasiveness of this assumption and the problems with it are discussed by John Kenneth Galbraith, *The Affluent Society* (1958), 2d ed. (Boston: Houghton Mifflin, 1969), 303–4.

15. For data, see Fred Block, "Technological Change and Employment: New Perspectives on an Old Controversy," *Economia & Lavoro* 18, no. 3 (July–September 1984): 3–21.

16. The same study calculated that nonmarket work contributed $295.4 billion to total value in 1965. W. Nordhaus and J. Tobin, "Is Growth Obsolete?" in Moss, ed., *Measurement of Economic and Social Performance*, 509–32.

17. Tobin and Nordhaus appear to have estimated the value of an hour of leisure—above the seven hours attributed to sleep—at the price of the average wage (ibid., 517). See also the comment by Dan Usher in the same volume, 540–45.

mists have argued that even those who are officially counted as unemployed are choosing leisure over the work available at existing wage rates, there is no obvious standard for making this critical demarcation. For example, how does one avoid attributing the same dollar value to the leisure of individual A, whose life has been made miserable by forced retirement, with that of individual B, who has been counting the days until she is eligible to receive retirement benefits. The effort to evaluate leisure time is closely linked to evaluating the nonpecuniary rewards of work.

Nonpecuniary Rewards of Work

Despite the tendency of economists to see work as a disutility, individuals derive many kinds of nonpecuniary rewards from work—companionship, a sense of meaning and purpose, intellectual challenges, social status, and so on.[18] With the growth of professional and managerial employment and the patterns in skill level described in chapter 4, it is arguable that some of these nonpecuniary rewards, such as on-the-job training and challenging work, have been growing in recent years. However, it is clear that some types of work provide more of these nonpecuniary rewards than others. Adam Smith suggested long ago that there would be a process of compensating differentials that would eliminate the advantages or disadvantages of particular types of jobs; by this theory, work with fewer nonpecuniary benefits would offer higher monetary compensation.[19] However, there is little evidence for this theory; on the contrary, jobs that provide high monetary rewards tend to provide high nonmonetary rewards as well.[20] Ignoring this dimension of output means that it is possible for two countries to have equal levels of GNP despite the fact that in one country most

18. The value of the economic security a job might provide is treated separately below.

19. Jerry A. Jacobs and Ronnie J. Steinberg, "Compensating Differentials and the Male-Female Wage Gap: Evidence from the New York State Comparable Worth Study" (paper presented at the Eastern Sociological Society Meetings, March 1988), 1.

20. This point is made by Arthur Okun, *Equality and Efficiency: The Big Tradeoff* (Washington: Brookings Institution, 1975), 72. Christopher Jencks, Lauri

work is boring and repetitious, while in the other the average individual experiences work as challenging and exciting.

The importance of this issue has been reinforced by several recent research findings. A study that sought to measure the intrinsic satisfactions of a broad range of activities that individuals engage in found that respondents in both 1975 and 1981 consistently reported that their jobs had higher process benefits than a wide range of leisure activities, including gardening, watching television, and playing sports. "The data . . . suggest that the *intrinsic* rewards from work are, on average, higher than the intrinsic rewards from leisure, a finding that creates considerable difficulty for the conventional analysis of well-being."[21] Moreover, F. Thomas Juster found that the challenge of the work and the capacity of individuals to use their skills were key determinants of how highly they ranked the process benefits of the job. Similarly, Christopher Jencks and his colleagues found that the availability of opportunities for on-the-job training was one of the strongest determinants of how respondents rated the overall quality of their jobs.[22]

These findings are supported by other studies on the willingness of people to work and to work long hours. When asked if they would continue working even if there were no economic need, 84 percent of American men and 77 percent of women in 1977 answered in the affirmative.[23] It is difficult to imagine that such responses can be entirely attributed to the strength of the work ethic. Moreover, Tibor Scitovsky draws on data on historical trends on working hours to argue that people who enjoy their work appear to have increased their working time, while those with less pleasant work have dimin-

---

Perman, and Lee Rainwater found that an index that incorporates nonmonetary characteristics as well as the monetary characteristics of jobs finds 2.8 times the inequality found by examining wages alone ("What Is a Good Job? A New Measure of Labor Market Success," *American Journal of Sociology* 93, no. 6 [May 1988]: 1322–57). See also Greg Duncan, "Labor Market Discrimination and Nonpecuniary Work Rewards," in F. Thomas Juster, ed., *The Distribution of Economic Well-Being* (Cambridge, Mass.: Ballinger, 1977), 355–78.

21. Juster, "Preferences for Work and Leisure," in Juster and Stafford, eds., *Time, Goods, and Well-Being*, 340.

22. Jencks et al., "What Is a Good Job?" 1339.

23. Joseph Veroff, Elizabeth Douvan, and Richard A. Kulka, *The Inner American: A Self-Portrait from 1957 to 1976* (New York: Basic Books, 1981), 295.

ished their hours.[24] His argument is given further support by Shirley Smith's data on working hours, which show that annual hours of work increase significantly with levels of education. She found that men who had attended any kind of post-baccalaureate graduate school worked an average of 8.3 percent more hours each year than men with only a high school diploma. She also reports that men who were managers in manufacturing worked 19.4 percent more hours than the average auto worker.[25] Finally, Jencks and his colleagues found in their 1980 survey that for those respondents in jobs of at least 35 hours a week, the more hours worked, the higher their rating of their job.[26] In short, where work has significant nonmonetary rewards, individuals tend to work longer hours to gain more of those rewards.

The Jencks findings also provide some indication of how large these nonpecuniary rewards loom relative to economic rewards. Employees reported on average that a 138 percent increase in compensation would be necessary to offset the shift from a job where a low proportion of work was repetitious to one with a high proportion of repetitious work. In other words, a nonrepetitious job at $10,000 a year was rated equal to a repetitious job at $23,800.[27] The authors indicate that this seems to be a high estimate of the relative importance of monetary and nonmonetary factors. Yet even if one discounts the finding considerably, it does not seem farfetched to imagine that the nonpecuniary rewards of work could be on an order of magnitude of half of the total income from wages and salaries.

Moreover, any effort to assess the aggregate value of both the nonpecuniary rewards of work *and* of leisure time would require an extremely complex calculation. A 25 percent reduction in working time—with no change in pay—might be an extraordinary gift to one person and a terrible deprivation for the next. Moreover, even for the same individual, maximizing utility might not involve simply

24. Scitovsky, *Joyless Economy,* 98–101.

25. Shirley J. Smith, "Estimating Annual Hours of Labor Force Activity," *Monthly Labor Review* 106, no. 2 (February 1983): 13–22.

26. Jencks et al., "What Is a Good Job?" 1332–33.

27. Ibid., 1339.

increasing leisure time or increasing work time, but some complex and flexible balance between the two.

The Externalities of Production

Another dimension of output that is not calculated directly in GNP are the multiple indirect effects of economic activity on various aspects of human existence. The most obvious part of this category are environmental effects—improvement or degradation of the quality of air, water, and other aspects of the physical environment. It has often been observed that while increasing expenditures for pollution control will raise GNP, there is no downward adjustment for the initial pollution. Moreover, arguments that expenditures on environmental improvements interfere with the efficiency of production rest on this failure to count environmental quality as a legitimate economic satisfaction.[28]

In the final years of the twentieth century, it is painfully obvious that the degradation of the natural environment has generated enormous economic costs, and that the continuation of current environmental practices threatens the continued existence of the human species. Cities in the United States are now struggling with the increasingly expensive problem of getting rid of solid waste, while the casual disposal of hazardous wastes has generated huge cleanup costs and serious threats to the quality of drinking water in many communities. The destruction of the ozone layer—linked to the use of hydrofluorocarbons—is expected to significantly raise the global incidence of skin cancer. The greenhouse effect that results from the continued exploitation of fossil fuels and the destruction of forests will produce droughts, extreme discomfort, and the loss of coastal areas as the polar ice caps melt. This list can be extended to include a broad range of specific threats to ecological systems that will ultimately have negative impacts on humans, such as the conse-

28. One of the classic discussions of the issue is F. Thomas Juster, "A Framework for the Measure of Economic and Social Performance," in Moss, ed., *Measurement of Economic and Social Performance*, 63–68. In the same volume, Tobin and Nordhaus discuss externalities in terms of the disamenities of urban life. They calculate these as a subtraction from total output equal to about 5 percent of GNP in 1965 ("Is Growth Obsolete?" 521).

quences of ocean dumping and commercial fishing technologies on the viability of marine life.

It is no easy matter to calculate the potential costs of any of these forms of environmental destruction.[29] Moreover, the key variable that cannot be pinned down precisely is the resilience of the earth itself—what level of strain on natural systems will lead to cumulative failures that affect human existence? How much carbon dioxide can be produced before the global temperature begins to rise? How much can the oceans be polluted before the supply of fish that is safe to eat begins to diminish markedly? Uncertainty about incurring costs of such magnitude should logically result in great caution and efforts to move back from the environmental brink. Thus far, however, the general response to uncertainty has been to pretend that the costs are not there and to continue the destructive environmental practices. This response is reinforced by GNP data indifferent to impending environmental crises.

A closely related category of such externalities is the impact of the economy on the health of the population. Environmental factors enter here as well, since various types of pollution and environmental destruction have an impact on rates of morbidity and mortality. The debased air quality in most of our major metropolitan areas has been calculated to have huge costs in sick days, medical bills, and diminished life expectancy.[30] Other factors, such as investments in medical research, the availability of health care to different population groups, and the effects of diet, are also involved. The point, however, is that with the existing GNP measure, it is theoretically possible for two different countries to have the same per capita GNP while in country A people live twenty years longer than in country B.[31]

29. Economists have had difficulty developing measures of the value of the environment. For a discussion of the different methods that have been used, see Horst Siebert and Ariane Berthoin Antal, *The Political Economy of Environmental Protection* (Greenwich, Conn.: JAI Press, 1979), 101–8. Moreover, these methods are particularly problematic for analyzing impending disasters. For a review of some of these studies, see Edwin S. Mills, *The Economics of Environmental Quality* (New York: Norton, 1978).

30. One study cited in Mills, *Economics of Environmental Quality*, 157, calculated annual benefits from improved health and longevity through a reduction of air pollution at $16.1 billion a year in 1973 dollars for the period from 1970 to 1978.

31. One would not expect this equality to remain for long, since the health of

Another related externality is the economic security or economic insecurity of the population. Again, it is theoretically possible for per capita GNP to be equal in two different countries in which most people live with radically different levels of economic security. In one country, citizens might face considerable anxiety that the loss of a job or of a spouse or a serious illness might reduce them to poverty, while in the other, citizens are significantly more secure because government programs protect them against a catastrophic loss of income.

Jencks and his colleagues found, for example, that the risk of job loss was one of the variables with the strongest impact on an individual's rating of his or her job. They calculate that the average worker would need a 157 percent increase in earnings to offset a shift from high job security to low job security.[32] Here again, even if these results are discounted considerably, it seems clear that the value of job security looms large relative to the value of earned income. Moreover, job security is only one component of overall economic security, since individuals also worry about medical problems and the availability of income in old age.

This list of externalities is hardly exhaustive, because there are many different factors that can have a bearing on people's sense of economic well-being. For example, it could be argued that increases in the instrumentalism of individual action, including opportunistic rule-breaking, leads to a misleading increase in measured GNP, since more security guards, accountants, criminal justice personnel, and jailers will have to be hired. However, people's experience of the declining trustworthiness of friends, co-workers, and neighbors would mean an actual decline in the utility that they receive from the economy. It is easy to caricature this mode of analysis, but the point remains that the GNP measure

---

the population has important economic effects as an input to the production process; one would expect a healthier labor force to be more productive. In one study designed to impute dollar values to gains in life expectancy, Dan Usher estimated the value of changes in life expectancy on Canadian growth rates from 1926–68, and found that the imputation raised the annual growth rate from 2.25 to about 2.8 percent ("An Imputation to the Measure of Economic Growth for Changes in Life Expectancy," in Moss, ed., *Measurement of Economic and Social Performance*, 192–232).

32. Jencks et al., "What Is a Good Job?" 1339.

omits much that is of critical importance in determining the quality of people's lives.

Whether output has been rising faster or more slowly than measured GNP when these four unmeasured dimensions of GNP are taken into account is a difficult question. The end result would depend almost entirely on the assumptions used for the imputations, such as the price used to value household labor or to value an hour of leisure. However, on almost any set of assumptions, these components of output would vastly exceed the measured utility reflected in the official GNP data. Hence, it becomes far easier to understand why studies of people's well-being fail to show a correlation between improvements in well-being and increases in GNP.[33] In a word, GNP measures only a fraction of the utility that the economy produces.

Measurement Problems in the GNP Data

Even for those parts of output that GNP measures, there are significant biases in the data that generally have the effect of understating GNP growth. One area of systematic bias in the GNP data has already been discussed at length—the issue of capital savings. The GNP figure adds together all purchases for final use whether by consumers, businesses, or government. Hence, purchases of capital goods and structures are directly added into the GNP totals. However, if technological advances are making possible significant capital savings, the dollar value of business and government purchases of capital goods will understate the total utility being produced in a given year.[34] Similar biases exist when costless quality changes occur in consumer goods and where quality improvements are mistakenly interpreted as simple price rises.

The failure to measure the output of government and nonprofit organizations independently of the inputs was also mentioned ear-

33. Scitovsky, *Joyless Economy*, 134–45.

34. Skeptics will insist that if there are systematic capital savings, the use of more effective capital will lead to increases in output in other sectors of the economy. Hence, there should be a visible decline in the ratio of capital to final output. However, this decline would not appear if measures of final output in many sectors of the economy are inadequate.

lier. Since government and nonprofit entities have been growing as a share of total employment and have been absorbing increasing quantities of investment, a technique that rules out in advance the possibility that outputs rise faster than inputs in these sectors is bound to understate the society's total production.

These biases are compounded by another one—the inadequacy of the GNP measures of output in the for-profit service industries. The GNP methods of measuring constant dollar output work best only for farming, fishing, mining, and manufacturing—industries that produce tangible products in stable and discrete units. Even in some sectors of manufacturing, these techniques are problematic because of costless quality changes and continuing innovation in product lines. Yet these goods-producing industries employed only 23.4 percent of all full-time equivalent employees in the domestic economy in 1984. In short, the great bulk of economic activity takes place in industries where the GNP measures are highly problematic.[35]

The construction industry produces a tangible product, for example, but the lack of standardization in the product creates severe problems in measuring the constant dollar output of the industry. During the 1970s and early 1980s, the official data indicated dramatic declines in the construction industry's productivity, but the problem was the deflators that were being used to calculate constant dollar output. The National Academy of Sciences' Panel to Review Productivity Statistics wrote in 1979: "Although expenditures on single-family houses and public roads are deflated by relatively good price indexes, some of the remaining portions of the construction industry are still deflated by input-cost price indexes, which are a weighted average of wage rates and materials costs that make no allowance for productivity change in construction activity."[36] Yet one can also raise questions about the quality of the "good deflators" used for single-family homes. Many new homes are

35. *Survey of Current Business*, July 1988, 81. For an extended discussion of some of these measurement problems, see Fred Block, *Revising State Theory: Essays in Politics and Postindustrialism* (Philadelphia: Temple University Press, 1987), ch. 8.

36. Panel to Review Productivity Statistics, *Measurement and Interpretation of Productivity* (Washington, D.C.: National Academy of Sciences, 1979), 91.

custom-built with many particular features to meet the specifications of their owners, and even in ordinary housing developments, new features are added each year as part of the basic package. To be able to make an accurate comparison between the new homes produced in 1984 and those produced in 1985 that can separate out pure price increases from changes in quality would require an awesome amount of data and new statistical techniques.

While the construction industry is relatively small compared to total GNP, it looms large in the analysis of productivity trends because these measurement problems result in data showing an absolute decline in construction productivity. One analyst reports that the construction industry alone accounted for 17 percent of the reported productivity slowdown of the 1970s.[37]

Services to individuals are another area of problematic measurement. These constitute a huge proportion of the economy—exclusive of housing, roughly 44 percent of all consumer purchases are services, and most of these are poorly measured in the GNP data because of the difficulty of defining clear units and adequate price deflators. For example, medical services constituted 9.7 percent of all personal consumption expenditures in 1984, but the deflators used are problematic. Payments to physicians are deflated by indexes of physician fees that fail to differentiate between purely inflationary price increases and changes in the quality of the service provided. Moreover, if advances in medical technology make it possible for a procedure to occur on an outpatient basis rather than with a hospital stay, this will be reflected in a slower rate of GNP growth, since the patient's medical expenditures will decline. Similar problems occur with consumer purchases of legal and other professional services.

Another example is consumer purchases of banking services. In the absence of any independent measure of output of this industry, the GNP accountants assume that the growth in output is proportional to growth in total banking employment, so that productivity is assumed to be the same as it was in 1948. This means that every year the data find that there was zero productivity growth in banking services to individuals, but other studies show that commercial

37. Lester Thurow, "Discussion," in Federal Reserve Bank of Boston, *The Decline in Productivity Growth* (Boston: Federal Reserve, 1980), 22–25.

banking productivity rose at a 6 percent annual rate during the 1970s with advances in computerization.[38]

Similar problems show up in other major components of individual purchases such as transportation services and restaurant meals. Government data on GNP by industry show that for the transportation sector as a whole, current dollar expenditures rose from $50.1 billion in 1973 to $114.9 billion in 1983. However, the constant dollar figures show an actual decline from $48.4 billion in 1973 to $47.3 billion in 1983.[39] Since a decline in transportation output across that ten-year period seems improbable, there is good reason to be suspicious of the deflators that are being used. Yet the measurement problems are formidable. Airfares have been extremely volatile, for example, and there are difficulties with a measure of output that fails to include such qualitative dimensions as the extent of travel delays. By the same logic, one would have to be suspicious of the techniques used to measure the constant dollar value of restaurant meals—an item that comprised 5.3 percent of all personal consumption expenditures in 1984.

The Deeper Problems of Measurement: Quality

Most of these problems of measuring service output cannot be solved simply by improving the amount and quality of the data collected. There are deeper issues at stake, which have to do with the nature of consumption as a developed society becomes wealthier. When the benefits of economic growth are shared by the majority of the population, there will be a steady decline in the share of individual income needed to buy necessities such as food and clothing. Many people will have a growing amount of discretionary income.

This growth in discretionary income has several predictable re-

38. *Survey of Current Business*, January 1976, 22; Horst Brand and John Duke, "Productivity in Commercial Banking: Computers Spur the Advance," Bureau of Labor Statistics, *A BLS Reader on Productivity* (Washington, D.C.: GPO, 1983), 58–66.

39. These data are drawn from figures for gross product by industries of origin, September 1984, provided to me by the Bureau of Economic Analysis. The coverage of transportation in this data series includes transportation services both to consumers and to businesses.

sults. In buying food and other necessities, individuals gradually shift their consumption toward products of higher quality. Since the gains in income are broad-based, the result is a steady shift of production in the direction of these new and better grades. For example, the minimum standard for an automobile ceases to be a machine that can get you from here to there and shifts to a relatively high level of comfort. Similarly, in purchasing housing, a larger percentage of consumers look for a variety of special features.

Individuals also expand their spending for a range of "luxury" goods or services. The appeal of some of these items, such as gourmet meals, concerts by string quartets, and fine jewelry, depends precisely on their *not* being produced on a mass basis. Also, when people travel, they look for higher levels of comfort on airplanes and in hotels and motels, and services are steadily upgraded to meet this shift in demand.

Similarly, people come to expect higher levels of comfort in a range of different environments. Retail stores are redesigned with carpets and soft lighting, and even moderately priced restaurants have hanging plants and hardwood tables. This shift in expectations also means that some employers upgrade the quality of their employees' work settings; some offices and other workplaces are designed or redesigned with greater concern for aesthetics and the comfort of personnel.

Finally, individuals acquiesce in the use of some of their discretionary income for expanded production of public goods designed to improve the quality of life. Spending for medical research provides ways of saving the lives of newborns who might otherwise die and of reducing cancer deaths. Similarly, certain types of spending on social services, such as increased public spending for the elderly and the disabled, are widely supported because all citizens are at risk of entering these categories.

To be sure, this upward shift in consumption patterns has been going on for some time. However, it is only relatively recently that the great majority of the population have become participants in this pattern of discretionary spending. In her study of consumption patterns in twentieth century America, Clair Brown argues that "nutritional standards were basically met by laborer families and equalized across class by 1950, with continued improvements made in diversity of foods and ease of preparation, including eating out, after 1950."[40] She also shows that it was not until 1973 that the majority of laborers' families owned their own homes.[41] Finally, she argues that "families' economic security increased dramatically across all four classes [white salaried, white wage earner, white laborers, blacks] between 1960 and 1973, as the ratio of expenditures to income declined and expenditures for personal insurance increased."[42] In short, it is only in the past twenty years that all but the poorest families have gained enough discretionary income to begin to emphasize the qualitative dimensions of consumption. The result is an increase in the importance of quality and a host of related measurement problems.

There are several analytically distinct dimensions to this growing emphasis on quality. First, there is the continuous upgrading of goods and services to meet a more discerning demand. In theory, these kinds of changes could be measured, but in practice it is extraordinarily difficult. The problem of measuring improvements in the average family home has already been mentioned. On a different scale, there are parallel measurement problems as consumer tastes shift to higher-quality foods. For example, how does one measure the dramatic improvements in the availability of fresh vegetables in many supermarkets and produce stores?

A second analytic dimension is that one can expect a wealthier society to make more choices that place qualitative goals over quantitative ones. In other words, decisions are made to sacrifice a quantitative increase in goods and services for other ends. Gourmet meals are far more labor-intensive than many other types of products, but when a growing number of people have bought their fill of appliances, they are likely to spend more of their discretionary income on these labor-intensive luxuries. Employing more people in this kind of labor-intensive activity leads to a slower growth of measured GNP than if the same people were employed in capital-intensive production. The dynamic is exactly the same if the social choice is to spend more money for the care of the aged and the disabled. Here, as well, other values are being placed ahead of

40. Clair Brown, "Consumption Norms, Work Roles, and Economic Growth, 1918–1980," in Clair Brown and Joseph A. Pechman, eds., *Gender in the Workplace* (Washington, D.C.: Brookings Institution, 1987), 40.
41. Ibid., 43.
42. Ibid., 45.

simple increases in measured GNP, since the workers involved could easily produce more dollar value per hour if they were making steel.

The choice to make stores and workplaces more comfortable reflects the same kind of decision. If the resources used for carpeting and attractive furniture were directed to the purchase of capital goods, the capacity of the economy to produce those goods that are measured by the GNP data would expand more quickly. Instead, people are trading off some potential increase in consuming power for greater comfort in other areas of their lives. This is really a shift of a portion of consumption from the home to the workplace or the marketplace, but this more collective form of consumption does not get counted in the official data as an increase in utility to individuals.[43]

A final element of society's choice to place other goals above increased output is the decision to invest increasing resources in reducing the negative externalities of production that are excluded from the GNP data. One way of thinking of such investments is that they are oriented toward achieving "priceless" outcomes. Viviana Zelizer argues that American society made a transition in the early twentieth century from an instrumental conception of children, in which their value came from their capacity to work, to a radically different conception in which their value lay in their being insulated from the market. Children in her view became priceless.[44] A parallel development is the increasing flow of resources to the elderly to improve their economic security and well-being. Similarly, increasing investments in health care and medical research are justified in terms of the priceless nature of human life. By the same logic, spending money to expand public parks, to clean up the environment, or to preserve the society's historical monuments represent further investments in priceless outcomes.

These different qualitative dimensions of consumption might

43. In fact, some of these expenditures for office and store design will be included as capital expenditures. However, they are capital expenditures that produce a flow of services—increased comfort levels—that are excluded from measures of final product.

44. Zelizer, *Pricing the Priceless Child: The Changing Social Value of Children* (New York: Basic Books, 1985). Whether it is possible to place a price on "priceless" goods is, however, a hotly debated issue. The question is closely linked to the limits one wants to place on economic calculations.

vary in importance over time, but it seems quite reasonable to imagine that they can contribute to a kind of law of diminishing returns of measured economic growth. As a society becomes progressively more affluent, it chooses to devote more of its increasing productive capacity to qualitative goals. The result is a slowdown in GNP growth. Since annual growth of real GNP in the United States has been on the order of 3 to 4 percent a year, a loss of measured GNP growth of half a percentage point per year attributable to shifts toward quality would be extremely significant. Yet the central point is that this measured slowdown in the rate of GNP growth does not indicate an actual slowdown in the growth of utility. Moreover, if the shift toward qualitative goals accelerates, it is conceivable that rates of GNP growth that are very low by historical standards could mask subtantial improvements in people's well-being.

The Deeper Problems of Measurement: Productive Consumption and Consumptive Production

Another aspect of the shift toward quality is sufficiently important to justify separate treatment. This is the growing importance of spending to increase human capacities. This creates a serious problem for the system of national-income accounting because that system requires that activities be either investment or consumption; they cannot be both. In this respect, the accounting system is consistent with economic theory that also insists on a hard and fast distinction between consumption and investment. That distinction has always been problematic,[45] and with postindustrial developments it can no longer be sustained.

The point is that many expenditures for enhancing individual capacities simultaneously produce two different kinds of utility— they produce a consumer good and they add to the individual's ability to be a productive employee. Educational expenditures are the obvious case, but they are not unique. Many types of spending

---

45. "Production, then, is also immediately consumption, consumption is also immediately production. Each is immediately its opposite" (Karl Marx, *Grundrisse: Foundations of the Critique of Political Economy* [New York: Random House, Vintage Books, 1973], 91). Marx discusses the complex relation between the two categories in the introductory section of the *Grundrisse* (90–94).

on medical care also have this dual nature. The same can be said of spending on certain types of psychological and social services where the goal is to enhance the individual's sense of well-being, which can also make him or her more productive as an employee. Drug and alcohol counseling and treatment programs, for example, often have these dual consequences. The same can be said of much spending on enhancing the individual's physical fitness—such as purchases of exercise equipment, health club memberships, and aerobics classes. Arguably even a significant portion of spending on travel and vacations should be seen not only as consumption but as a way of restoring people's productive capacities.

These forms of productive consumption constitute a growing share of GNP, but they are generally counted only once in the official data, and in some cases they are not counted at all. If a firm provides alcohol or drug counseling to its staff, that will be treated as a cost of doing business, not as an increase in investment or consumption. Moreover, the value of education is included in the national accounts in terms of its costs, not in terms of the much greater value that it adds to the economy.[46] Yet if we are trying to track all of the utility that the society produces, there is a strong case to be made for counting both the productive and the consumptive nature of these expenditures. In short, as the proportionate role of productive consumption increases, the GNP figures will more severely understate the actual growth of utility.

The growing importance of productive consumption is mirrored by the increased weight of what might be called consumptive production. As was noted earlier, economic theory treats work as a disutility, but there is reason to believe that the nonpecuniary rewards of work have been increasing, particularly learning and the satisfaction of problem-solving. When a national sample of employ-

46. Some economists have sought to calculate the value of each year's addition to the "human capital" stock that can be traced to educational expenditures. These studies work backwards from data for individuals on economic returns to additional education. One study calculates that the value of schooling investment in 1967 was $403.8 billion, compared to $120.8 billion for gross private domestic investment in the same year in the national accounts (Eugene Kroch and Kriss Sjoblom, "Education and the National Wealth of the United States," *Review of Income and Wealth* 32, no. 1 [March 1986]: 87–106).

ees was asked, "Do you feel that a person on your job learns new things that could lead to a better job or to a promotion?" 85 percent of the respondents said yes.[47] Here again, we have a case of two types of utility being produced at the same time; employees produce goods and services and they also produce the utility of interesting work. This pattern is currently captured in the seemingly contradictory image of the "Yuppies," or young urban professionals, who received much media attention in the early 1980s. Yuppies are supposed to work long hours in their professional and managerial jobs, but they are also supposed to be eager consumers of high-quality goods. What reconciles the contradiction is that their long hours of work also represent a form of consumption, which they pursue with great intensity.[48]

The heightened importance of productive consumption and consumptive production does not just cast doubt on the accuracy of GNP data; it represents significant anomalies in economic theory in general. As the distinction between productive and consumptive activities breaks down, it is clear that new concepts and a new conceptual map are required to make sense of our economic activities. If it is possible for people to combine consumption and investment in the same activity, then even without capital savings, it is possible to consume more today *and* have more tomorrow. Furthermore, if interesting work becomes a kind of consumer good, then it is hard to see the rationale for paying people who do interesting work at much higher rates than those who do boring work. The classic argument in defense of such inequalities—the need to induce people to suffer through a prolonged period of training—loses its persuasiveness when the highly educated can also look forward to a lifetime of challenging work.[49]

47. Jencks et al., "What Is a Good Job?" 1326.
48. "Few would describe today's upper-status groups as a leisure class; they are a class of 'workaholics' instead. A good many of its members are always complaining about not knowing the difference between weekdays and Sundays, and not having a holiday for years; but in fact such complaints are another form of conspicuous consumption, of displaying the new wealth of work" (Ralf Dahrendorf, *The Modern Social Conflict: An Essay on the Politics of Liberty* [New York: Weidenfeld & Nicolson, 1988], 144).
49. Kingley Davis and Wilbert Moore, "Some Principles of Stratification," *American Sociological Review* 10, no. 2 (April 1945): 242–49.

GNP and Perceptions of Well-being

The argument to this point is that there is a growing gap between what the GNP data report and the actual output of the economy. Some of this discussion has emphasized ways in which the official data understate the actual growth in utility in recent years, such as improvements in quality and the growth of productive consumption. Such an argument flies in the face of the popular perception, which has been exactly the opposite—that if anything, the official data exaggerate the growth of utility in recent years. In 1980 Ronald Reagan was elected on the basis of a widespread perception that economic growth had slowed dangerously during the 1970s. And even during the 1988 election, the unsuccessful Democrats were able to tap a widespread sentiment that economic growth in the Reagan years had not been as rosy as the official data seemed to indicate. At the very least, most people would be astonished to learn that they are actually much better off than the GNP data indicate.

This gap between popular perception and economic reality has been explored by Christopher Jencks in an analysis of the 1970s.[50] He shows that the popular perception of economic slowdown in the 1970s was reinforced by the Census Bureau's annual report on family income, which indicated that "real" family income rose 38 percent during the 1950s, 34 percent during the 1960s, but only 0.4 percent in the 1970s. Jencks points out a number of different problems with these data. First, reports on trends in family income ignore the growing fraction of the population who live on their own and whose median income rose faster than that of families during the 1970s. Moreover, the average family size fell from 3.6 people in 1970 to 3.3 in 1980, so that the slow improvement for families conceals more rapid income improvement for family members during the 1970s. Second, Jencks points out that a more appropriate price deflator than the Consumer Price Index used by the Census Bureau "reduces the apparent difference between the 1970s and the two previous decades by a third."[51] Third, he argues that some

50. Jencks, "The Hidden Prosperity of the 1970s," *The Public Interest* 77 (Fall 1984): 37–61.
51. Ibid., 51.

of the same inadequacies with the GNP measure that have been discussed here understate the value of the output received by families in recent years. Finally, he examines trends in aggregate consumer income and shows that when appropriate adjustments are made for taxes and changes in government services to individuals, there is no significant difference between trends in the 1970s and earlier decades.[52]

Jencks's essay ends by posing the critical puzzle: "The reader may wonder why, if the material standard of living really rose significantly during the 1970s, so few people noticed."[53] Why if actual standards of living were rising faster than the official data indicated, were people so easily persuaded that economic growth had slowed?

To be sure, the relationship between economic growth and survey results about feelings of happiness or well-being have always been problematic. A number of scholars have shown that changes in personal income in the post–World War II period do not produce comparable increases in reported happiness.[54] Also, popular perceptions of the strength or weakness of the economy can be strongly influenced by messages from politicians and the media. FDR, for example, was able to create a popular perception by 1936 of dramatic economic improvement even though unemployment rates remained at very high levels in the late 1930s. Similarly, public perceptions of the economy's poor performance in the 1970s were heavily influenced by a sustained business propaganda campaign and by the way politicians defined the situation.[55] Nevertheless,

52. Ibid., 53. Jencks's measure of the average annual increase in aggregate after-tax income, including government services, rose 3.1 percent between 1950 and 1960, 4.3 percent between 1960 and 1970, and 3.3 percent between 1970 and 1980.

53. Ibid., 60.

54. Scitovsky, *Joyless Economy*, 133–45; Easterlin, "Does Economic Growth Improve the Human Lot? Some Empirical Evidence," in Paul A. David and Melvin W. Reder, eds., *Nations and Households in Economic Growth: Essays in Honor of Moses Abramovitz* (New York: Academic Press, 1974): 89–125; Frank Levy, "Happiness, Affluence and Altruism in the Postwar Period," in Martin David and Timothy Smeeding, eds., *Horizontal Equity, Uncertainty, and Economic Well-Being* (Chicago: University of Chicago Press, 1985), 7–29.

55. The subjective dimension of perceptions of economic success or failure is stressed in Joel Krieger, *Reagan, Thatcher and the Politics of Decline* (New York: Oxford University Press, 1986).

the ability of politicians to shape perceptions is limited; they generally need something real on which to build.

Jencks's answer to this puzzle is that inflation in the 1970s distorted people's perceptions of their economic well-being. He invokes the argument, popularized by Lester Thurow, that high rates of inflation led to dramatic increases in people's nominal wages, but people experienced significant disappointments when their actual purchasing power did not increase proportionately.[56] Although most people were better off at the end of the 1970s than at the beginning, the improvement was far smaller than what people imagined they were due, given the growth in their nominal incomes. The result was a sense of disappointment that clouded people's perceptions of their actual well-being.

While this ingenious argument probably exaggerates individuals' inability to account adequately for inflation, it serves as a reminder that perceptions of well-being are always relative to other things, such as where one expects to be. Hence, perceptions of other people's well-being have a significant impact on how one perceives one's own situation.[57] By linking this insight to the shift toward quality in consumption, it is possible to develop an even more persuasive explanation for the puzzle Jencks identifies.

Positional Goods

One important dimension of the shift toward quality in consumption is the growing importance of what Fred Hirsch has called "positional goods."[58] As individuals have more discretionary income, they are able to increase their consumption of positional goods—goods and services inherently in scarce supply because their attractiveness derives from their relative scarcity. Examples include houses in exclusive neighborhoods, admission to Ivy League colleges, and seats on the fifty-yard line for championship games. Although small increases can be made in the supply of some

---

56. Thurow, *The Zero-Sum Society: Distribution and the Possibilities for Economic Change* (New York: Basic Books, 1980), 49.

57. See also Easterlin, "Does Economic Growth Improve the Human Lot?"

58. Fred Hirsch, *Social Limits to Growth* (Cambridge, Mass.: Harvard University Press, 1976). For commentaries on Hirsch, see Adrian Ellis and Krishan Kumar, *Dilemmas of Liberal Democracies* (London: Tavistock Publications, 1983).

of these kinds of goods, large increases are self-defeating, because they strip the goods of their valued exclusivity. Such positional goods have always existed, but they become progressively more important to the economy as income levels rise.

Concerns about positional goods that were once the exclusive domain of upper classes have now trickled down to large segments of the broad middle class. In buying or renting housing, more and more people are sufficiently well off to be worrying about what the quality of a particular neighborhood says about their relative status position rather than simply thinking of getting a roof over their heads. In purchasing health care, the most prestigious specialists are in great demand, not just because of the promise of better performance, but also because of status considerations. Similarly, going on vacation is for many not a question simply of getting away from home but of finding a resort that is not overcrowded with other tourists. The same can be said for restaurants and cultural events. In New York City it has become a fact of life that the most popular nightspots are those that have doormen who refuse entry to large numbers of prospective clients.

Positional goods have two insidious characteristics from the point of view of increasing economic well-being. First, it is by definition impossible for supply to keep up with demand; there will always be people unable to consume goods and services that they have the income to purchase. Second, it is almost always the case that whatever one attains, there will be positional goods that are even more exclusive and valuable. It is difficult to find complete satisfaction in the pursuit of positional advantage, because there are constant reminders that there are others who are enjoying positional goods from which one is still excluded. A grotesque illustration of this dynamic is "Feeling Poor on $600,000 a Year," a *New York Times* article that details how young investment bankers in New York City have trouble making ends meet because their pursuit of such positional goods as co-op apartments, beachfront houses, designer clothes, and exclusive private schools for their children absorbs huge quantities of money.[59] In short, the pursuit of positional goods

59. April 26, 1987, Business Section, 1. In the case of these investment bankers, it could be argued that the maintenance of this extravagant lifestyle is necessary to reinforce their professional credibility. The last thing they want a prospective client to say or think is, "If you are so smart, why ain't you rich?"

tends to produce disappointment because most people find that they cannot secure the status advantage they initially sought.[60]

When this argument is joined to Thurow's analysis of inflation, the result is a more plausible account of what happened to the more affluent parts of the middle class in the 1970s. As more of their increased incomes were devoted to the purchase of positional goods, they felt disappointed with the progress they were making. They judged their well-being both in relation to what their nominal earnings were and in relation to the well-being of the more affluent Joneses, and they perceived themselves as progressing at a slower rate than the latter.

The Disappearance of Utility

Positional goods and money illusion, however, are not sufficient to explain the broad public perception of slowing income growth, since the more affluent groups are only a fraction of the whole. Another factor that contributed to the perception of slowing growth of family income during the 1970s and 1980s is the disappearance of some of the value historically produced by unpaid family members. It was earlier noted that the GNP data omit the output in the home of family members or produced in the community by volunteers. Yet the increasing participation of married women in the labor force in recent years has meant that some of this utility is no longer produced at all, or is produced under conditions that place great stress on families.[61]

The obvious example of this is child care. From 1970 to 1985, the

---

60. Albert Hirschman makes a persuasive argument for the inherent dissatisfactions in many types of consumption (*Shifting Involvements: Private Interest and Public Action* [Princeton: Princeton University Press, 1982]). However, it seems plausible that the frustrations of positional goods are greater than those connected with ordinary consumer durables.

61. Another interpretation of these same developments is that the increasing labor-force participation of wives was an indication that working-class families had to contribute more hours of market labor to maintain their historic standards of living. This argument has been elaborated in Elliott Currie, Robert Dunn, and David Fogarty, "The New Immiseration: Stagflation, Inequality, and the Working Class," *Socialist Review* 54 (November–December 1980): 7–32. The difficulty of this line of argument is it implies that the most recent cohorts of wives to enter the labor force are doing so only because of family income needs.

participation of mothers with children under six in the labor force increased from 32.3 to 53.5 percent, and the increase for mothers of children under three was equally dramatic.[62] Although some of the child care that had previously been provided in the home was now provided by the market, the high cost of privately provided child care made complete replacement unlikely. Moreover, the public sector in recent years has failed to expand its provision of child-care services. The result is that families have had to improvise to meet their needs; it is common to develop complicated arrangements that combine formal child care, informal arrangements, and reliance on relatives and friends.[63]

It often takes considerable effort to make these packages work, since the schedules of a variety of people must be coordinated closely. Moreover, such systems are often subject to further disruption because of illness. Small children are particularly vulnerable to colds and flu, and few child-care centers will accept sick children. The result is a situation where many of the advantages that mothers gain from working—more income and the rewards of engaging in a socially valued activity—are eroded by the economic costs of child care and reduced leisure time, as well as by the psychic costs of balancing work and family life.

A similar story can be told with aging adults. When most married women worked in the home, it was assumed that they would bear the burden of caring for aged and sick relatives. This was another important utility that was generally provided outside of the market. Yet as participation of women in the labor force rises, it becomes much more difficult to combine paid work with these kinds of familial obligations. Yet with continuing gains in life expectancy, it is also more likely that adults in midlife will have aging parents to care for. Some families can meet these needs by hiring additional help or by relying on social service agencies. Often these expedients are not available, however, and when they are, there are still considerable demands on family members. The result is a loss of discretionary leisure and considerable stress.

62. Barbara R. Bergmann, *The Economic Emergence of Women* (New York: Basic Books, 1986), 25.

63. Some data on the tension between child-care arrangements and work schedules are provided in John P. Fernandez, *Child Care and Corporate Productivity: Resolving Family/Work Conflicts* (Lexington, Mass.: D.C. Heath, 1986).

It is less often recognized that parallel problems exist in the social lives of communities. There were many voluntary roles in the community that housewives tended to fill in the normal course of events. Youth groups, church groups, parents' associations, local political parties, social service organizations, and a variety of other voluntary associations tended to rely disproportionately on the voluntary labor of housewives. As the population of housewives has diminished, many of these organizations have been seriously weakened. Many working women continue their voluntary efforts, but they are generally not able to volunteer for large blocks of time. It was often the case that one or two energetic housewives devoted a large amount of time to coordinating the efforts of many others, and the loss of people to play that coordinating role can be extremely serious. The point, however, is that organizations that rely on voluntary labor produce services that are significant in determining the quality of life.

There are alternative ways for the society to produce the output historically provided by unpaid labor in the home and in the community. However, since these services were historically produced outside of the market economy, they have generally been invisible and undervalued, and the society has been slow to respond to their disappearance. Yet this disappearance, or the production of these services under conditions that place severe stress on families, has a real impact on the well-being of families. A family's real purchasing power may increase, but people might still have the perception that they are worse off, because they have lost some of their highly valued discretionary leisure time.

The Mismatch of Production and Demand

The failure of the society to replace services that were historically produced in the home or by voluntary labor is one case of a larger problem; the existence of institutional obstacles to an effective matching of production and demand. In the market model, needs are almost automatically turned into demand that will be met by entrepreneurs, but in actual economies the situation is much more complex. There are many factors that can prevent a timely adjustment of supply to fit demand, especially when one is considering elements of output that are not directly produced for sale on the market. If these mismatches become particularly severe in a particular period, they can contribute to people's perception that income growth is too slow.

One type of mismatch that was particularly important in the 1970s and 1980s occurred in the market for low- and moderate-income housing. Although the official data probably exaggerate the inflationary increases in the cost of new family homes, such costs nonetheless rose quickly enough to price many people out of the market.[64] At the same time, public spending for low-income housing also slowed considerably, and gentrification and the abandonment or destruction of older units further contracted the housing available for moderate- and low-income families. One result of these trends has been the return of a historic pattern in which adult children—even when married—continue to live with their parents while they accumulate savings to find a place of their own. Another result was the rapid bidding up of prices for the existing housing stock, since scarcity created strong price pressures, which were a significant factor in the inflation of the 1970s.[65] These developments provide the background for the reemergence of the problem of homelessness on a mass scale in the 1980s.

The society's failure to add more units to the low- and moderate-price end of the housing stock has multiple roots, which include the greater profitability of building higher-priced housing and office units, the slow diffusion of new production technologies in construction, the rising price of suburban land in close proximity to jobs, and the politics of race. The latter factor is important in the limited public initiatives to produce more low- and moderate-

64. While the percentage of all households owning their own home increased during the 1970s, the increase was more rapid among more affluent families. Christopher Jencks reports that "in 1970 home owners' median income had been only 53 percent higher than that of renters. By 1980 the difference was 89 percent" ("Hidden Prosperity," 40). Data on deterioration in the housing market since 1975 are provided in David C. Schwartz, Richard C. Ferlauto, and Daniel N. Hoffman, *A New Housing Policy for America: Recapturing the American Dream* (Philadelphia: Temple University Press, 1988), 6–34. They report that among renter families—constituting 35 percent of all households in 1980—the percentage whose rent burden was more than 25 percent of income rose from 40 percent in 1974 to 60 percent in 1983 (p. 17).

65. Data on family budgets showed that for all population groups the percentage of family income spent on housing was higher in 1980 than it had been in 1960, while housing's share had diminished from 1935 to 1960 (Brown, "Consumption Norms, Work Roles, and Economic Growth," 24–25).

priced housing. Despite the society's adoption of an ideology of racial equality, there has been little progress in reducing racial segregation in housing. This means that when new public-sector housing is created, it will generate controversy regardless of whether it is used to reinforce or transform existing patterns of residential segregation. The path of least resistance has been to avoid the controversy by not building the housing.

The other important mismatches of the 1970s focused on non-market goods. It was argued earlier that with rising income levels, individuals were choosing to place more emphasis on the qualitative dimension of consumption. However, it is a mistake to assume that all such choices are effective. People might place a greater value on clean air and clean water, but they still might not be able to afford to move away from a toxic waste dump. And even when they press their demands through the political process, they might find that they are unable to get existing toxic hazards cleaned up or to prevent new hazards from being created.

In short, people were predisposed to believe that their incomes were not rising quickly enough in part because the economy's production of certain public goods trailed behind people's expectations. There was a tremendous growth in the 1970s in people's consciousness about such dimensions of output as environmental quality and occupational health and safety, and if there were improvements in these areas, they were not enough to meet people's rising expectations. Similarly, there was considerable evidence in the early 1970s of rising expectations about the quality of work, particularly among young people. It seems probably that many of these expectations were not met, as many jobs continued to provide little scope for personal autonomy.

Although this argument about rising expectations for nonmarket utility is necessarily speculative, it points to an indisputable reality. On the one hand, income—as it is conventionally measured—is only one among a broad variety of factors that determine people's perceptions of their well-being, even of their "economic" well-being. On the other hand, these perceptions are formed in a society preoccupied with the GNP concept and related measures of income. The main language that people have for thinking about the question, "Are we better off now than we were four years ago?" is the language of money income. It follows that perceptions about income can condense a whole range of other satisfactions and dissatisfactions.

Conclusions

In sum, it is very difficult to know whether Americans were economically better off in 1988 than they were in 1970. The point is rather that the rate of growth of GNP has very little to do with answering that question. Moreover, the mindset that assumes a close fit between GNP growth and economic well-being also imagines that more investment is uniformly the solution to inadequate GNP growth. Yet the real issue is not rates of investment, but the institutional arrangements through which people's needs are met or remain unmet. It is entirely possible that popular perceptions of inadequate growth result from the society's failure to shift resources quickly enough toward the more qualitative dimensions of consumption, such as increased leisure time, the reduction of externalities, and the replacement of services previously performed by unpaid family members.

However, this still leaves the problem of the growing importance of positional goods—a problem that cannot be solved simply through reallocating resources or even through faster growth. In fact, the struggle over positional goods represents another instance where the instrumentalization of economic activity is subversive of economic rationality. When people come to see their well-being as depending on the possession of goods and services that others cannot attain, the marketplace becomes a war of each against all, where each person's satisfactions are few and fleeting. Vast resources are diverted for the purposes of providing a few with a quick consumer high that will quickly pass, requiring even further efforts the next time.

The only solution to the problem of positional goods is to attempt to minimize the competition. The concentration of the quest for positional goods at the higher end of the income continuum makes the problem eminently manageable. A more equitable distribution of income would dampen the struggle over positional goods by reducing the discretionary income of the rich and the upper middle class. For example, the prestige value of certain academic credentials is closely linked to the large income disparities in the society.

A more egalitarian distribution of income would make possible a flatter and more rational prestige hierarchy among such institutions and ease the positional struggle for admission to the "best" schools. The expanded provision of public goods could also help reduce the competition for positional goods. If beachfront land were organized into public parks, it would be possible to avert the race to build the most magnificent beachhouse and the attending pattern of over-development that characterizes fashionable resorts.[66] To be sure, there will always be those who compete to appear better or more sophisticated than their neighbors, but different institutional arrangements—such as greater income equality and greater reliance on public goods—can help sublimate part of that competition into realms other than an economically wasteful struggle over positional goods.

In sum, both the case of positional goods and the examples of mismatch reinforce the insight that institutional variables intervene between economic growth and improvements or deterioration in the utility people receive. Moreover, when we examine the full range of utility or satisfactions produced in the society, it is not at all difficult to imagine zero GNP growth in a highly dynamic economy that is producing progressively higher levels of human satisfaction. It is this idea of qualitative growth that is elaborated in the next chapter.

66. In the case of medical care, it is possible also to imagine public-sector interventions that would reduce the competition for access to high-prestige physicians and facilities. If more resources were devoted to the improvement of primary-care facilities, they could serve as screening mechanisms for access to the more prestigious facilities.

Chapter Seven

Alternatives:
Qualitative Growth

It is far easier to point to the inadequacies of an existing set of categories than to develop a persuasive set of alternative categories and concepts. Making sense of social possibilities that are still only emergent in the present stretches the sociological imagination to its limits. Moreover, even when such alternatives are imagined, they usually appear abstract and utopian because they are divorced from people's experiences. Yet the problem is circular, since people experience reality through the lenses of the earlier set of categories. In some historical transitions, an extended period of social learning is necessary before an alternative set of concepts begins to appear concrete and practical.

Despite these difficulties, it is still important to attempt to move beyond critique. Even if it is not possible to generate a whole new set of categories, some minimal idea of alternative is preferable to disembodied critique. Critique divorced from any idea of alternative can, at best, be an academic exercise, and, at worst, may reinforce the idea that existing arrangements are inevitable and unchangeable.

The critiques elaborated in previous chapters do point to an alternative way of organizing the economy—an economy organized around qualitative growth. This chapter will elaborate the concept of qualitative growth and show how it emerges directly out of the specific critiques of market, labor, capital, and GNP. The intention is to persuade the reader that a different set of principles than those embedded in the neoclassical tradition can make sense out of the potential of an economy that has been transformed in a postindustrial direction. The second part of this chapter is necessarily far more speculative. It explores some of the specific ways economic institutions could be reorganized to facilitate qualitative growth. The suggestions are not exhaustive and represent only one of many possible reform programs. The idea is simply to make the case that when one shifts from neoclassical to qualitative growth principles, all assumptions about how an economy should be organized must be reexamined.

Thinking about Alternatives

It is necessary, however, to begin with a discussion of the kind of alternative that qualitative growth represents. This is important for several reasons. First, it was argued in chapter 1 that the concept of postindustrialism can and should be cleansed of the elements of nineteenth-century evolutionary thought. It is important that qualitative growth not be thought of as a new form of economic organization inevitably developing within the womb of industrial capitalism. Second, there are different dimensions or levels embedded in the concept of qualitative growth that need to be distinguished. Finally, the alternative developed here has to be situated in terms of the historic conflict between capitalism and socialism.

Qualitative growth is simply an intellectual construct; it is not a new stage of historical development or an emergent form of social organization. The claim is only that qualitative growth is a logical or rational alternative to present institutional arrangements because it can be constructed out of many of the visible tendencies identified in the previous chapters. However, other alternatives can also be constructed and some might appear more or less rational to different people. Moreover, the path that the society actually takes will depend only secondarily on logic; the key determinant will be the relative political power of contending forces struggling over different visions of the future.

It is also useful to distinguish between what can be termed "Qualitative Growth I" and "Qualitative Growth II." "Qualitative Growth I," described in the first part of the chapter, embodies new principles of economic organization. These principles are analogous to such principles of industrialism as standardized mass production and the systematic shift of economic surplus from agriculture to industry. These principles can be pursued within a variety of institutional forms, just as industrialism was organized through such diverse arrangements as Anglo-American laissez-faire and Stalinist statism. Qualitative Growth II, as elaborated in the second part of the chapter, is a specific set of institutional arrangements for pursuing these principles that is consistent with the goal of greater democracy, equality, and freedom. Qualitative Growth II is simply one of many possible ways of organizing an economy around these new principles.

How do these different dimensions of qualitative growth connect to the issue of capitalism and socialism? The question is complicated because of the ideological uses of these categories. For over a hundred years, advocates of quite diverse plans for economic reorganization have either been labeled socialists by their opponents or have proudly proclaimed themselves to be socialists. Both supporters and opponents of capitalism have often assumed that there are inherent limits to the mutability of capitalism, so that exceeding the limits will bring one automatically to the qualitatively different world of socialism. This notion of inherent limits has been used by revolutionaries when they insist on the inherent impossibility of winning critical reforms within capitalism, and by conservatives when they claim that certain reforms will result in the inevitable triumph of socialism.

This doctrine of the limited mutability of capitalism is deeply flawed. To insist that certain changes are not possible within this particular set of economic arrangements, it is necessary to know what exactly is meant by the term *capitalism*. Yet a term that has been used to describe societies from seventeenth-century England to contemporary Sweden, Japan, South Korea, and Chile appears to lack a high degree of specificity. Even if one argues that the sine qua non of capitalism is private ownership of the means of production, private property rights can be organized in very different ways. Firms can be required to have employees on their corporate boards of directors, they can be legally compelled to carry out certain public purposes, and so on. The range of different institutional possibilities is sufficiently broad that a notion of inherent limits loses its credibility.

Furthermore, the actual institutional arrangements within societies that are considered capitalist have changed significantly over the past two hundred years largely as a result of popular struggles for improved living standards, greater economic security, and the extension of democratic rights. The actual scope and sovereignty of property rights have been altered by a whole series of different reforms. Moreover, there is good reason to imagine that the continuation of such struggles will lead to significant changes in the future. The broad differences at present among the developed capitalist countries in their provisions for economic security or for employee influence in the workplace provide strong evidence of the possibility of future change. In short, arguments that the principles of qualitative growth are inherently incompatible with continued private ownership of the means of production are unpersuasive.

At the same time, the concept of socialism has also become problematic. The experience of Soviet-style socialism has made it obvious that centralized state ownership and planning of the economy has a disastrous impact on economic efficiency and democratic rights. As a result, both socialist theorists and socialist leaders have increasingly been experimenting with concepts of "market socialism."[1] Yet once socialism is redefined to include profit incentives at the level of the firm and competitive markets for goods, it becomes clear that "market socialist" societies and "developed capitalist" societies are not polar opposites. They represent different degrees of marketness in the organization of economic life, and they encounter parallel problems in deciding on the proper mix between markets, state action, and other forms of regulation.

Consequently, it is no longer clear what it means to define an alternative form of economic organization as socialist. The goal that Marx envisioned of a society beyond scarcity has become unpersuasive with the recognition that time will always remain scarce and there will always be those who fail to achieve the status and recognition they desire.[2] Defining socialism in terms of the abolition of

1. See Alec Nove, *The Economics of Feasible Socialism* (London: George Allen & Unwin, 1983). Since the publication of Nove's volume, the shift toward market socialism in the Soviet Union and China has clearly accelerated.

2. Critical contributions on these points have been made by Carmen Sirianni, "The Self-Management of Time in Post-Industrial Society: Towards a Democratic Alternative," *Socialist Review* 88, no. 4 (October–December 1988): 5–56, and

private property or of private profits leads back to the choice between central planning and "market socialism."[3] The former places
so much power in the hands of state managers that they are able to
pursue their interests against those of the rest of society. The latter
involves vesting property rights and the control of profits in collectivities, but there is no necessary reason that these collectivities will
act better than capitalists. A worker-owned tractor factory is likely
to have the same incentive to place profits over product safety as a
typical private corporation. In both cases, outcomes will depend on
the institutional and cultural mechanisms developed to minimize
conflicts between private and public interests.

At one time, it was possible to define socialism in terms of the
guaranteed provision of minimum levels of well-being, but the
advanced welfare states of Western Europe have made it clear that
this can be done with private ownership of the means of production.
More recently, a number of theorists have sought to redefine socialism in terms of the extension of democracy and democratic rights.[4]
This is an attractive strategy, but it leads away from the traditional
Marxist emphasis on the primacy of property rights. In developing
that kind of argument, the distinction between the form and the
substance of democracy becomes a central part of the critique of
Western democracies. If people have the formal right to make
critical decisions, but they remain passive and uninvolved in governance, there is little content to democracy. It follows, however,
that formal rights—including property rights—can be less important in guaranteeing democratic practices than people's capacity
and willingness to engage in democratic decision-making.

This means, for example, that a worker-owned plant can be
significantly less democratic than a privately owned firm with a
highly developed system of employee participation despite the
differences in the formal rights of each group of workers. Moreover,

---

Michael Walzer, *Spheres of Justice: A Defense of Pluralism and Equality* (New
York: Basic Books, 1983).

3. Another theme in the socialist critique of capitalism is the abolition of all
forms of commodification, but it is difficult to envision this occurring without
centralized control of all allocation.

4. Joshua Cohen and Joel Rogers, *On Democracy: Toward a Transformation
of American Society* (New York: Penguin Books, 1983); Ernesto Laclau and Chan-
tal Mouffe, *Hegemony and Socialist Strategy: Towards a Radical Democratic
Politics* (London: Verso, 1985).

even within the constraint of private property, it is possible to provide employees in the privately owned firm with significant formal rights that would provide a solid foundation for their democratic practices. They could, for example, be granted rights of free speech, protection from arbitrary actions by their employers, and a guarantee of a certain number of votes on the corporate board of directors.[5]

The outline of Qualitative Growth II developed here builds on this reinterpretation of the socialist tradition to place primary emphasis on expanding democracy. The central question becomes not capitalism or socialism, but how a society can create economic institutions that give maximum scope to democratic participation. Qualitative Growth II represents a vision of an advanced economy in which steady progress could be made to expand popular sovereignty over all critical social and economic decisions.

Qualitative Growth I

The principles that underlie Qualitative Growth I exist in the present economy, but they operate in the background; they are subordinate to the intravenous model of capital and to the drive to expand commodity output. If these principles came to the foreground—if they were elevated to the central principles of economic organization—the result would be a significantly different kind of economy.

The first principle is the positive feedback between the development of human capacities and expanded future production. This was discussed earlier in terms both of the growing importance of organizational variables and of the concept of productive consumption. Marx, writing more than one hundred and twenty years ago, analyzed the positive feedback in an advanced economy. In a passage in the *Grundrisse* in which he anticipated a high level of automation, Marx argued that advanced technologies transform the economy:

In this transformation, it is neither the direct human labor he himself performs, nor the time during which he works, but rather the appropria-

5. See Karl E. Klare, "Workplace Democracy and Market Reconstruction: An Agenda for Legal Reform," *Catholic University Law Review* 38, no. 1 (Fall 1988): 1–68.

tion of his own general productive power, his understanding of nature and his mastery over it by virtue of his presence as a social body—it is, in a word, the development of the social individual which appears as the great foundation-stone of production and of wealth.[6]

This passage suggests that as economic output is used to expand individual capacities—through more education, through more creative leisure activities, and through the diffusion of scientific and technological understanding—the collective capacity to produce utility of all kinds is further enhanced, and a virtuous cycle of expanded wealth is created.

This is not simply the familiar argument about the value of investing in "human capital"; the specificity of Marx's argument is the link between the development of human capacities and the particular tasks imposed by advanced production technologies. In the same section of the *Grundrisse*, Marx writes that "labour no longer appears so much to be included within the production process; rather, the human being comes to relate more as watchman and regulator to the production process itself."[7] It is in the context of this specific change in the nature of the human input into production that the development of human capacities becomes of such critical importance.

The key element in the argument has been conceptualized recently in terms of "dynamic flexibility." Burton Klein contrasts "static flexibility" with "dynamic flexibility." The former refers to the ability of a firm to adjust its operations to shifts in the market, while the latter "means the ability to increase productivity steadily through improvements in production processes and innovation in product."[8] At the core of dynamic flexibility is the ability to make rapid use of new technologies; "the central preoccupation is to get ideas into action quickly."[9]

Positive feedback is the ability of a society to maximize dynamic

6. Karl Marx, *Grundrisse: Foundations of the Critique of Political Economy* (New York: Random House, Vintage Books, 1973), 705.
7. Ibid.
8. Stephen S. Cohen and John Zysman, *Manufacturing Matters: The Myth of the Post-Industrial Economy* (New York: Basic Books, 1987), 131. In this section, Cohen and Zysman draw heavily on Burton Klein, "Dynamic Competition and Productivity Advances," in Ralph Landau and Nathan Rosenberg, eds., *The Positive-Sum Strategy: Harnessing Technology in Economic Growth* (Washington, D.C.: National Academy Press, 1986), 77–88.
9. Klein, quoted in Cohen and Zysman, *Manufacturing Matters*, 132.

flexibility by developing the capacity of individuals to solve problems and by developing organizations that are able to make use of those solutions. For example, individual breakthroughs in computer programming have the capacity to eliminate millions of hours of repetitive labor, while also increasing employees' capacities for higher-level tasks. Think of the hours of typing saved by the development of word-processing programs or the effect of spreadsheet programs on the effectiveness of managers.[10] Yet as the society uses its wealth to expand the pool of people who are capable of developing and using these innovations in programming, the possibilities for further productive advances increase, and so on.

The problem, of course, is that there is nothing automatic about positive feedback. There are many institutional and cultural variables that intervene between the expansion of human capacities and their effective utilization. For example, a society might spend millions of dollars to produce a generation of new computer programmers, who may nonetheless lack the creativity to develop effective innovations. Additional money spent on education might only produce more individuals who suffer from "trained incompetence." Even when creative ideas are in abundance, institutional or organizational rigidities can stand in the way of dynamic flexibility.

At present, positive feedback is often serendipitous; it happens to varying degrees, but there is no systematic societywide effort to expand it. There are also important ways in which existing institutional structures interfere with positive feedback. In a society organized around qualitative growth, positive feedback would be seen as *the* key wealth-producing dynamic, and institutions would be reformed to increase their contribution to it.

The second key principle is the expansion of the qualitative dimensions of output, including satisfactions that are not directly embedded in commodities. As was argued earlier, there are critical dimensions of economic output that are inadequately measured or even totally ignored, but which have a very significant impact on the well-being of individuals. The items that fall into this category include work that is intrinsically satisfying, voluntary leisure time, economic security, a safe and clean environment, and a plenitude of

10. To be sure, these are extreme examples, but there are thousands of smaller innovations, such as tailoring a program to the needs of a specific industry, that have substantial consequences.

community and voluntary services. Qualitative growth would seek to reverse the underproduction of these satisfactions, while also systematically increasing the quality of all kinds of commodity outputs.

To be sure, this emphasis on noncommodity satisfactions and product quality is not cost-free; protecting the environment, providing individuals with greater economic security, encouraging the production of community and voluntary services, and improving the quality of goods and services costs money. However, most of the growth dividend from the positive feedback dynamic would be used to increase not the quantity of economic output but the quality. Moreover, these improvements in quality would, in turn, contribute to the expanded development of human capacities that makes the economy more productive.

In this sense, qualitative growth is a response to the ongoing debate about the limits of growth. All too often, that debate has been polarized between those who argue about the necessity of continuing growth along established lines and those who insist that such continued growth is either impossible because of resource constraints or undesirable because of the environmental damage it entails. The result is a deadlock between those who demand more of the same and those who appear to believe in a steady-state economy that lacks any dynamism. Qualitative Growth I is an alternative in which economic priorities are reorganized, but the economy would remain highly dynamic.[11]

There are two factors that make it possible to reconcile continued growth with environmental concerns. First, shifts in the nature of consumption and technological advances make possible a reduction in the pressures on the environment. Government data show that services now constitute the bulk of consumer purchases, and when one adds government-provided services, the dominance of services is even greater.[12] Since the production of services generally de-

11. Another way to make the point is to distinguish between growth—which is quantitative—and development—which is qualitative. See Herman Daly, "The Economic Growth Debate: What Some Economists Have Learned but Many Have Not," *Journal of Environmental Economics and Management* 14 (1987): 323–36.

12. Fred Block, "Rethinking the Political Economy of the Welfare State," in Fred Block, Richard A. Cloward, Barbara Ehrenreich, and Frances Fox Piven, *The Mean Season: The Attack on the Welfare State* (New York: Pantheon Books, 1987), 143–46.

pends less on the use of material resources—both raw materials and energy—than manufacturing does, it becomes easier to sustain growth without reaching resource limits or overloading the environment. Moreover, microelectronic technologies have already contributed to energy savings, and developments in superconductivity promise to accelerate those trends.

Second, qualitative growth's focus on expanding the noncommodity components of output means that environmental improvement is one way in which continued growth could occur. Improvements in air quality or reductions in ocean dumping would be recognized as a material contribution to greater economic welfare. To be sure, there would be no automatic assurance that the society would make environmentally correct choices. There would be continuing political struggles to encourage resource-conserving technologies and to discourage the imposition of environmental externalities by both manufacturing and service industries. However, the idea is that people operating within the framework of qualitative growth would have available an accounting scheme that no longer treated the environment as something completely external to economic production.

The third principle of qualitative growth is the recognition that neither market nor planning is adequate as an exclusive organizing principle for regulating the economy. Both unconstrained competition and centralized planning have repeatedly demonstrated that they are incompatible with considerations of product quality. Moreover, the various noncommodity satisfactions tend to be underproduced in systems with high levels of marketness, as well as in systems where central planning suppresses individual choice. The pursuit of qualitative growth requires hybrid institutional arrangements that combine individual choice, social regulation, and extensive state action. The fantasy of one royal road to rational decision-making must give way to recognition of the need for constant adjustment and adaptation to find effective ways to make choices.

The logic behind these hybrids is that the price mechanism operating alone is often ineffective in optimizing several simultaneous goals, such as efficiency within the firm and a reduction of environmental externalities. At the same time, centralized rule-making can be inflexible and unresponsive to people's actual needs. Moreover, certain types of hybrid forms can take advantage of the knowledge and understanding in different organizations to produce effective choices.

There are many current institutional arrangements that reflect experimentation with hybrid forms that go beyond plan or market. Examples include the Japanese model of interfirm and public-private cooperation, the corporatist forms of bargaining developed in some of the smaller countries of Europe, and various types of public-private partnerships developed in U.S. cities.[13] While these alternatives differ markedly in the amount of scope they provide for democratic participation, they can be seen as efforts to find new organizational arrangements to facilitate economic decision-making.

Qualitative Growth II

The recognition of these new principles of economic organization makes it possible to think of ways of organizing economic life that contribute both to economic efficiency and to greater democracy, equality, and freedom. The institutional alternative offered here does not represent a complete blueprint; it is intended only to show specific ways in which some areas of economic life could be reorganized to fit better with the principles of Qualitative Growth I.

Organizing the Workplace

The critical issue in organizing the workplace is how to institutionalize the positive feedback on productivity of expanded human capacities. It was argued in chapter 4 that the efficient use of labor increasingly depends on cooperative arrangements between employees and employers that sustain employees' motivation, encourage them to be heard, and assure high levels of investment in the development of their skills. Not coincidentally, these are the same problems that must be solved in order to strengthen the positive feedback dynamic—the continuing flow of productivity gains from expanded human capacities.

Some of the institutional arrangements that might solve these problems are already visible in the recent innovations in workplace

13. Many of the new market reforms in Eastern Europe, the Soviet Union, and China also belong on this list because they produce hybrid arrangements. However, it is too soon to evaluate their effectiveness.

management being used by some U.S. firms.[14] First, the firm must commit itself to providing its employees with career-development opportunities and greater employment security. This is essential if employees are to perceive technological innovations as positive rather than as a threat to their livelihood. If a particular worker is made redundant by technological change, the firm should not fire him or her, but should attempt to train the person for an equally or more demanding job. There are some limits to what the individual firm can do to assure employee security; in extreme circumstances a firm might have no choice but to cut the size of its labor force. However, if the society had an adequate system of social support in place, such layoffs would be less traumatic than at present. Moreover, there is considerable evidence that under normal circumstances, firms can do a great deal to avoid layoffs.[15] In a period of slack demand for particular products, multiskilled employees can be shifted to other tasks, or they can be provided with training for entirely new jobs.

Employers' concern with career development also involves creating a meaningful internal job ladder that provides the employee with the possibility of movement into more challenging work. This is essential, because when an individual has been trained to be a problem-solver, but is then stuck in a job that has become almost entirely routine, his or her motivation is likely to suffer. This concern for career development also requires that management create incentives for individuals to raise their skill levels. These incentives can then operate to overcome the normal bias toward an underinvestment by individuals in skills. These incentives can take a variety of forms; employers can use pay-for-learning compensation schemes that reward workers for learning new skills,[16] they can provide subsidies for tuition for education or training; they can have a policy of attempting to provide existing employees with new jobs to match their newly acquired skills; or they can commit themselves

14. Thomas Kochan et al., *The Transformation of American Industrial Relations* (New York: Basic Books, 1986).

15. For an extended discussion of how a number of American firms have adopted no-layoff policies and other measures to improve employment security, see Jocelyn F. Gutchess, *Employment Security in Action: Strategies That Work* (New York: Pergamon Press, 1985).

16. Larry Hirschhorn, *Beyond Mechanization: Work and Technology in a Postindustrial Age* (Cambridge, Mass.: MIT Press, 1984), ch. 11.

to an active policy of helping employees find jobs with other employers in the event that the employee's skills cannot be utilized by the firm.[17]

A second set of changes in the workplace centers on the greater democratization of decision-making. The expression of workers' views can be a central mechanism for moving the firm toward the more efficient use of resources. Even in the case of decisions about appropriate investments in physical capital, employees' opinions can be an effective countervailing force to management's tendency either to exaggerate or to minimize the possible benefits of investment in new technologies.

As noted earlier, many firms have sought to systematize the expression of their workers' opinions by establishing institutions for collective problem-solving. The common intent of quality circles and similar arrangements is to facilitate both individual and collective problem-solving. In many contemporary work settings, particularly those that depend on computer-based technologies, issues of coordination among different work units have become increasingly central. However, it is often impossible to impose coordination from above because tasks are too fluid and unpredictable. Yet the failure to work out the problems of coordination can have dire consequences for the organization's effectiveness. Hence, there is a real need for institutional settings in which employees can discuss these problems openly and fully and find better ways to synchronize their efforts. Once such institutions are in place, it is costly for management to ignore the proposals suggested by employees.

The full mobilization of workers' opinions requires something more than quality circles or discussion groups. There must also be a structure of governance at the workplace that assures that employees' views will be taken seriously and protects them from the arbitrary exercise of management power. It is futile to expect employees to speak out in a context where they feel powerless or think they might be punished for doing so. The necessary quid pro quo for the effective mobilization of collective problem-solving is a structure that is democratic enough to give workers the sense that their input will be taken seriously. The extent of democratization will vary over time, but the firm's commitment to democratic participation must be more than lip service and the protection of rights of free speech must be real.

However, both the commitment to the development of employees' careers and the democratizing of decision-making will be unstable unless they are supplemented by steps to establish the employees as genuine stakeholders in the firm. Now that the buying and selling of corporations or units of corporations is routine, employees must have some awareness that any institutional commitments— whether to career development of employees, democratic procedures, or whatever—could be torn up from one day to the next if the unit is sold. Such a prospect erodes the effectiveness of all of the current management's commitments and hence interferes with the firm's capacity to develop efficient responses to problems of motivation, voice, and investments in training. The alternative is to provide employees with some power to influence takeovers, so they can block undesirable takeovers or negotiate appropriate terms with potential purchasers. This could be done under present law by providing employees with a significant quantity of the corporate stock, or it could be done through a reorganization of the entire system of corporate governance to provide votes on the board of directors to a variety of different stakeholders and require employees' consent to hostile takeovers.

On a day-to-day basis, either of these solutions would give employees a greater stake in the firm. Since employees would be more likely to reap benefits from the firm's successes, both individual motivation and the expression of their collective voice would be strengthened. It seems logical that the best way to overcome the sense of distance between the employees' interests and those of management is to make employees full stakeholders in the firm. This is precisely why stock distribution plans have been so common among managerial employees, but as skill becomes ever more important for lower-level workers, the case for broadening such schemes becomes stronger.

In addition, giving employees significant power over the corporation represents a positive solution to the current crisis in corporate governance. Despite the ideology of shareholder democracy, it is well known that the diffusion of ownership makes it possible for a firm's management to become entrenched. An entrenched management, in turn, has considerable freedom to pursue its own self-interest—golden parachutes, excessive levels of executive compensation, and so forth—rather than the efficient use of resources. It is precisely this potential for an ineffective management team to entrench itself that has led many to see the emergence of corporate "raiding" as a positive step. In this view, those who engage in hostile takeovers of corporations are giving new life to the idea of shareholder democracy, while also assuring that the firm's resources are used more efficiently. Yet, as we have seen, such takeovers can be highly disruptive to firms, and there is little evidence that such financial maneuvers actually increase the long-term efficiency of the economy. In short, the current choice is between entrenched managements and a highly irrational free market in corporations. Employee stakeholding could help reduce the likelihood of an ineffective management team entrenching itself without all of the added costs of the takeover game.[18]

Each of these changes in the organization of the workplace—commitment to employment security and career development, democratization of decision-making, and the establishment of employees as stakeholders—can be thought of in terms of a process of organizational learning that develops over time. To be sure, legislative changes would be necessary to provide employees with expanded rights, but firms would not be magically transformed from one day to the next. On the contrary, expanded employee rights would serve as the foundation for an ongoing process of change. This process will be driven forward by the need to motivate employees. At first, employees who are used to the old ways of organizing work will be responsive to small reforms, but as they become accustomed to these new practices, they will develop new frustrations. Overcoming these frustrations will then require further changes, pushing the process of democratization further.

18. This scenario is discussed as a possibility in John C. Coffee, Jr., "Shareholders versus Managers: The Strain in the Corporate Web," in John C. Coffee, Jr., Louis Lowenstein, and Susan Rose-Ackerman, eds., *Knights, Raiders, and Targets: The Impact of the Hostile Takeover* (New York: Oxford University Press, 1988), 112.

Organizing the Labor Market

It is difficult to shift toward the cooperative workplace without supporting changes in the way the labor market is organized. In particular, the labor market needs to be substantially tighter, so that employers are deprived of some of the coercive power that the threat of unemployment provides. One way to do this that also achieves other objectives is to create a system of basic income supports available to all members of the society.[19] All citizens, whether employed or not, would receive a monthly grant large enough to sustain a minimal standard of living, including housing, food, and other basic necessities. Such grants could substitute for the elaborate systems of welfare, unemployment insurance, and social security that exist in developed capitalist societies. The difference is that while many of those income transfers are not available to people who receive some income, the basic-income grant would still be available to those who choose to work.

The basic-income grant would contribute to dynamic flexibility both by underwriting a more cooperative workplace and by giving individuals maximal opportunity for their own personal development. Individuals would have much greater opportunity to pursue additional education and training in midlife because they could afford either to take off from work altogether or to shift from full-time to part-time status. The result could be much more rapid diffusion of new ideas and new technologies into the workplace.

As conservatives have insisted, such a guaranteed-income scheme would have a work disincentive effect.[20] It would be harder for employers to fill poorly paid jobs that offer few intrinsic rewards

19. The basic-income idea has a long and rich history, and it has reemerged as a lively topic of discussion in Western Europe in the 1980s. For some of the history and references to the recent debate, see Philippe van Parijs, "Quel destin pour l'allocation universelle?" *Futuribles* 106 (January 1987): 17–31. For other recent defenses of the idea, see Bill Jordan, *The State: Authority and Autonomy* (Oxford: Basil Blackwell, 1985), and Robert J. van der Veen and Philippe van Parijs, "A Capitalist Road to Communism," *Theory and Society* 15 (1987): 635–55. Lewis Mumford advocated the idea in *Technics and Civilization* (1934; reprint, New York: Harcourt, Brace & World, 1963), 400–406, and Robert Theobald argued for it in the 1960s in a series of books including *Free Men and Free Markets* (New York: C. N. Potter, 1963).

20. Work disincentives are discussed in Frances Fox Piven and Richard A. Cloward, "The Historical Sources of the Contemporary Relief Debate," in Fred Block et al., *Mean Season,* 3–43.

because individuals would have an alternative source of income. But the work disincentive effect would have a benign consequence. Employers would have a strong incentive either to automate those jobs out of existence or to make them more attractive—by raising pay levels, improving working conditions, raising the problem-solving component of the work, or integrating the jobs into a career line that leads to more attractive jobs.

A basic-income system would also contribute to the production of a range of nonmarket satisfactions. It would contribute to people's sense of economic security, since they would have a reliable source of income independent of their ability to work or find employment. This would be especially significant for women, who are often in a position of extreme economic dependence on their spouses, particularly during childbearing years.

The basic-income system could also reverse the tendency in this society to underproduce voluntary leisure time. The length of the full-time work week has remained relatively unchanged since the 1930s despite continuing advances in labor-saving technologies.[21] This has meant a halt in the kinds of dramatic increases in voluntary leisure that occurred from the 1880s to the 1930s as a result of limits on the length of the working day. Across that period, the average work week in the United States fell from 64 to 44 hours,[22] but there has been little subsequent change in full-time hours. This is a problem because the total number of hours of paid labor tends to grow only slowly, if at all, while an ever-larger percentage of the population has been seeking to enter the labor force. Between 1940 and 1979, hours of paid labor per man, woman, and child actually fell overall from 855 to 814, while the labor-force participation rate rose from 55.3 to 63.7 percent.[23] This means that more people are

21. This is the central theme of an important book by Benjamin Hunnicutt, *Work without End: Abandoning Shorter Hours for the Right to Work* (Philadelphia: Temple University Press, 1988).

22. F. Dewhurst and Associates, *America's Needs and Resources: A New Survey* (New York: Twentieth Century Fund, 1955), 40.

23. Data on hours are from Fred Block, "Technological Change and Employment: New Perspectives on an Old Controversy," *Economia & Lavoro* 18, no. 3 (July–September 1984): 3–21. Unfortunately the U.S. government discontinued publication of the series on hours worked by persons engaged in production by industry, so it is not possible to trace this series into the 1980s. However, published data limited to hours worked by employees show that employee hours per capita have failed to rise in the 1980s. Data on participation rates are from Depart-

pursuing a limited number of hours of work, and this tends to result in more involuntary leisure, such as unemployment, involuntary part-time work, and decreased access to the labor market for some demographic groups, such as older workers. In theory, these outcomes could be avoided if the substitution of part-time jobs for full-time jobs occurred at a pace that exactly matched the preferences of the labor force. However, the government's data tracking the growth of involuntary part-time work indicate that this has not been the case.[24]

The basic-income system can counter these trends by facilitating an expansion in voluntary leisure, reducing the necessity for involuntary leisure. With a basic-income grant, more individuals would find that they could manage a satisfactory standard of living by working only part-time.[25] For others, part-time work might make sense at particular stages of the life course—during childrearing or as an alternative to retirement with advancing age. Still others might simply want to work only part-time to free time for other activities, such as volunteering or artistic pursuits. Furthermore, if the basic-income grant were financed through progressive taxes, the marginal return on longer hours of work would be reduced. Some of those who work full-time could be expected to press for shorter hours when they realized that the benefits of increased leisure would outweigh marginal increases in income.

Finally, the basic-income system could facilitate the growth of different types of nonmarket work. Individuals comfortable with

---

ment of Labor, *Handbook of Labor Statistics* (Washington, D.C.: GPO, 1985), 18, and Bureau of the Census, *Historical Statistics of the United States, Colonial Times to 1957* (Washington, D.C.: GPO, 1960), 71. Note that in 1940 the labor-force participation rate was given for the population fourteen years of age and over, while the later data are for the population sixteen and over.

24. The number of people reported working part-time for economic reasons rose from 2.6 million in 1973 to 5.2 million in 1988. Department of Labor, *Handbook of Labor Statistics* (Washington, D.C.: GPO, 1985), 58, and *Employment and Earnings* 36, no. 1 (January 1989): 199.

25. Currently, many part-time jobs lack the employee benefits of full-time work and provide few opportunities for career mobility over time. Even in the absence of specific social policies designed to upgrade part-time work, the implementation of a basic-income system would create some pressures for such upgrading. Employers of part-time workers would have to make increased efforts to make those jobs attractive to individuals with the alternative of living on their grants alone.

the basic-income standard of living might decide to devote all of their energies to nonwage activity such as child-rearing, caring for elderly relatives, or engaging in a variety of community or voluntary activities. Moreover, people would also have the option of working for nonprofit organizations as volunteers or at relatively low wages to carry out a wide variety of service activities. In short, the fact that individuals were guaranteed a minimal level of income would increase the attractiveness of relatively poorly reimbursed service activities relative to formal employment.

One of the advantages of the growth of this nonmarket work is that it creates virtually unlimited possibilities for expanding the supply of interesting work. For example, people who wanted to start a community newspaper, a local theater company, or a child-care center could subsidize the start-up of the effort with their own basic-income grants. Even if they encountered initial resistance from the community, they could probably persist for some time as long as they were content with a low level of income. And if the community came to appreciate and support their service, they would be likely to gain an increase in income.

It has been suggested that basic-income grants might serve to subsidize low-wage employers and encourage the growth of unattractive jobs.[26] However, this need not be the case so long as two conditions are met—that the grant provides a decent level of support and that trade union rights are effectively protected. By giving employees a genuine alternative to paid employment, the basic-income grant would tighten the labor market, giving employees greater leverage vis-à-vis employers. The combination of this greater leverage and trade union rights would make it possible for employees to force an improvement in wages and working conditions. This weakening of employer coercion could contribute to economic efficiency by encouraging a more cooperative organization of the workplace.

A system of basic income would not exhaust the institutions needed to organize the labor market under Qualitative Growth II. There is also a need for further measures to facilitate what Carmen Sirianni calls "the self-management of time." A rich array of subsi-

---

26. See John Myles, "Decline or Impasse? The Current State of the Welfare State," *Studies in Political Economy* 26 (Summer 1988): 73–107.

dized educational opportunities would be necessary to provide individuals with both broad and specific skills at different stages of the life course. While the basic-income system would make it easier for an individual to study either part-time or full-time in midlife, that alone is not sufficient. Without arrangements to finance the costs of education and to assure that the content met the needs of adult learners, there would be no guarantee of the expansion of individual capacities required for dynamic flexibility.

It is also essential to create greater flexibility in the structure of careers within firms and within occupations. In particular, individuals need the option of moving back and forth between part-time and full-time work without sacrificing the possibility of mobility into higher-level positions. It is often the case now that individuals who choose to work less than full-time must abandon any hope of moving into more responsible or more interesting positions. Yet such penalties for the choice of part-time work arbitrarily restrict the ability of the society to make full use of workers' capacities, while also discouraging individual investments in retraining.

The Decommodification of Intelligence

Since dynamic flexibility depends on the rapid development and utilization of new ideas, the society's arrangements for organizing intelligence are of critical importance to qualitative growth. Changes in the organization of work will have significant bearing on the speed and effectiveness with which firms are able to take advantage of innovative ideas. Yet there are also other institutional arrangements that would have to be modified to achieve dynamic flexibility.

It is widely recognized that there is a fundamental tension between the privatization of innovative ideas and the diffusion of those ideas into the economy.[27] The case of computer software is instructive. When a new program is placed in the public domain, it can circulate very quickly and thousands of programmers can offer improvements that help perfect it. When a program is proprietary,

27. For an overview of current dilemmas in the social organization of intellectual property, see Office of Technology Assessment, *Intellectual Property Rights in an Age of Electronics and Information* (Washington, D.C.: GPO, 1986).

diffusion tends to be slower, and fear of legal action discourages individuals from circulating improved versions. The pace of change slows, as programmers must develop and market an entirely new program in order to get the improvements into circulation. Moreover, as the software industry comes to be dominated by giant firms with strong distribution systems, small start-up firms that offer only slightly better mousetraps might find nobody beating a pathway to their doors.

Parallel problems emerge in many other arenas. In fields such as biotechnology and artificial intelligence, research scientists have become acutely aware that their laboratory research can have significant economic payoffs. However, as these scientists rush to set up their own corporations or affiliate with existing corporations, the conflict between the traditional values of the scientific community and proprietary control of information intensifies.[28] How can you risk publishing your innovative findings when their proprietary use is worth millions? Yet without publication, the diffusion of ideas slows dramatically.

These dilemmas are almost always discussed in terms of the trade-off between speed of diffusion and retaining adequate economic incentives for those who develop the ideas. The argument is that if individuals or firms are denied the ability to capitalize on their innovations, there will be no incentives to invest in innovation. Moreover, it is also claimed that problems of slow diffusion can be minimized through licensing agreements that allow nonowners to exploit proprietary ideas.

There are, however, several difficulties with these arguments. The development of the personal computer industry in the 1970s provides ample evidence of the costs of current arrangements. While the development of a personal computer was not a particularly great technological challenge for the established computer companies, they showed little interest in innovating along those lines until hobbyists proved that there was a potentially huge market for these devices. Moreover, those hobbyists did not begin as a group of entrepreneurs trying to exploit a technology that the established firms were neglecting. On the contrary, the hobbyist subcul-

28. See Dorothy Nelkin, *Science as Intellectual Property: Who Controls Scientific Research?* (New York: Macmillan, 1984), esp. chs. 2 and 7.

ture had strong links to the anti-establishment counterculture of the 1960s and 1970s.[29] It was from this counterculture that the hobby-ists developed an ethic of free sharing of information that was a critical element in their ability to develop the personal computer and personal computer software in a remarkably short period of time. Ironically, as the businesses the hobbyists built in their ga-rages turned into major corporations, the free flow of information stopped. Moreover, as the stories of these hobbyist-entrepreneurs are assimilated into the culture's rags-to-riches mythology, their successful examples could well further slow the pace of innovation. Even more individuals are encouraged to horde innovative ideas as they fantasize about starting their own businesses and making for-tunes.

This narrow focus on economic incentives ignores all of the other reasons that individuals have for developing new ideas. For centu-ries, both artists and scientists have innovated for reasons that have had little to do with the desire to make more money.[30] Moreover, the Silicon Valley hobbyists were only the most recent incarnation of a long tradition of tinkerers, who are often motivated by a love of gadgets and a desire to make sense of the world. It is important to remember the rich variety of incentives that have facilitated innova-tion, because a society that makes money the exclusive motivating force in all spheres of activity cuts itself off from what have histori-cally been vital streams of human creativity.

In fact, it remains the case that in the arts—even those that have become big business—proprietary rights in ideas are extremely limited. One can get into trouble by literally copying the text of a play or a television script or large portions of a popular song, but there is no problem in copying the innovative ideas behind a par-ticular artistic work. On the contrary, it can be argued that this freedom to borrow and comment on the work of predecessors is at the core of the artistic endeavor.

The fact that the Bauhaus architects were not able to gain pro-prietary control over their stylistic innovations or that Andy Warhol

---

29. Paul Freiberger and Michael Swaine, *Fire in the Valley: The Making of the Personal Computer* (Berkeley: Osborne, 1984).

30. The tension between these traditional motivations and financial incentives is discussed in Office of Technology Assessment, *Intellectual Property Rights*, 130–32.

could not license the idea of Pop Art has not appeared to diminish artistic creativity. That the arts have flourished without proprietary control of ideas suggests that the artistic model could be extended further. Software "artists" or computer-design "artists" could be commissioned by a particular firm to produce a work that meets certain specifications. If the work incorporated significant innovations, then other "artists" would be free to develop variations on those themes. Such a model would, in fact, retain economic incentives, since the more successful "artists" would win larger and more lucrative commissions, but their ideas would circulate freely.

Moreover, the argument for preserving incentives to innovate ignores the fact that even when proprietary rights in ideas are uncertain, firms have clear economic incentives to invest in research for both process and product innovations. Process innovations can make the firm more efficient and increase profits, and new or improved products can expand markets even when rival firms are not constrained from developing imitations of these innovations.[31] In highly competitive industries where technologies are changing quickly, even a six-month head start in marketing a new product can provide significant rewards. In short, firms would continue to have strong incentives to innovate even if ownership of ideas were sharply limited.

To be sure, it makes no sense to eliminate all notions of intellectual property; such a step would enormously disadvantage individuals and small firms relative to larger ones. However, a number of steps can be taken to protect the society from too high a level of marketness in the organization and production of ideas. First, the duration of legal protection for ideas through patents or copyrights could be significantly shortened, so that ideas entered free circulation sooner and firms faced increased pressures to exploit innovations quickly. Second, the range of ideas that fall under the model of artistic innovation should be expanded rather than contracted. Third, the places in society where individuals develop ideas independent of a concern with commercial exploitation need to be protected and expanded. The academic or government scientist

---

31. Even with the current legal arrangements for protecting proprietary ideas, many product innovations are easily copied by competitors. Since the focus of patent law is on technical processes, it is often possible to imitate a new product by using a differently designed mechanism to achieve the same ends.

who develops an AIDS vaccine should be rewarded with fame and recognition, but the patent rights should enter the public domain. Those scientists who want to benefit from the commercial exploitation of their ideas should be required to leave the university community if they cannot comply with the requirement for rapid publication of their findings. Joint financing of academic research by private firms—with proprietary strings attached—is a poor substitute for greater public investment in the creation of the public good of greater knowledge.

The goal, in fact, should be a greatly expanded public and non-profit domain of knowledge production that extends its research scope to include production processes. For example, publicly funded research institutes that address the human and technological problems of industrial automation could produce innovative ideas freely available to a whole range of different firms.[32]

The Coordination of Production and Investment Decisions

Perhaps the most challenging problem in delineating Qualitative Growth II is to figure out how to coordinate production and investment decisions. What are the specific mechanisms for moving beyond plan or market in determining what is to be produced? How are firms to be prevented from imposing externalities such as pollution or dangerous products on the wider community? Most important, how is it to be decided what qualitative goals will be pursued and who is to bear the cost?

One point can be made with certainty. There can be no single mechanism for accomplishing these tasks; the society must rely on a diverse combination of markets, state action, and other forms of regulation. There is no route to effective coordination that bypasses complex combinations of different institutional arrangements. In

32. The Japanese have developed a kind of manufacturing extension service that is equivalent to the agricultural extension services in the United States (Stephen S. Cohen and John Zysman, *Manufacturing Matters: The Myth of the Post-Industrial Economy* [New York: Basic Books, 1987], 226). There is also a need for public and nonprofit institutions to play a larger role in assuring broad access to information. What is needed are high-technology equivalents to the role historically played by public libraries.

increasing noncommodity outputs, for example, the basic-income scheme would make possible a quasi-market dynamic in which individuals would have increased opportunities to produce various collective goods. Yet one would also want increased governmental provision of certain collective goods as well. The precise mix between public and voluntary provision would have to be negotiated on an ongoing basis.

Beyond that, it is possible to outline some of the devices that could be used for economic coordination. One step is to expand the role of the private firm as an instrument of public purpose. This has already been done in cases such as affirmative action, where the firm is required to operate not just to make profit but to reduce racial and gender inequalities in the society. In a society organized around qualitative growth, this could be extended to include a variety of different social goals. Firms could be required to pursue such public goals as the production of more interesting work, the improvement of occupational health and safety, and the protection of the environment.

This is not simply a question of having government regulators impose requirements on firms. The idea is that as employees become stakeholders in a firm, with greater input into its decision-making, they can help to assure that the firm's actions are consistent with certain broad social goals. There would still be a need for a regulatory apparatus to penalize firms that violate certain agreed-upon standards. However, the primary emphasis would be on getting firms to internalize a set of goals as part of their basic definition of purpose. Then employees could operate as whistle blowers or as a pressure group against management when the firm deviated from these goals. Since all firms in the society would be subject to the same constraints, there would be less competitive pressure to violate the standards.

The possibility of using the firm to achieve broader social purposes rests on the idea that the search for profits is always socially constructed; it occurs within a framework of understandings as to what is appropriate and legal behavior. In the absence of the perfect competition of economic theory, the firm has considerable leeway in shaping its goals. Even the definition of what constitutes an appropriate level of profits is the outcome of accounting conventions and understandings within particular societies. Since the firm is a social construction, it can be reconstructed to place more emphasis on nontraditional goals. Critics complain that nonprofit corporations behave no differently than profit-making firms, but the very success of these nonprofit entities is an indication of the potential for change in the corporate form. This malleability of the corporate form means that profitability and broader social goals can be reconciled.

At the level of the government, two other changes are necessary. The first is the provision of services by the public sector in ways that are not traditionally bureaucratic. Just as the private corporation need not be structured to place profit above any other goals, so, too, it is not necessary that public-sector service delivery be inefficient and unresponsive to the varying needs of consumers. It was earlier argued that market arrangements by themselves have failed to produce some of the services that people need most—housing, child care, information services, and so on. The government needs to develop the capacity to produce these satisfactions in adequate quantity and quality.

This can be done through the debureaucratizing of state agencies. Debureaucratizing is the equivalent process in the public sector to changes in the private sector that make workers problem-solvers and stakeholders in the organization. This means giving lower-level workers more discretion and more input in shaping the goals of the agency and creating incentives for the agency to be responsive to public concerns. It can also mean the growing use of public-private partnerships in which high-quality services are delivered through a collaborative effort amongst government agencies, nonprofit organizations, and even profit-making firms. Such collaborations can assure a pluralistic approach to the service-delivery problem. Moreover, through careful supervision of the contracting arrangements, public-sector employees can see to it that the goals of public policy are being met.

A second necessary change is the expansion of the role of democratic politics in shaping government decisions about investments in social infrastructure and the production of public goods. An embryonic form of this change is visible in certain public debates about transportation and urban development plans for cities and regions. The familiar form of these debates is that an alliance of powerful private and public interests develops a plan for the region. The plan is subject to some public debate and then is either accepted or rejected by the legislative bodies that must vote the funding to implement it. In some cases, however, there has been the development of counterplans by community groups or by other public-sector entities, and then the debate has centered on the relative merits of the two different approaches to the area's problems.

Such debates point to the possibility of creating democratic planning mechanisms. The key is to provide nonelite groups with the resources to develop counterplans that reflect broad popular concerns. With a system of basic-income grants in place, alternative planning groups could easily be sustained, but some additional public-sector subsidies might be necessary to assure that such groups would be able to hire the services of experts with highly specialized knowledge. Then, when both plan and counterplan existed, a broad public debate could begin that would reveal strengths and weaknesses in the different approaches. Referenda might be utilized to gauge public sentiment, and the legislative bodies would proceed to formulate a final plan that attempted to combine the strengths of plans and counterplans.

Through such a process, the society could begin to collectively make the most important decisions about processes of social and economic development. Rather than simply being passive victims of either market processes or elite planning, citizens could begin to address the basic questions of how to live and how the society's resources should be used. This democratization of economic life would not happen overnight; it would be a process of learning and institutional innovation that would progress over time.

The potential for such democratic decision-making is closely linked to the rejection of the intravenous view of capital. As long as the intravenous view of capital is hegemonic, debates about the expansion of public goods will be dominated by fears that new productive investment would have to be sacrificed and increased taxes on the wealthy would slow growth. The rejection of the intravenous model makes possible a more realistic sense of the trade-off between different types of expenditure and different means of financing them. Moreover, recognition of the costly consequences of the struggle for positional goods provides a firm rationale for redistributive taxation as a mechanism for financing the production of public goods.

To be sure, ample room will remain for intense conflicts over which public goods to produce and over the appropriate mix between public and private consumption. Struggles will continue over how much additional money is to be devoted to medical research as opposed to protection of the environment. And there will be persistent debate over how much discretionary income individuals need or deserve. The point, however, is that such conflicts would take place in a political context in which it is taken for granted that these are decisions to be made collectively, not through the invisible hand of the market.

In sum, Qualitative Growth II would not eliminate ongoing conflicts between social groups over income, power, and status. It would not mean the end to inequality or the end of hierarchy. But it would change the terrain on which such conflicts occur. It would create more democratic institutional structures and would provide a higher level of protection for those with less wealth and less power. It would bring us closer to a world in which "the free development of each is the condition for the free development of all."

Obstacles to Qualitative Growth

There is no question that the kinds of institutional changes envisioned in Qualitative Growth II will remain far outside the mainstream of American politics until and unless it comes to be widely understood that new economic principles—those of Qualitative Growth I—can assure the efficient organization of production and consumption. However, even then, the obstacles to economic reform will be considerable. International economic competition with Japan, Western Europe, and the Newly Industrialized Countries, and political-military competition with the Soviet Union pose formidable hurdles to domestic reform.[33] Domestically, political and

33. At this moment—September 1989—it seems far more possible to negotiate a Soviet-American understanding that would substantially reduce military spending than at any time since 1945. The key question appears to be whether U.S. political leadership will have the courage to seize an opportunity to end the Cold War.

economic elites can be expected to mobilize intensively against the redistribution of power and wealth that Qualitative Growth II implies. Most critically, the continuing debasement of American politics makes it difficult to see how significant reforms could even be placed on the political agenda. The restriction of the electorate to barely half of the eligible population, the dominant role of big money raised from corporate political action committees, and the triumph of advertising and packaging in political campaigns block any serious political debate.

The point, however, is that each of these obstacles is fundamentally political and therefore potentially surmountable. Even in the case of international economic competition, the problem is the political will to change the rules governing the international market. Under current conditions, it is obvious that a nation that forced its firms to adopt broader social purposes, such as a greater commitment to protection of the environment, would place those firms at a significant disadvantage in international trade. However, it would certainly be possible to negotiate international environmental rules that limit the access to the international market of firms that violate certain environmental standards. In fact, without the creation of such international environmental rules, there will be strong pressures for environmental practices to sink to the level of the least-regulated countries, with the possibility of irreparable damage to the earth.

Similarly, the rules that govern the international economy could be rewritten to place restrictions on the movement of money capital across national boundaries. Such restrictions were envisioned in some of the early drafts of proposals for the post–World War II international monetary order, and they could be revived in order to protect nations from the negative consequences of volatile movements of liquid capital. Such restrictions would be a logical extension of the rejection of the intravenous model of capital.[34]

Other obstacles, such as the resistance of powerful elites and the

34. In the case of the Third World, development requires infusions of money capital to finance plants and infrastructure. However, the international debt crisis provides formidable evidence that the market mechanism has not organized these flows effectively. A part of the envisioned renegotiation of the international economic order would be agreements on new mechanisms for transferring resources between developed and developing nations.

debasement of American politics are even more clearly remediable. At earlier moments in American history, powerful social movements have emerged—usually unexpectedly—to transform both the form and the content of domestic politics. Such movements have also been able to win significant reforms even in the face of considerable elite resistance. The fact that considerable time has passed since the last such occurrence is no reason in itself to doubt the possibility that this could happen once again.

Conclusions

Change along the lines of Qualitative Growth II requires the emergence of broad social movements that struggle to find new ways to organize economic and social life. Whether such movements actually will emerge depends on many factors, but one that looms large is the way people think about the society in which they live. The problem is that if these popular understandings continue to be rooted in the economic categories and concepts of industrial society, social choice will be constrained and popular movements will be disempowered. This book was written in the hope that a critique of these obsolete ideas may help expand the possibilities of change.

Index

Accounting, 31–33; capital, 120, 129–31, 146–52, 154; national-income, 125n, 129n, 133, 136, 155, 175, 176; organizational, 146–52, 154. *See also* Gross National Product

Adler, Paul, 105–6

Advertising, 23, 61–62, 157

African-Americans, in agriculture, 9, 57

Agriculture, 6; African-American slaves in, 9, 57; decline in, 10, 59–60, 191; marketness of, 56–58, 59

Akerlof, George, 78

Artificial intelligence, 209

Arts, 210–11

Atleson, James, 81

Attention, employee, 10, 112–13

Authority, employer, 79–81

Automation, 10, 13, 14, 18, 44; and capital, 131, 141–44, 146–51; in factories, 10, 44, 93–103, 108, 131, 141–44, 146, 148–49; flexible, 95–101, 102, 131, 142–49 passim; and motivation, 112–13; in offices, 103–8, 146, 148–49, 150; and skill levels, 86, 89, 93–108, 149. *See also* Computerization; Robotics

"Background conditions," 29, 30–33, 43, 44, 116

Badham, Richard, 9

Banking: central, 39; GNP and, 170–71; and skill levels, 104, 105–6; technology in, 105–6, 128, 148

Baran, Barbara, 105

Basic-income system, 204–8, 213, 215

Becker, Gary, 37

Beliefs: as "background" factor, 31, 33. *See also* Religion

Bell, Daniel, 5, 7, 11

Bluestone, Barry, 108–10

Board of directors, employee votes on, 202

Bounded rationality, 25

Bourgeois society: as anthropological culture, 27; historical materialism and, 29n. *See also* Middle class

Brand names, 61–62

Broadcasting: equipment, 140; in GNP, 157

Brown, Clair, 172–73, 185n

Buildings: factory, expenditures for, 144. *See also* Homes

Bureau of Economic Analysis (BEA), 129, 137, 138, 139, 140, 171n

Bureau of Labor Statistics, 133, 136, 139n

Business services, 127n, 130

Capital, 120–54; conceptualizing, 122, 128–32, 152; defining, 120, 121–28; economic theory on, 16, 22, 24, 45, 47, 121, 122–23, 128–29, 152; intangible, 121, 129–31; international flows of, 17–18, 217; intravenous model of, 152–53, 154, 194, 215–16, 217; older and newer, 121; and output, 120–28, 129, 136, 139–40, 143, 147, 168n; qualitative growth and, 194, 215–16. *See also* Capital savings

Capitalism, 46–47, 152, 193; defining, 191–92; "disorganized," 9n; "economistic fallacy" and, 27; industrial, 40, 190; and labor, 76, 120–32 passim, 147, 149, 150, 153, 154; limited mutability of, 191; and marketness, 61, 66, 69n, 192; Marx and, 6, 29–30, 40; "organized," 9n; Polanyi and, 27, 39–41; qualitative growth and, 190, 191

cal, 94, 103–8, 149, 150; "contingent,"
109, 110; and democracy, 193–94, 201–
3; dualism in, 108–12; economic theory
on, 16, 22, 24, 30, 45, 47, 75–76, 118–
19, 122–23; efficiency of, 76–85, 87,
112–19, 120, 199; factory, 9, 10, 18, 40,
58, 94–103, 108, 131, 149; female paid,
10, 11, 40, 86, 103, 107, 110, 159, 182–
83; female unpaid, 30, 36, 58, 182–84;
GNP and, 158, 161, 167n, 173; household manufacturing, 58, 59; and implicit
contract, 51n, 64, 77; industrial capitalism and, 40; in international economics,
18, 19; layoffs, 200; male, 11, 40, 86;
and marketness, 57–72 passim; nonpecuniary rewards of, 158, 162–65,
176–77; in nonprofit sector, 60, 207 (*see
also* Volunteer work); positive feedback
and, 194–96, 199–200; problem-solving
by, 113–15, 131, 176–77, 201–2; in
public sector, 60, 214; qualitative
growth and, 194–96, 199–208, 213, 214;
slave, 9, 57; Third World, 18; turnover,
69–72, 87–88; unions, 39, 47, 76, 80n,
119, 207; unpaid, 30, 36, 58, 60, 158,
159–61, 182–84, 206–7. *See also* Automation; Employee-employer relations;
Internal labor market; Job. . . ; Professionalism; Security; Skill levels, labor;
Training
Labor-force participation rates, 111–12,
205–6
Laissez-faire, 39, 191
"Laws of motion," of capitalism, 29–30
Layoffs, 200
Learning: as nonpecuniary reward of
work, 176–77; qualitative growth and,
200; work intertwined with, 13, 14. *See
also* Education; Training
Leftism, 3, 35. *See also* Marxism;
Socialism
Legality: economics and, 24, 30–31; ideas
protected by, 210, 211; and managerial
authority, 81
Legislation: employee rights, 203; patent/
copyright, 211
Leibenstein, Harvey, 45, 122n
Leisure: basic-income system and, 205–6;
GNP and, 158, 161–62, 164–65, 183,
184
Liberalism: economic, 2–3, 27, 41; political, 3, 12
Life course: basic-income system affect-
ing, 204, 206, 208; developmental, 14;
linear, 10–11, 13, 14; weight of paid
labor on, 161

Life expectancy: and care of elderly, 183;
GNP and, 156, 167n
Linear life course, breakdown of, 10–11,
13, 14
Loyalty, and marketness, 69–73

Machines: and capital, 121–22. *See also*
Technology
Machine tools, numerically controlled,
98–100, 141–44, 148, 149
Machinists, 94, 96, 98–100, 149
Managers: and capital for technology,
148–49, 154; entrenched, 202–3; and
marketness, 69–70, 71–73; and motivation, 112–15; qualitative growth and,
201–2, 213; and skill levels, 85, 87–88,
93, 112; in Soviet-style planning, 41;
stock distribution among, 202; and takeovers, 71–73, 202–3; training for, 117.
See also Employee-employer relations
Manufacturing, 10; and craft skills, 82–83,
94–103; in international economy, 18–
19; just-in-time inventory control in,
18, 44n; marketness of, 58–61, 67–68;
output data and, 139, 169; small, 58–60.
See also Factories; Flexible manufacturing systems
Marginalism: and capital, 22, 24, 47; and
labor, 22, 24, 47; and market, 22, 47,
48–49, 53–55, 65; and output, 158–59.
See also Neoclassical economics
Marginal utility, 24, 49
Marglin, Stephen, 31
Market, 2, 3–4, 8n, 30, 39–40, 46–74, 184;
and capital, 125, 126, 128, 130, 147;
defined, 50–51; economic theory on,
16, 22, 46–55, 65; and GNP, 157, 158;
and international economy, 217n;
Polanyi on, 41; problems with model
based on, 22–23, 66–73; "pure," 66n;
qualitative growth and, 198–99, 213,
214. *See also* Capitalism; Free market;
Labor; "Marketness"
"Marketness," 51–66; of "developed capitalist" and "market socialist" societies,
192; high, 51–52, 55, 59, 66–73; lower
levels of, 51, 52–53, 57–58, 59, 63–64;
qualitative growth and, 198, 211. *See
also* Commodification
"Market socialism," 192, 193
Marx, Karl, 6, 29–30, 34, 192; and capital,
121–22, 132; and coercion in labor market, 79; and consumption, 175n; and
positive feedback, 194–95; and production, 175n; and working day length, 40

Compositor: Interactive Composition Corporation
Text: 11/13 Caledonia
Display: Caledonia
Printer: Maple-Vail Book Mfg. Group
Binder: Maple-Vail Book Mfg. Group